Department of Economic and Social Affairs
Statistics Division

Guidelines for Producing Statistics on Violence against Women—
Statistical Surveys

United Nations
New York, 2014

Department of Economic and Social Affairs

The Department of Economic and Social Affairs of the United Nations Secretariat is a vital interface between global policies in the economic, social and environmental spheres and national action. The Department works in three main interlinked areas: (i) it compiles, generates and analyses a wide range of economic, social and environmental data and information on which States Members of the United Nations draw to review common problems and take stock of policy options; (ii) it facilitates the negotiations of Member States in many intergovernmental bodies on joint courses of action to address ongoing or emerging global challenges; and (iii) it advises interested Governments on the ways and means of translating policy frameworks developed in United Nations conferences and summits into programmes at the country level and, through technical assistance, helps build national capacities.

Note

The designations employed and the presentation of material in the present report do not imply the expression of any opinion whatsoever on the part of the Secretariat of the United Nations concerning the legal status of any country, territory, city or area or of its authorities, or concerning the delimitation of its frontiers or boundaries.

The term "country" as used in the text of this report also refers, as appropriate, to territories or areas.

The designations "developed" and "developing" countries or areas and "more developed" and "less developed" regions are intended for statistical convenience and do not necessarily express a judgement about the stage reached by a particular country or area in the development process.

Symbols of the United Nations documents are composed of capital letters combined with figures.

ST/ESA/STAT/SER.F/110
ISBN: 978-92-1-161567-8
United Nations publication
Sales No. E.13.XVII.7
Copyright © United Nation, 2014
All rights reserved

Preface

The Guidelines for Producing Statistics on Violence against Women: Statistical Surveys have been prepared to assist countries in assessing the scope, prevalence and incidence of violence against women. These Guidelines respond to the need to provide methodological advice regarding selection of topics, sources of data, relevant statistical classifications, outputs, wording of questions and all other issues relevant for national statistical offices to conduct statistical surveys on violence against women.

The publication was requested by the United Nations Statistical Commission at its fortieth session, in 2009, to comply with United Nations General Assembly resolution 61/143 on the intensification of efforts to eliminate all forms of violence against women, which requested the Statistical Commission to develop a set of possible indicators to assist States in assessing the scope, prevalence and incidence of violence against women. To assist in this work, the Friends of the Chair of the Statistical Commission on indicators on violence against women[1] was established by the Statistical Commission at its thirty-ninth session, in 2008. In 2009, this group developed a list of core indicators for which data should be compiled through population-based surveys. These indicators reflect the complex nature of violence against women which can have psychological, physical, sexual and economic dimensions.

The publication aims to provide national statistical offices with detailed guidance on how to collect, process, disseminate and analyse data on violence against women. It lays out the role of statistical surveys in meeting policy objectives related to violence against women, the essential features of these surveys, the steps required to plan, organize and execute these surveys, the concepts that are essential for ensuring the reliable, valid and consistent measurement of women's experiences in accordance with core topics and a plan for data analysis and dissemination. These Guidelines should be used in conjunction with other manuals, such as the United Nations Statistics Division publications Designing Household Survey Samples: Practical Guidelines (United Nations 2008) and Household Sample Surveys in Developing and Transition Countries (United Nations 2005a) and Manual on victimization surveys (UNODC and UNECE 2010), and others as they are referenced in the text.

The contribution of Ms. Holly Johnson, University of Ottawa, to the drafting of the Guidelines is gratefully acknowledged. Appreciation is also extended to the members of the Friends of the Chair of the Statistical Commission on indicators on violence against women of the UN Statistical Commission, who conducted an in-depth technical review of proposed indicators for measuring violence against women, reviewed the draft Guidelines and provided valuable comments with respect to finalizing the publication. Lastly, gratitude is expressed to Henrica A.F.M. (Henriette) Jansen for her significant review of the final version of these Guidelines.

The drafting of the Guidelines was partly financed by the World Bank.

---

1 Members of the Friends of the Chair of the United Nations Statistical Commission on indicators on violence against women include Australia, Bangladesh, Botswana, Bulgaria, Canada, Chile, China, Costa Rica, Egypt, Ghana, Italy, Mexico, Thailand, Turkey and the United States of America.

Contents

Preface iii

Introduction 1

Chapter I 5
Role of statistical surveys on violence against women 5
    The need for surveys on violence against women 5
    The role of national statistical agencies 7
    Essential considerations for surveys on violence against women 7
    The use of survey modules for collecting data on violence against women 8

Chapter II 11
Concepts, definitions and data requirements 11
    Definition of violence against women 11
    Focus of the current Guidelines 11
    Target population, time frame and unit of observation 12
        Target population 12
        Time frame of violence 13
        Count of persons versus count of incidents 13
    Topics for inclusion in surveys on violence against women 14
        Physical violence 15
        Sexual violence 16
        Psychological violence 16
        Economic violence 17
        Female genital mutilation 18
        Attitude towards violence against women 18
        Reporting to authorities/seeking help 18
    Descriptive variables 18
        Severity of violence 19
        Relationship of victim to perpetrator 20
        Frequency of violence 21
        Location of violence 22
    Core topics and core descriptive variables: Summary 22
    Personal characteristics of respondents 22
        Marital/relationship status 23
        Age 23
        Age at first marriage 24
        Educational attainment and literacy) 24
        Economic activity status 24

Place of residence..24
Ethnicity..24
Religion...25
Language..25
Personal characteristics of intimate partners..............................25
Age..25
Educational attainment and literacy......................................25
Economic activity status...25
Substance abuse..25
Witnessing partner violence or experiencing childhood violence in the family of origin..25
Personal characteristics of non-intimate partners perpetrators...........25
Sex..25

Chapter III 29
Planning a survey on violence against women 29
Establishing the legal basis...29
Consultation with stakeholders...29
Specifying the objectives of the survey......................................31
Choosing the mode of data collection...31
Interviewer-assisted methods...32
Self-administered methods..37
Combination of methods...38
Budget and timeline..38
Establishing the organizational structure....................................42
Sample design..42
Sample size determination..43
Structure of the sample..44
The sampling frame...47
Selection of interviewers..48
Study protocol...50

Chapter IV 53
Questionnaire design 53
Background qualitative research..54
Important aspects of questionnaire development...............................55
Questionnaire content..56
Questions aimed at measuring experiences of violence.....................56
Questions aimed at producing statistics on the core indicators identified by the Friend of the Chair of the United Nations Statistical Commission on indicators on violence against women 57
Types of violence against women..58
Classification and characteristics of violence against women.............60
Personal characteristics of respondents..................................62
Questions aimed at producing statistics on additional variables..........63
a. Personal characteristics of respondents...........................64
b. Experiences of violence...66
c. Personal characteristics of intimate partners.....................67
d. Personal characteristics of non-intimate partners.................68

    Sequence of questions 68
    Use of skips and filters 70
    Other aspects of questionnaire design 72
    Testing a questionnaire 73
        Informal testing/pretesting 73
        Split samples or alternatives test 74
        Expert revision 75
        Cognitive testing 75
        Behavioural coding of interviews 77

Chapter V 79
Survey implementation 79
    Training of interviewers 79
        Basic training 79
        Specialized training for surveys on violence against women 80
        Training manuals 87
    Ethical issues in the implementation of violence against women surveys 90
        Safety of respondents 91
        Safety and well-being of interviewers 92
        Confidentiality and anonymity 93
        Minimizing and responding to emotional distress 94
        Ethical conduct of statisticians 95
    Quality control during the data collection phase 95
        Overseeing interviewers' work and performance 96
        Reducing unit non-response 97
        Reducing item non-response 100
    Pilot testing 101

Chapter VI 103
Data processing and analysis 103
    Data coding and editing 103
        Data capture and coding 103
        Data editing and verification 105
    Data imputation 107
    Weighting of data 109
    Computing sampling error 111
    Data analysis and tabulation 112
    Dissemination of results 114
        Production of metadata 115
        Creation of a data file 116
    Evaluation of the survey processes 116
    Final Steps 116

Annex I
    International instruments that aim to strengthen the collection of data on
        violence against women 119

Annex II
    Other sources of statistics on violence against women 121

Annex III
Selected countries that have conducted violence against women
surveys since 2000. 127

Annex IV
Example of a public campaign: Violence prevention in Italy. 135

Annex V
Design components of selected surveys on violence against women 137

Annex VI
Recommended tabulations for the core indicators identified by the
Friends of the Chair of the United Nations Statistical
Commission on indicators on violence against women 141

Annex VII
A model questionnaire for producing statistics on the core indicators
identified by the Friends of the Chair of the United Nations
Statistical Commission on indicators on violence against women 171

Annex VIII
Good practice for survey questions on additional variables/topics 197

References 205

Introduction

1. Violence against women is an obstacle to the achievement of the objectives of equality, development and peace. It both violates and impairs or nullifies the enjoyment by women of their human rights and fundamental freedoms. In all societies, to a greater or lesser degree, women and girls are subjected to physical, sexual and psychological abuse that cuts across lines of income, class and culture.[2]

2. A call to end all forms of violence against women was made in the Declaration on the Elimination of Violence against Women,[3] in 1993, and the Beijing Declaration and Platform for Action,[4] in 1995. Both instruments recognize that efforts to end violence against women must be accompanied by reliable statistics on such violence. Intergovernmental bodies, including the United Nations General Assembly, have on many occasions reiterated the critical importance of collecting and improving statistics on violence against women as important components towards its eradication and have mandated work on this issue (see annex I). There is a broad consensus among policymakers, legislators and civil society concerning the need for reliable data on the prevalence of different forms of violence against women and on the causes, nature and consequences of such violence.

3. The collection and dissemination of data on the prevalence and incidence of various forms of violence against women, as well as on the causes and consequences of such violence, is the starting point for developing effective mechanisms, at the policy level, for eradicating this phenomenon. Accurate and comprehensive data serve to increase societal awareness of violence against women and call attention to the accountability of States to act against such violence. Information needed by policymakers and advocates may include the number of women affected by various types of violence and the short- and long-term consequences thereof, the personal characteristics that leave certain women particularly vulnerable to victimization, the barriers to seeking help and the responses of criminal justice, health and social services to women who seek help. Detailed data are required to gauge the magnitude and dimensions of the problem, to establish baselines, to identify groups at high risk, to focus intervention and prevention efforts where they are needed most, to monitor change over time, to assess the effectiveness of interventions and to address the harm to victims of violence. In the absence of accurate information, efforts to track progress in terms of policy responses to the problem are severely compromised (Saltzman and others, 1999).

4. Information and statistics regarding violence against women are potentially available from a variety of sources. These sources include, but are not limited to, health and medical services, agencies of the criminal and civil justice systems, social services, legal aid services, research and documentation centres, and services designed specifically to respond to women who have experienced violence, such as shelters or refuges, rape/sexual assault centres, crisis

---

[2] See Report of the Fourth World Conference on Women, Beijing, 4-15 September 1995 (United Nations publication, Sales No. E.96.IV.13), chap. I, resolution 1, annex II, para. 112.

[3] See General Assembly resolution 48/104.

[4] See Report of the Fourth World Conference on Women, Beijing, 4-15 September 1995 (United Nations publication, Sales No. E.96.IV.13), chap. I, resolution 1, annexes I and II.

telephone line and women's groups and advocacy organizations. Some of these agencies or organizations are specifically mandated to respond to intimate partner violence or sexual violence, while others serve women fleeing from violence as part of their mandate to provide other related services. These agencies may collect information about the women who seek their help, including their experience of violence and other information that is necessary for the performance of their work. The records collected by such agencies and organizations in the course of the execution of their functions fall under the category of administrative records. The statistics compiled from administrative records are often by-products of administrative processes. The reliability of statistics derived from administrative records depends on the completeness of the records and the consistency with which definitions and rules are applied.

5. It is widely accepted—but cannot be underlined enough—that administrative data cannot provide an estimate of the prevalence of violence against women taking place within a population. Acts of violence against women are underreported, especially when violence is perpetrated by an intimate partner or other family member. Furthermore, acts of violence that are brought to the attention of agencies and services often are among the most severe and affect the most disadvantaged women. In short, cases of violence against women recorded in administrative systems do not represent the full extent and nature of the problem. Nevertheless, administrative data can be useful in providing an indication of both the societal response to reported cases of violence against women and serviced available for victims. (For more on the utility of administrative data as a source of information on violence against women, see annex II.)

6. If conducted properly, with due consideration for quality and ethics, population-based surveys are the best source of data for estimating the prevalence of violence against women. Surveys can reach nearly all women, regardless of whether or not they have reported violence to the police or sought help from health or social service agencies. Women in the population are interviewed about their experiences of violence and additional information, such as on the circumstances of the violence, the health consequences thereof and the actions they took to seek help can easily be collected. When properly designed and executed, dedicated surveys on violence against women produce the most reliable data on the prevalence of such violence and shed light on the scope, nature and consequences of most types of violence against women.

7. Over 70 countries have conducted surveys specifically dedicated to measuring the prevalence and nature of various forms of violence against women. At least 40 of them have done so at the national level. (See annex III for information on selected countries that have conducted violence against women surveys since 2000.) Some of the surveys focused specifically on intimate partner violence, while others were broader and encompassed a wide range of physical and sexual violence and threats of violence perpetrated by intimate partners, other family members, other known men and strangers.

8. In some countries, national statistical agencies have been responsible for conducting surveys on violence against women, while in others such efforts have been led by, or have involved, other Government ministries, university researchers and non-governmental organizations. The involvement of various organizations and stakeholders reflects the recognition across a wide range of sectors of the need for reliable data in order to raise awareness of violence against women and to develop policies and programmes to eliminate it.

9. Yet significant gaps in the availability of data remain. Many countries do not have any data, let alone reliable data, on violence against women. Among those that do have data, the quality and reliability vary. Many surveys do not provide the detail necessary for policy development or monitoring purposes. Very few national statistical authorities conduct surveys on violence against women on a regular basis to allow for comparisons over time.

10. In addition, survey results are often not comparable across settings or over time because the methodologies used differ with respect to concepts and definitions of violence, time frame and population groups. Some efforts have been made in the past decade to conduct surveys using standardized methodologies in a diverse set of countries in order to arrive at comparable statistics. The best known of these multi-country surveys are the World Health Organization (WHO) Multi-country Study on Women's Health and Domestic Violence against Women, which was initially conducted in 10 culturally diverse countries and later replicated in dozens of countries and the International Violence against Women Survey, which was coordinated by the European Institute for Crime Prevention and Control, to study violence against women.

11. These efforts reflect recognition of the importance of both improving and standardizing methods for collecting, processing and analysing statistics on violence against women. At the international level, the Secretary-General's study on all forms of violence against women (United Nations, 2006) recommends that the United Nations system should undertake to support the development of unified methods and standards for data collection, provide technical support to countries and build capacity of national statistical offices, and promote existing methods and good practices to ensure that the principles of sound data collection are met.

12. The present publication provides national statistical agencies with guidance on collecting, processing, disseminating and analysing data on violence against women. While the focus is on a stand-alone, dedicated (or specialized) survey, guidance is also provided on how to introduce a module on violence against women into another survey. These Guidelines introduce the concepts, definitions and data requirements for measuring violence against women and provide guidance on planning, organizing and implementing a survey on violence against women as well as on planning for data analysis and dissemination.

13. Several methodological materials provide valuable complements to the present Guidelines and are extensively referenced in the text. The Manual on Victimization Surveys (UN Office on Drugs and Crime (UNODC) and UN Economic Commission for Europe (UNECE), 2010) provides guidance on all aspects of victimization surveys; the publication Designing Household Survey Samples: Practical Guidelines (United Nations, 2008) is a practical guide to sample survey design, data processing and analysis of large-scale household surveys; and the publication Household Sample Surveys in Developing and Transition Countries (United Nations, 2005a) covers important aspects in the conduct of household surveys, including sample design, survey implementation, non-sampling errors, survey costs and data analysis.

14. The Guidelines are organized as follows:

- Chapter I specifies the need for, and the essential features of, statistical sample surveys on violence against women.
- Chapter II introduces the concepts and definitions relating to violence against women and outlines data collection requirements.
- Chapter III outlines the steps in planning a survey on violence against women.
- Chapter IV elaborates on the design of the questionnaire, including the specific wording of questions.
- Chapter V covers the implementation of surveys on violence against women, including the specialized training of interviewers, ethical issues and quality control.
- Chapter VI provides guidance on data processing, analysis and dissemination.

- Recommended tabulations for the core indicators identified by the Friends of the Chair of the UN Statistical Commission on indicators on violence against women are presented in annex VI.

- A model questionnaire for producing statistics on the core indicators identified by the Friends of the Chair of the UN Statistical Commission on indicators on violence against women is included in annex VII.

- Examples of good practice for survey questions on additional topics are presented in annex VIII.

Chapter I
Role of statistical surveys on violence against women

15.   This chapter elaborates on the need for statistical surveys on violence against women and the role of national statistical agencies in producing the data required to address this issue. It outlines a number of essential considerations for surveys on violence against women, discusses the merits of surveys specifically dedicated to measuring such violence and discusses the drawbacks of survey modules vis-à-vis dedicated surveys.

The need for surveys on violence against women

16.   The need for accurate and reliable statistics on the extent of violence against women has increasingly been recognized and emphasized at the national and international levels (see Introduction). Without a full understanding of the scope, dimensions and correlates of violence against women, it is not possible to design appropriate responses aimed at properly addressing or preventing such violence at any level of government or civil society. (For an example of how survey results were used in Italy to launch a violence prevention campaign, see box I.1.)

> **Box I.1**
>
> **Lessons for policymakers: The experience of Italy**
>
> In 2006, ISTAT, the national statistical agency of Italy, conducted the Italian Women's Safety Survey with a random sample of 25,000 women aged 16 to 70. The survey provided the data needed to effectively counter a number of false assumptions about the prevalence and nature of various types of violence against women and to launch a campaign to prevent such violence.
>
> The survey focused on physical and sexual violence perpetrated by intimate partners and other known men, and male strangers. Intimate partner violence also included psychological and economic violence and stalking. In addition to the prevalence of each type of violence, the survey measured the severity of violence and its consequences for victims and where victims sought help.
>
> The survey results and the campaign messages developed therefrom are set out below. The campaign posters are presented in annex IV.
>
> First result: Intimate partners commit the most severe acts of violence.
>
> - The most serious acts of violence were perpetrated by intimate partners, followed by relatives, friends and colleagues.
> - Repeated violence was more common by partners than by non-partners (67 per cent compared to 53 per cent). Sexual violence was most likely to be repeated among current partners (91 per cent).
>
> Campaign message: *Violence has many faces. Let's face the nearest one.*

> Second result: Psychological abuse by partners is common and is linked to an escalation of violence.
>
> - Forty-three per cent of women currently with partners were victims of psychological violence.
> - Acts of psychological violence included isolation and attempted isolation (47 per cent), control (41 per cent), financial abuse (31 per cent), berating (24 per cent) and intimidation (8 per cent)
>
> Campaign messages: *There's only one way to change a violent boyfriend…Change boyfriends. If your dream lover starts to whack you, WAKE UP! A violent partner will get you nowhere: or rather, he'll get you to a hospital bed.*
>
> Third result: Few victims speak up about violence and very few report it to the police.
>
> - Ninety-six per cent of cases of non-partner violence, 93 per cent of cases of partner violence, 92 per cent of rapes and 94 per cent of attempted rapes were not reported to the police.
> - Thirty-four per cent of victims of partner violence and 24 per cent of victims of non-partner violence did not talk about the violence with anyone.
> - Only 3 per cent of victims reported to a shelter or contacted another agency offering support to women.
>
> Campaign message: *A violent man doesn't deserve your love. He deserves to be denounced.*
>
> - Only 27 per cent of women raped by their partner considered the violence a crime.
> - Twenty per cent of victims of partner violence said they feared for their life.
>
> Campaign messages: *You know he'll bang you up. If he bangs on the door, don't open it. Mistaking slaps for love might hurt you easily.*
>
> Fourth result: There is a cycle of violence.
>
> - Men who were witnesses to or victims of violence in childhood were more likely to assault their intimate partners than men without such experiences (30 to 35 per cent compared to 6 per cent). Sixty-two per cent of women who suffered repeated violence by their partner said that their children witnessed the violence, while 16 per cent said that their children were victims of violence by the same man (their fathers).
>
> Campaign message: *Don't marry a violent man. Children learn very fast.*

17. Statistical sample surveys are relied upon to gather information on violence against women and to produce statistics on the prevalence of various types of violence. Surveys on violence against women are most effective when conducted as dedicated surveys, that is, surveys designed primarily, if not exclusively, to gather detailed information on the extent of different forms of violence against women. Such surveys have the potential to produce high-quality statistics, since they use interviewers who are trained specifically for that purpose and who are well equipped to deal with this sensitive topic.

18. Dedicated surveys provide the most reliable and comprehensive statistics on violence against women for several reasons. An important factor is that dedicated surveys can employ and train interviewers specifically to deal with the highly sensitive topic material; such measures should minimize underreporting. Furthermore, specialized surveys can accommodate a large number of detailed questions on the different types of violence experienced by respondents. In addition, the data on the sociodemographic characteristics of respondents and their intimate partners collected in these surveys allow for an analysis of the ways in which the risks and impacts associated with the violence vary according to the social characteristics of the women and their partners. A disadvantage of specialized surveys is that they are costly and are difficult for countries to repeat on a regular basis.

19. A less costly approach is to add a dedicated module on violence against women to an existing survey, such as a health survey or a crime victimization survey. The limitations of such an approach are discussed at the end of this chapter.

The role of national statistical agencies

20. Today, all forms of violence against women, including intimate partner violence, are considered by most States to be a social and public health problem that concerns Government agencies, legislators, medical professionals, police and legal professionals, community agencies, schools and all community members. As part of the process of eliminating violence against women, every State has an obligation to ensure that data on violence against women are systematically collected and disseminated under the framework of official statistics. A State can demonstrate its strong commitment to this obligation by embedding statistical sample surveys on violence against women in the strategic plans of its national statistical system.

21. National statistical agencies have a central role to play in producing the data needed to address violence against women. Together with the relevant Government ministries, they have a responsibility to assist States in meeting their international obligations, in particular that of achieving the goal of strengthening the collection of data on the prevalence of violence against women and girls under the Declaration on the Elimination of Violence against Women, the Beijing Platform for Action and subsequent General Assembly resolutions (see annex I). If possible, national statistical agencies should establish a clearly defined periodicity for surveys so that changes can be monitored over time.

22. National statistical agencies also have a responsibility to ensure that the concepts, definitions and methods used are consistent with international recommendations.

Essential considerations for surveys on violence against women

23. Given the sensitivity of the topic, ethical considerations are of utmost importance when implementing a survey on violence against women. In addition to ensuring that all the fundamental principles for conducting statistical sample surveys are applied, care must be taken when conducting such surveys, to consider how each aspect of the survey design and implementation will affect the safety and well-being of the respondents and, indeed, of the interviewers. Important considerations include ensuring the safety of respondents and interviewers, protecting the confidentiality and anonymity of the data during collection and processing, minimizing and responding to emotional distress, providing information on sources of support and ensuring the ethical conduct of statisticians (see paragraphs 377-378).

24. Dedicated surveys on violence against women—with specialized training of interviewers—are the preferred approach for acquiring detailed and reliable data on women's experiences of violence. Since they focus specifically on issues relating to violence against women, such surveys have the advantage of being able to elicit from respondents detailed information regarding the circumstances and consequences of the violence they experienced and their use of health, legal and other services, as well as descriptive information regarding the perpetrators. They are also excellent at providing detailed information on the prevalence and experience of different types of violence, including economic and psychological violence, which are often missed otherwise.

25. However, there may be situations in which it is not feasible to undertake a dedicated survey on violence against women owing to a lack of funding or other resources. In such situations, consideration should be given to collecting data on violence against women through survey modules. This entails introducing a specially designed module of questions into an existing, and appropriate, survey.

The use of survey modules for collecting data on violence against women

26. Before a decision is made to insert a module of questions on violence against women into an existing survey, it must be ascertained that the sampling design does not systematically exclude subgroups of the population that are important for the study of such violence. Inserting a module of questions on violence against women into a survey that covers only certain population subgroups, such as married women of childbearing age or women who speak the dominant language, may exclude the experiences of large groups of women.

27. As a general rule, surveys on unrelated topics are not good candidates for the incorporation of a module of questions on violence against women. Health surveys, safety surveys and crime victimization surveys tend to be more appropriate vehicles for this purpose. The sensitivity of the topics addressed in health surveys, in particular those examining women's health, make them a feasible vehicle for a module relating to women's experiences of violence. Examples of such surveys are the Multiple Indicator Cluster Surveys (MICS) and the Demographic and Health Surveys (DHS)[5] (see box I.2).

> **Box I.2**
>
> **Domestic violence module in the Demographic and Health Surveys (DHS)**
>
> The Demographic and Health Surveys (DHS) are carried out primarily in low- and middle-income countries using standardized questionnaires and methodologies. They cover a wide range of topics, including reproductive health, maternal and child health, sexual behaviour and nutrition. DHS are nationally representative statistical surveys of between 5,000 and 30,000 households. All women aged 15 to 49 in sample households are eligible to be interviewed.
>
> In 2000, a standardized module of questions and methodology was developed for the collection of data on intimate partner violence. This module has now been added to DHS in 40 countries. Known as the domestic violence module, it is typically administered in a subsample of selected households to one randomly selected woman per household, aged 15 to 49, who is currently married or cohabiting. The surveys are conducted in accordance with WHO ethical and safety guidelines.

28. Surveys designed to address a broad array of crime- or health-related or other issues cannot accommodate the broad range of questions needed to study violence against women in all its complexity. Certain drawbacks are evident when a module on violence against women is inserted into an already lengthy questionnaire on other topics. For example, the question wording and ordering may not facilitate disclosures of violence, especially if introductory statements or questions that cue respondents to think about violence occurring in private

---

[5] The MICS, conducted by the United Nations Children's Fund (UNICEF), monitor infant and child health and the reproductive health of mothers through face-to-face interviews in nationally representative samples of households. DHS are nationally representative statistical surveys covering a broad range of topics including reproductive health, maternal and child health, sexual behaviour and nutrition.

settings or incidents involving intimate partners have not been introduced. Compared to dedicated surveys, the breadth of questions that can be included in surveys on other topics is also limited, thereby reducing the opportunities for disclosure of experiences of violence. Finally, less attention is usually paid to the sensitization of interviewers to violence-related issues during their training, the need for interviewers to develop a rapport with respondents, privacy and confidentiality issues surrounding the interview and other ethical and safety issues, all of which can have a significant negative impact on the willingness of respondents to report violence.

29. Such limitations may result in the underreporting of violent experiences, particularly if a few questions related to violence against women are inserted between lengthy questions on unrelated issues (Ellsberg and Heise, 2005). In contrast, dedicated surveys allow multiple opportunities for respondents to disclose their experiences of violence and are designed to enable interviewers to establish a rapport with respondents. As a consequence, dedicated surveys generally yield higher prevalence rates than a module of questions incorporated into large-scale surveys on broader topics.[6] The estimates produced by dedicated surveys are considered to be a more accurate reflection of the true prevalence of such acts of violence.

30. Nevertheless, well-designed and well-implemented modules provide an inexpensive way to obtain reasonable statistics on aspects of violence that would otherwise be unattainable. The best results are obtained when the principles and guidelines for dedicated surveys are taken into consideration. Examples of crime victimization survey that include special modules of questions on intimate partner violence, sexual violence and stalking include the British Crime Survey[7] and Statistics Canada's General Social Survey on Victimization. In both instances, the survey instruments and protocols were significantly refined to incorporate many of the fundamental principles, learned from dedicated surveys, for interviewing women about their experiences of violence in a safe and ethical manner.

31. Table I.1 provides a comparison of dedicated surveys on violence against women versus modules on violence against women incorporated into other surveys in relation to several important aspects.

Table I.1
Comparison of dedicated surveys on violence against women versus modules on violence against women

Aspect	Dedicated surveys	Modules
Budget	As a stand-alone survey, costs for all aspects of survey development and implementation must be borne. In addition to standard costs associated with any sample survey, there are additional costs associated with consultations with stakeholders, testing of the questionnaire, selection and training of interviewers and other special considerations necessary for meeting ethical requirements.	Costs are considerably reduced. Thoroughly testing the module on violence against women within the context of the host survey is an important budget item. The budget must allow for additional training of interviewers in order to meet ethical and safety considerations of conducting interviews on violence against women.
Questionnaire content and design	The questionnaire content is broad and flexible. It can include detailed questions required to meet the survey objectives, such as questions on experiences of violence, consequences of violence and help seeking.	Questions on violence against women must be adjusted to fit within the host survey. Introductions are particularly critical to ensure accurate disclosures of violence. The depth and breadth of relevant questions may be limited.
Sample size and design	The sample size and design are tailored to the survey objectives. This can ensure that the sample size is sufficient to meet the survey objectives and that the sample design appropriately includes specific subgroups of interest.	The sample size and design depend on the host survey. The sample size may be too small to meet the survey objectives and the sample design may omit certain geographical areas or subgroups of the population that are of interest to users.

---

6 The Women's Safety Survey conducted by the Australian Bureau of Statistics, for example, estimated rates of physical assault to be three times higher than Australia's generic Crime and Safety Survey (Walby and Myhill, 2001).

7 On 1 April 212, the British Crime Survey was renamed the Crime Survey of England and Wales.

Table I.1
Comparison of dedicated surveys on violence against women versus modules on violence against women (cont'd)

Aspect	Dedicated surveys	Modules
Selection of interviewers	Interviewers are specially selected according to specific criteria. All interviewers are female.	In addition to the requirements of the host survey, interviewers must be selected according to specific criteria for conducting interviews on violence against women. Interviewers for the host survey may be male. This must be strictly avoided for modules on violence against women.
Training of interviewers	Interviewers are trained to implement specific measures to ensure that respondents can participate safely, to respond to emotional reactions on the part of participants and to recognize emotional reactions in themselves.	In addition to general training related to the host survey topic, interviewers must be given specialist training on ethical and safety guidelines.
Data analysis	Detailed data analysis on the prevalence, nature and impacts of violence against women is possible.	Data analysis is typically more limited.

Chapter II
Concepts, definitions and data requirements

32. This chapter provides guidance on the topics to be investigated in a statistical sample survey on violence against women. It lays down concepts, definitions and data requirements.

Definition of violence against women

33. The United Nations Declaration on the Elimination of Violence against Women defines violence against women as "any act of gender-based violence that results in, or is likely to result in, physical, sexual or psychological harm or suffering to women, including threats of such acts, coercion or arbitrary deprivation of liberty, whether occurring in public or in private life". This definition encompasses physical, sexual and psychological violence occurring in the family, physical, sexual and psychological violence occurring within the general community and physical, sexual and psychological violence perpetuated or condoned by the State.[8]

34. The Beijing Platform for Action further specifies that acts of violence against women include violation of the human rights of women in situations of armed conflict, such as systematic rape, sexual slavery and forced pregnancy, as well as forced sterilization, coercive/forced use of contraceptives, female infanticide and prenatal sex selection. The definition also encompasses acts of violence particular to specific contexts, such as dowry-related violence and female genital mutilation.[9]

Focus of the current Guidelines

35. As a long-term objective, violence against women in all its forms and manifestations should be measured. Various mechanisms are needed to accurately measure the different forms of violence against women. However, methodological development has not advanced far enough to capture all such violence. Collecting data on the trafficking of women, on violence against women in situations of armed conflict and on violence against women that results in death (e.g., dowry-related deaths, honour killings, femicide and female infanticide) is particularly challenging. It is recognized that statistical sample surveys that interview women in their households are not an appropriate method for measuring such types of violence.

36. Nevertheless, many forms of violence against women can be measured with a good degree of reliability through household sample surveys. The present Guidelines focus on these

---

[8] See General Assembly resolution 48/104, articles 1 and 2.
[9] See Report of the Fourth World Conference on Women, Beijing, 4-15 September 1995 (United Nations publication, Sales No. E.96.IV.13), chap. I, resolution 1, annex II, paras. 113-115.

forms of violence and use the list of core indicators identified by the Friends of the Chair of the United Nations Statistical Commission on indicators on violence against women[10] as a guide when recommending the types of violence and associated variables to be covered in a survey on violence against women. (See box II.1 for the list of core indicators.)

37. Before presenting recommendations on the types of violence to be included (topic coverage) in a dedicated sample survey on violence against women, a number of basic conceptual and measurement issues that have a direct bearing on the scope of such a survey will be considered.

Target population, time frame and unit of observation

38. There are three key conceptual or measurement issues that should be considered in a survey on violence against women: the population group to be studied (target population), the period of time to be covered (time frame of violence) and the unit to be counted (persons or incidents). Recommendations are given below for each.

Target population

39. The target population for a survey on violence against women is the population of women who could be victims of violence. Since all women could potentially be victims of violence, the target population would ideally be all women. Depending on the objectives of the survey, however, the target population may be narrower. For example, if the objective is to study intimate partner violence, the target population will be all women who have or have ever had an intimate partner.

40. In many cases, a survey on violence against women will be conducted as a household sample survey, thereby excluding women who do not live in households. Examples of such women include homeless women and women living in institutions such as school dormitories, nursing homes, jails or military installations. Women living in institutions may have a greater or lesser chance of being subjected to violence, depending on the type of violence. It is important that excluded subgroups are clearly identified and described for users.

41. For a dedicated survey on violence against women, the recommended target population is all women living in households aged 15 or older, regardless of marital or relationship status. Unless the survey is looking exclusively at intimate partner violence, respondents should not be preselected on the basis of marital or relationship status. Doing so will eliminate groups of women who are at risk of violence in other contexts, such as those involving perpetrators who are family members other than spouse or intimate partner, acquaintances or strangers.

42. An age limit lower than 15 is NOT recommended for surveys on violence against women for three reasons: to prevent the blurring of gender-based and other types of violence against children; to ensure the quality of data; and for methodological, legal and ethical reasons.

43. Girls younger than 15 may also be subjected to physical violence by family members and other persons. Lowering the age limit would blur the distinction between physical violence against women that is due to gender stereotypes and male control over female partners

---

10 For details on the work and responsibilities of the Friends of the Chair of the Statistical Commission on statistical indicators on violence against women, see unstats.un.org/unsd/demographic/meetings/vaw/default.htm.

on the one hand, and other phenomena such as disciplinary violence inflicted by parents or teachers or fighting among siblings or playmates on the other.

44. Interviewing girls younger than 15 also presents particular difficulties relating to ethics, suitability of research methods and reliability of recall.

45. In addition, young people in many countries are unable by law to provide consent independent of their parents or guardians. To acquire such consent would jeopardize the confidentiality and possibly the safety of the young person in question as the topic of the survey would become known to her parents or guardians, who might also be her abusers. Furthermore, many countries have a legal requirement to report incidents of child abuse to the authorities. This would require interviewers to violate guarantees of confidentiality. It is therefore recommended that 15 should be the minimum age for respondents in surveys on violence against women.

46. Nonetheless, in the case of violence by intimate partners, it is also important to consider intimate partner violence experienced by women and girls who were married or in other intimate relationships before the age of 15. This goal can be accomplished by asking respondents to report all incidents of intimate partner violence, irrespective of when they occurred in the relationship.

47. Some countries have opted to set an upper age limit for respondents, the reasons being that an older age category may be too small to allow for separate analysis. Should a country decide to collect information specifically on violence against women in older age groups, appropriate measures including the sampling phase will need to be taken into account.

Time frame of violence

48. A dedicated sample survey on violence against women should be able to shed light on current levels of violence as well as on women's lifetime experience of violence. Thus it is recommended that each woman's experiences of violence both in the 12 months prior to the survey (sometimes referred to as "current violence") and during her lifetime should be recorded. Data covering the past 12 months provide an indication of the extent and nature of current levels of violence and an estimate of the number of women who may require assistance. Lifetime experience provides an indication of the total number of women ever affected by such violence.

49. The lifetime reference period will literally refer to a woman's whole lifetime with respect to intimate partner violence only. That is to say information on intimate partner violence should be included even if it occurred before the woman reached the age of 15. For all other physical and sexual violence, the lifetime reference period will refer only to events occurring at age 15 and above. For a further explanation of why it does not always make sense to combine violence that occurred before the age of 15 and violence that occurred after the age of 15, see paragraphs 43 to 46.

Count of persons versus count of incidents

50. The extent of violence against women may be measured in terms of the number of women in a given population who have experienced violence or the number of incidents of violence that have been perpetrated against them.[11] In practical terms, the count of persons

---

11 Attention needs to be paid to the difference between "incidence" and "incidents". "Incidence" is a concept used in the health field to refer to the number of new cases within a given time period. "Incidents" is a concept often used in the criminal justice field to refer to the number of incidents (e.g., crimes) that are reported in a given population within a given time period.

is typically expressed as a prevalence rate, defined as the proportion of the population that has experienced violence within a given time period, while the count of incidents is often expressed in terms of the number of incidents of violence within a given time period per 100 or 1,000 women in the population, also referred to as "frequency".

51. Technically, there is no difference between prevalence rate and incident rate if each victim suffers one and only one incident within a given time period. However, it can be expected that many women will experience repeated victimizations, in which case, the incident rate will be higher than the prevalence rate. In the context of a survey on violence against women, it is harder to count the number of incidents of violence than it is to count the number of women affected, since women who experience ongoing or frequent acts of violence may have difficulty providing an exact count of separate occurrences of violence.

52. For a survey on violence against women, it is intuitive, and recommended, to measure the extent of violence in terms of the prevalence rate, since the unit of enumeration in the survey is the woman. In contrast, the count of incidents or incident rate tends to be the more convenient measure when administrative data sources are involved, since the unit of recording is a reported incident or case, rather than the victimized person (woman). Examples of such sources include police reports and victim service utilization records. Nevertheless, it is important to attempt to obtain a measure of frequency in a survey, as this allows for a better understanding of the extent, severity and patterns of violence. Examples of how this can be done will be given later.

Topics for inclusion in surveys on violence against women

53. The Guidelines present recommended topics for inclusion in surveys on violence against women according to two levels of priority. The first priority is a set of core topics. These topics are based on the data requirements of the list of core indicators identified by the Friends of the Chair of the United Nations Statistical Commission on indicators on violence against women (see box II.1). The core topics are recommended for inclusion in all dedicated surveys on violence against women.

54. Lower priority is given to a small set of suggested optional topics. This set consists of topics that may be important only in certain regions of the world and topics that, while not of primary concern, can both expand the overall knowledge and understanding of violence against women and enhance the value of the information collected. Countries have the option of including any of the optional topics suggested, as well as any other topic not listed in these Guidelines that they deem necessary based on their specific circumstances and policy needs. When considering including a topic not listed in these Guidelines, care should be taken to ensure that the topic can be measured with a reasonable degree of reliability and that the methods used are sound.

55. The Guidelines recommend the following four core topics:

- Physical violence (see paragraphs 57 to 59)
- Sexual violence (see paragraph 60)
- Psychological violence (see paragraphs 61 to 63)
- Economic violence (see paragraphs 64 to 66).

56. The Guidelines also suggest the following three optional topics:
- Female genital mutilation (see paragraph 67)
- Attitude towards violence against women (see paragraph 68)
- Reporting to authorities/seeking help (see paragraph 69).

> **Box II.1**
>
> **Core indicators for measuring violence against women identified by the Friends of the Chair of the United Nation Statistical Commission on indicators on violence against women**
>
> In 2009, the Friends of the Chair of the United Nations Statistical Commission on indicators on violence against women identified the following core set of statistical indicators for measuring violence against women:
>
> I. Total and age-specific rate of women subjected to physical violence in the past 12 months by severity of violence, relationship to the perpetrator and frequency
>
> II. Total and age-specific rate of women subjected to physical violence during their lifetime by severity of violence, relationship to the perpetrator and frequency
>
> III. Total and age specific rate of women subjected to sexual violence in the past 12 months by severity of violence, relationship to the perpetrator and frequency
>
> IV. Total and age-specific rate of women subjected to sexual violence during their lifetime by severity of violence, relationship to the perpetrator and frequency
>
> V. Total and age-specific rate of ever-partnered women subjected to sexual and/or physical violence by current or former intimate partner in the past 12 months by frequency
>
> VI. Total and age-specific rate of ever-partnered women subjected to sexual and/or physical violence by current or former intimate partner during their lifetime by frequency
>
> VII Total and age-specific rate of ever-partnered women subjected to psychological violence in the past 12 months by an intimate partner
>
> VIII. Total and age-specific rate of ever-partnered women subjected to economic violence in the past 12 months by an intimate partner
>
> IX. Total and age-specific rate of women subjected to female genital mutilation (see paragraph 67).

Physical violence

57. In a survey situation, a detailed list of different acts of physical violence (without using the term "violence") is better able to capture physical violence than a general question about physical violence, the interpretation of which is dependent on subjective perceptions. The list of acts of physical violence provided below comprises the most common acts of physical violence against women and is a recommended minimum list for use by countries. This list is not exhaustive or closed-ended for any country and may be expanded as appropriate in each context.

58. A minimum list of acts of physical violence consists of the following:
- Slapping her
- Throwing something at her that could hurt
- Pushing or shoving or pulling her hair
- Hitting her with something
- Hitting her with fists or other objects
- Kicking, biting or dragging her

- Beating her
- Choking or burning her
- Threatening her with a knife, gun or other weapon
- Using a knife, gun or other weapon against her
- Other (leave open for the respondent to specify).

59. Other acts of physical violence that are known to be carried out or attempted against women in a specific country should be added to the list developed for that country. For example, in certain countries it might be appropriate to add such violent acts as stoning or throwing acid.

Sexual violence

60. Sexual violence is any sort of harmful or unwanted sexual behaviour that is imposed on someone. It includes acts of abusive sexual contact, forced engagement in sexual acts, attempted or completed sexual acts with a woman without her consent, sexual harassment, verbal abuse, threats, exposure, unwanted touching, incest, etc. A minimum list of acts of sexual violence, which should be expanded depending on the specific country context, consists of the following:

(a) *Rape*: Refers to engaging in the non-consensual vaginal, anal or oral penetration of a sexual nature of the body of another person with any bodily part or object, including through the use of physical violence and by putting the victim in a situation where she cannot say no or complies because of fear;

(b) *Attempted rape*: Refers to attempting to have non-consensual sexual intercourse through the use of force or threats;

(c) *Other sexual acts*: Refers to:

- Intimate touching without consent
- Sexual acts other than intercourse forced by money
- Sexual acts other than intercourse obtained through threats of physical violence
- Sexual acts other than intercourse obtained through threats to the well-being of family members
- Use of force or coercion to obtain unwanted sexual acts or any sexual activity that the female partner finds degrading or humiliating
- Other acts of sexual violence.

Psychological violence

61. Psychological violence includes a range of behaviours that encompass acts of emotional abuse and controlling behaviour. These often coexist with acts of physical and sexual violence by intimate partners and are acts of violence in themselves. Studies have shown that the use of multiple types of psychological violence is associated with an increased risk of physical and sexual violence against female partners and can have serious impacts on such women, regardless of whether or not other types of violence occurred.

62. Examples of behaviours that fall within the definition of psychological violence include the following:

(a) Emotional abuse:

- Insulting her or making her feel bad about herself
- Belittling or humiliating her in front of other people
- Deliberately scaring or intimidating her
- Threatening to hurt her or others she cares about.

(b) Controlling behaviour:

- Isolating her by preventing her from seeing family or friends
- Monitoring her whereabouts and social interactions
- Ignoring her or treating her indifferently
- Getting angry if she speaks with other men
- Making unwarranted accusations of infidelity
- Controlling her access to health care
- Controlling her access to education or the labour market.

63. Owing to concerns about the reliability of reports of psychological violence over the duration of a relationship, it is recommended that information collected on this form of violence should be limited to the past 12 months. It is further recommended that experience of psychological violence should be limited to psychological violence perpetrated by current and former intimate partners.

Economic violence

64. Economic violence is said to occur when an individual denies his intimate partner access to financial resources, typically as a form of abuse or control or in order to isolate her or to impose other adverse consequences to her well-being. Economic violence involves the following:

- Denying her access to financial resources
- Denying her access to property and durable goods
- Deliberately not complying with economic responsibilities, such as alimony or financial support for the family, thereby exposing her to poverty and hardship
- Denying her access to the labour market and education
- Denying her participation in decision-making relevant to economic status.

65. The above examples should be considered illustrative only. Psychological and economic violence, in particular, can vary significantly according to cultural context and country circumstances and should be developed with this in mind. As with data on psychological violence, the collection of data on economic violence should be limited to the past 12 months in order to avoid problems related to the ability to accurately recall events.

66. Economic violence takes many forms. As a core topic it is limited to economic violence committed by intimate partners. A further restriction is that economic violence is not relevant in the case of dating partners or boyfriends who do not reside with the woman. In

such relationships, the man is not likely to be in a position to exert control over the woman's financial situation or to limit her access to her own financial resources.

Female genital mutilation

67. Although female genital mutilation is the subject of one of the core indicators identified by the Friends of the Chair of the United Nations Statistical Commission on indicators on violence against women (see box II.1), it is not a widespread phenomenon in many countries. Consequently, it is listed as an optional topic in these Guidelines and will be discussed on briefly. Furthermore, it may be more appropriate to collect information and calculate indicators on this practice through specialized health surveys such as the Demographic and Health Surveys or the World Health Survey. That being said, female genital mutilation is an extreme form of physical, sexual and psychological violence and should not be ignored.

Attitude towards violence against women

68. An important aspect of understanding the risks associated with experiencing violence is the extent to which this violence is tolerated in the wider community. The attitudes or beliefs of respondents can be used as a proxy indicator of the level of tolerance for the use of violence against women in intimate relationships, although in certain cases surveys may not be measuring attitudes or tolerance but rather a reflection of personal experience and thus normalization. One way to measure attitudes supportive of violence against women is to ask respondents if they think a husband is justified in hitting or beating his wife under certain circumstances, for example if she goes out without telling him, neglects the children, argues with him, refuses sex with him or burns the food.[12] If an analysis of these variables and the core topics demonstrates that women who adhere to these beliefs experience higher rates of intimate partner violence, efforts to reduce violence against women will have to address women's attitudes and beliefs through public education campaigns. Caution should be used when interpreting quantitative attitudes data, however. Indeed, as norms and attitudes are often more effectively researched through qualitative methods (Jansen, 2012).

Reporting to authorities/seeking help

69. An important topic that may be included in a survey on violence against women concerns the avenues that women take to obtain assistance or gain protection when they encounter violence. It is recommended that the act of reporting physical and sexual violence to the criminal justice or legal authorities, seeking assistance from health agencies and telling others in the family and the local community should be included so that they can be analysed together with the core topics. Indeed, estimating unreported physical and sexual violence is an important aspect of estimating the overall prevalence of violence.

Descriptive variables

70. Several variables further describe, differentiate or characterize the different types of violence experienced by women. The first three variables are recommended for inclusion in all surveys on violence against women for most types of violence, while the fourth variable is an optional variable to be collected only for non-partner violence only. The variables are as follows:

---

12 These questions were included in DHS and MICS. For further information, see www.childinfo.org/attitudes_methodology.html and annex VIII.

- Severity of violence (paragraphs 71 to 76)
- Relationship of victim to perpetrator (paragraphs 77 to 79)
- Frequency of violence (paragraphs 80 to 83)
- Location of violence (paragraph 84).

Severity of violence

71. The core variable "severity of violence" attempts to qualify and quantify how severe, strict or harsh an act of violence is thought to be by the victim. Because of its multidimensional nature, it is difficult to measure severity by asking the victim directly. Both a woman's past experiences of violence and the level of risk of injuries associated with certain acts of violence need to be taken into consideration when determining how severe an act of violence is. It is therefore necessary to assess severity separately, not only according to the consequences suffered by the victim, including frequency, injury and other impacts that may make it difficult for her to carry out her usual daily activities, but also according to the nature of the acts that she has experienced.

72. It is essential during the survey to obtain some indications of severity that can be used individually or jointly to assess the severity of the violence and the impact of the violence on the women concerned. This will help to provide clarity about the nature of these experiences, to guide the development of prevention programmes and to serve as inputs in the training programmes of agencies seeking to provide appropriate responses and interventions. The impacts and consequences of each type of assault include the following:

- Physical injury
  - ◊ Small cut or bruise
  - ◊ Sprain
  - ◊ Broken tooth
  - ◊ Broken bone
  - ◊ Internal injury
- Miscarriage as a result of violence
- Need for medical treatment or hospitalization
- Medical treatment obtained
- Mental health consequences
- Violence during pregnancy
- Fear of perpetrator as a result of the violence.

73. Degrees of physical injury should be specified so that small cuts and bruises can be differentiated from serious wounds, broken bones or broken teeth, internal injuries and miscarriage. Respondents may also be given an opportunity to indicate that medical treatment was required even if it was not obtained, since isolating the woman from medical and other assistance is a frequent tactic of violent partners. In other instances, medical services are not easily obtainable in the local community; therefore, the fact that a woman did not receive medical attention cannot be assumed to indicate that her injuries were not serious enough to warrant such attention.

74. Mental health consequences can include depression, anxiety, suicidal thoughts, inability to perform paid or unpaid work and use of drugs or alcohol to help cope with the impact of the violence. Collecting information about all aspects of the severity of violence including physical injury, use of medical services and mental health consequences is important in terms of helping States to adequately plan and provide necessary services and to develop relevant policies to address the consequences of violence.

75. It is also important to identify violence that took place at specific life stages, such as during pregnancy. Violence during pregnancy is an indicator of severe violence, since it suggests a callous disregard not only for the woman but also for her unborn child.

76. "Moderate physical violence" refers to acts that did not result in bruises, cuts, broken bones, miscarriage, and/or a need for medical treatment or hospitalization, acts that did not cause the woman to be afraid of her partner or to fear for her life, and acts that took place when the woman was not pregnant. "Severe physical violence", meanwhile, refers to acts that did result in bruises, cuts, broken bones, miscarriage and/or need for medical treatment or hospitalization, acts that did cause the woman to be afraid of her partner and/or to fear for her life and acts that did take place when the woman was pregnant. In addition, acts of hitting with a fist or object, kicking, dragging or beating up, choking, deliberately burning and threatening with or using a knife, gun or other weapon are de facto considered acts of severe physical violence regardless of the consequences owing to their much higher associated risk of injuries and mental health consequences. These multiple indicators of severity can be used separately or in combination depending on the objectives of the analysis.

Relationship of victim to perpetrator

77. The relationship of the victim to the perpetrator is a key variable of discrimination in any study of violence against women. To understand women's risks of and vulnerability to violence, it is imperative to clearly identify the perpetrator and to determine whether they are related in any way or known to the victim.

78. At the very minimum, perpetrators of violence against women should be categorized so that intimate partners can be isolated from other perpetrators. Indeed, it is recommended that partner violence questions and non-partner violence questions should appear in separate sections of the survey. Studies have shown that partner violence is underestimated if questions are asked without first cueing respondents about the domestic context. In a survey on violence against women, information on the relationship of victim to perpetrator must be sufficiently detailed in order to identify and cover violence occurring in a wide range of settings and time periods. The following categories are recommended for the variable "Relationship of victim to perpetrator":

- Intimate partner[13] – A person with whom a woman maintains an intimate relationship, whether formally (marriage), through a cohabiting relationship or by regular or steady dating. These relationships must be clearly differentiated as current marital partner, current de facto partner and current steady dating partner, and former marital partner, former de facto partner and former steady dating partner. If a woman does not have a current partner, the most recent partner may be distinguished from other former intimate partners in the analysis, as needed. Occasional dating partners should not be considered intimate partners, but rather friends or acquaintances.

---

13 In some cultural settings it is entirely appropriate to frame questions about women's marital/relationship history to include steady dating and de facto relationships, prior intimate relationships and divorced partners. It may be inappropriate in other cultural settings. Countries should adapt the definition of intimate partner accordingly.

- Relative – A person within the immediate or extended family, such as a son, parent, brother, sister, grandparent, aunt, uncle, cousin or in-law. Relationships within this category must be clearly specified so that violence by fathers, for example, can be differentiated from violence by mothers, siblings or in-laws.

- Acquaintances and friends from the community – Persons that belong to the same circle of friends within a community (neighbourhood, village).

- Supervisors, co-workers – Persons in the workplace.

- Teachers, school officials, schoolmates – Persons in educational settings.

- Civil and military authorities – Officers or civil servants serving in their capacity as representatives of civil or military authorities.

- Stranger – A person unknown to the victim.

79. As much as possible, this detailed listing of relationships must be applied to all types of physical and sexual violence disclosed by respondents in order to provide an accurate profile of women's experiences of violence and to help target necessary interventions. It is recognized that relationship types will vary according to country contexts. For example, in some contexts violence involving civil and military authorities is less prominent and may be omitted; in other contexts, it may be essential to include subcategories such as mother-in-law.

Frequency of violence

80. Frequency of violence refers to the number of occurrences (1, 2, 3, 4) of violent acts or events experienced by a woman during a specific time period, such as in the past 12 months or during her lifetime.

81. When the frequency of violence is high, obtaining precise counts over a lengthy period such as during a lifetime or even in the past 12 months can be difficult. For example, violence perpetrated by a spouse or other intimate partner or by a co-worker may be ongoing or may occur on such a frequent basis that it is difficult, if not impossible, for the respondent to provide an accurate count of separate incidents. In such cases, other ways of describing frequency should be considered.

82. In the case of women who have experienced violence many times in the past 12 months or during their lifetime, it may be preferable to ask whether the specific type of violence occurred once, a few times or many times. Another alternative is to ask whether the violence occurred on such a regular basis that it can be counted as occurring every day or nearly every day, once or twice a week, once or twice a month or less than once a month. This can be combined with information on when the violence first occurred and when the violence most recently occurred in order to gauge the duration of the violence, if such information is collected as part of the survey.

83. The concept of frequency is not straightforward in the case of psychological violence. While frequency of emotional abuse may be estimated in the same way as frequency of physical or sexual violence, controlling behaviour cannot be counted as separate incidents. For example, if a woman is prevented by her partner from seeing her family or friends or must always tell her partner where she is and to whom she has spoken, it is not necessary for her partner to tell her this every time. In this sense, she is controlled by fear of the possible consequences of defying him. It is therefore recommended that questions should seek to determine whether the various controlling behaviours have occurred in the past 12 months, rather than seeking to determine the frequency of violent acts.

Location of violence

84. Information concerning the location of non-partner violence is important for prevention and strategic planning purposes and in terms of improving women's security at work and in public spaces. Examples of locations include schools, public transport, the workplace, bars and cafés, parks, deserted streets or areas, and public buildings. The list of possible locations where non-partner violence may occur will vary according to country context.

Core topics and core descriptive variables: Summary

85. Table II.1 lists the core indicators for measuring violence against women and, for each indicator, identifies the time frame, core topic(s) and descriptive variable(s) for which data should be collected.

Table II.1
Required classifications for the United Nations core set of statistical indicators for measuring violence against women [a]

	Core indicator	Time frame	Core topics				Descriptive variable		
			Physical violence	Sexual violence	Psychological violence	Economic violence	Severity of violence	Relationship of victim to the perpetrator	Frequency of violence
All women	I	Past 12 months	x				x	x	x
	II	Lifetime	x				x	x	x
	III	Past 12 months		x			x	x	x
	IV	Lifetime		x			x	x	x
Ever-partnered women	V	Past 12 months	x	x					x
	VI	Lifetime	x	x					x
	VII	Past 12 months			x				
	VIII	Past 12 months				x			

[a] The core set of indicators identified by the Friends of the Chair of the United Nations Statistical Commission on indicators on violence against women contain nine indicators, but these Guidelines cover only indicators I-VIII. See paragraph 67 for information on indicator IX.

Personal characteristics of respondents

86. Although women are vulnerable to violence in all settings and contexts, some groups of women are affected disproportionately. In order to effectively guide policies, surveys on violence against women must include sufficient detail about the personal characteristics of respondents so that factors associated with different types of violence can be identified.

87. The two most important personal characteristics that should be ascertained from respondents in a survey on violence against women are as follows:

- Marital/relationship status
- Age.

These two variables constitute the minimum, or core, set of personal characteristic variables for which data should be collected in a survey on violence against women.

Marital/relationship status

88. Surveys on violence against women must ascertain the marital or relationship status of respondents at the time of the survey and identify any relationships they may have had in the past. This information is critical for identifying women at risk of intimate partner violence.

89. Marital/relationship status refers to the living situation of a person in relation to the marriage laws and customs of the country. The variable for current living situation may, depending on the context of the country, include the following four categories: married, de facto married (living with a man but not formally married to him), involved in a regular or steady dating relationship (involved with a man, but not living together) and not in a relationship (not married, living with a man or involved in a regular or steady relationship). The same categories should be used to identify previous relationships. The category "involved in a regular or steady dating relationship" is included because women in this category are at risk of violence from their steady dating partners. This category may not be needed in countries where women do not have relationships with men prior to marriage. However, the need to be as inclusive as possible when classifying women's relationship status cannot be emphasized enough.

90. Many women will report previous relationships that ended in separation, divorce or widowhood in addition to their current relationship. It is a woman's current relationship status that is important, not her current legal marital status. For example, a woman may be separated from a marital partner and at the same time living in a de facto relationship with another man. In this example, the woman's current marital/relationship status is de facto married (living with a man but not formally married to him), while her previous marital/relationship status is married.

Age

91. Age is the interval of time between a person's date of birth and the date of the survey, expressed in completed years. Every effort should be made to ascertain the exact age of each respondent. In situations in which respondents do not know or are reluctant to provide their age, their approximate age in terms of a range (e.g., 25 to 29 years of age) may be obtained.

92. Studies have found age to be an important correlate of experience of violence, both inside and outside the home. Partner violence in the 12 months prior to the survey is generally more prevalent among younger women, while lifetime partner violence is generally more prevalent for older women because of their longer exposure to the risk of violence.

93. Data on other personal characteristics are often collected as part of a survey on violence against women in order to better understand whether, and to what extent such characteristics make women more vulnerable to violence. This additional information is helpful when developing appropriate responses and designing targeted prevention strategies.

94. The list of additional personal characteristics to be included in a survey on violence against women depends on the heterogeneity of the target population, the national context and the objectives of the study. The personal characteristics for which data may be collected in such a survey include the following:

- Age at first marriage
- Educational attainment and literacy
- Economic activity status
- Place of residence

- Ethnicity
- Religion
- Language.

Age at first marriage

95. The prevalence of early marriage in a society is indicative of the low status of women in society. In a society characterized by male dominance over women, young wives are particularly vulnerable to violence by their husbands.

Educational attainment and literacy

96. Educational attainment and literacy is an important correlate of experience of violence and the existence of barriers that prevent women from seeking help or accessing resources. Low educational attainment may result in a lack of awareness among women of their legal rights, and may limit their ability to access resources or other support systems, to escape a violent partner and to obtain paid employment and live independently. That said, some studies have suggested that the relationship between education and experience of violence is not straightforward.

Economic activity status

97. Women are considered to be economically active if they work for pay or profit for a business or enterprise, on a family farm or service undertaking or in self-employment. Economically active women have access to economic resources; this may give them status in the family. Being economically active may also increase their ability to escape violence in the home and to live independently of a violent partner, though this will also depend on control of resources.

Place of residence

98. This variable refers to a respondent's place of usual residence; that is, the place where she has lived continuously for most of the past 12 months or the place where she intends to live for at least the next six months. Place of usual residence may be categorized as urban or rural. This is important when studying the differential risk of violence among rural women and urban women, as well as differences in women's access to support services and barriers that prevent them from obtaining help. Women living in rural areas may face barriers that prevent them from fleeing an abusive relationship or accessing available resources owing to limited mobility or transportation options. Additionally, fewer resources and less support may be available to rural women owing to sparse and widely dispersed populations, the costs associated with service delivery or other characteristics of rural communities that warrant examination.

Ethnicity

99. Ethnicity refers to the ethnic group with which the respondent identifies. An ethnic group is a group of individuals who share a common heritage, language, identity, culture or ancestry. Identification of the ethnicity of respondents is important when assessing differential levels of violence among groups such as indigenous populations and ethnocultural minorities and can help identify the special needs of these groups.

Religion

100. Religion refers to the respondent's spiritual beliefs or religiosity. Typically, religion is classified in terms of the dominant categories of religion in the study area. Religion is associated with cultural and strongly held personal beliefs that can affect the social status of women and their willingness to report partner and non-partner violence to the authorities. Some studies have shown religious beliefs to increase the likelihood of violent victimization by intimate partners, while others have shown religiosity (i.e., frequent attendance at organized religious practices) to reduce the risk of violent victimization. In contexts where religion is a sensitive issue, a question on religion should not be included.

Language

101. Language refers to languages currently spoken by the respondent. Depending on the country context, language, religion and ethnicity may reflect equivalent characteristics and may not therefore all be needed. Language may be a barrier that prevents women who experience violence in the home or elsewhere from obtaining help.

Personal characteristics of intimate partners

102. While a knowledge of the situation of respondents is important for many purposes, including identification of risk factors and provision of support services and other resources, the introduction of legislative changes and the development of strategies to prevent partner violence depend to a large degree on an in-depth understanding of the root causes of violence, which in turn depends on a knowledge of the correlates of violence as they relate to partner characteristics.

103. In order to better understand the risks associated with intimate partner violence, the following partner characteristics should be included:

- Age
- Educational attainment and literacy
- Economic activity status
- Substance abuse
- Witnessing partner violence or experiencing childhood violence in the family of origin.

104. Given the complexity of gathering this information for multiple partners and the burden this implies for respondents, it is recommended that the collection of data on intimate partner characteristics should be restricted to the current or most recent partner.

105. Data on personal characteristics should be obtained for intimate partners regardless of whether or not the partner was violent, in order to ascertain whether and how specific characteristics predispose men to violence.

Age

106. In the same way that age is a correlate of experience of violence, so too is age a correlate of perpetration of intimate partner violence. Every effort should therefore be made to ascertain the exact age of intimate partners. Where age can be accurately reported or estimated, it should be recorded either as age in completed years or as year of birth. Where age cannot be reported with precision, age groups (e.g., 25 to 29 years of age) can be used.

Educational attainment and literacy

107. Educational attainment and literacy may be an important correlate of perpetration of intimate partner violence. Low educational attainment may affect men's awareness of legal codes and women's rights. It may also limit their ability to seek support such as income support for the family, or to obtain and retain paid employment, leading to frustration and low self-esteem.

Economic activity status

108. Economic activity status is an indicator of the economic resources available to the family. Employment is also an important social resource for men in societies where participation in the labour market is an essential indicator of traditional masculinity. Lack of paid employment may therefore be associated with intimate partner violence owing to associated stresses in the family or efforts by the man to use violence to exert control over his female partner.

Substance abuse

109. Substance abuse is commonly identified as a correlate or predictor of perpetration of intimate partner violence. Substance abuse includes excessive or problematic consumption of alcohol (whether commercial or home-brewed), consumption of illegal drugs, misuse of prescription medications and misuse of consumer products in order to achieve an altered state (e.g., sniffing petrol). Measures of substance abuse may include frequency of consumption or intoxication, and amount consumed within a typical consumption period. Studies have shown that the most important predictor of intimate partner violence related to substance abuse is not frequency of consumption but frequency of intoxication.

Witnessing partner violence or experiencing childhood violence in the family of origin

110. Many studies have confirmed an association between early experiences of violence in the home and use of violence later in life. Male children who witness their mothers being abused by their fathers have a greater propensity for using such behaviours against their own female partners later in life. Men's early experiences of violence can be measured by asking women whether their partners witnessed domestic violence as a childhood. Experience in various countries has shown that women can reliably report on their partners' childhood experiences of violence (including their partners' own experience of being beaten as a child).

Personal characteristics of non-intimate partners perpetrators

111. In the case of non-intimate partner perpetrators, women may not be able to provide information on many of the characteristics that would be of interest. Data on the relationship of the victim to the perpetrator should be collected as a core variable (see paragraphs 77 to 79).

Sex

112. In most circumstances, the sex of the perpetrator is accurately known and can be recalled by respondents. Data on this variable should be collected in addition to data on the relationship of the victim to the perpetrator.

113.   In some instances, the sex of the perpetrator will be evident from the relationship category selected (e.g., mother or sister). For other responses, it will be necessary to include an additional question in order to ascertain the sex of the perpetrator or perpetrators, when there are more than one.

Chapter III
Planning a survey on violence against women

114. Careful planning is critical to the success of any survey or survey module on violence against women. General principles and rules for all statistical sample surveys are applicable to these specialized surveys but, in addition, specific considerations should be taken into account in order to ensure the quality and reliability of the results as well as the ethical and safe conduct of the survey throughout all phases. Topics addressed in this chapter include preparatory processes and the detailed steps required to plan such surveys in compliance with international statistical standards. Attention is given to the following steps: establishing the legal basis; consultation with stakeholders; specifying the objectives of the survey; choosing the mode of data collection; budget and timeline; establishing the organizational structure; sample design; selection of interviewers; and study protocol. The essential steps in planning a survey on violence against women are listed in table III.1. Some of the steps will be addressed in subsequent chapters.

Establishing the legal basis

115. Establishing the legal basis for a survey on violence against women is particularly important given the sensitivity of both the topic and the information to be collected. All entities involved in the process must have an unambiguous mandate to undertake the survey and collect the sensitive and personal information required with the highest consideration for quality and safety.

116. The mandate for collecting official statistics typically emanates from national statistical legislation, such as a law on official statistics. Steps will need to be taken to include the topic of violence against women in the appropriate legislation. Once the legal basis has been established, surveys on violence against women must be incorporated into the national statistical system's programme as a regular data collection activity. The periodicity of violence against women surveys will depend on the capacity of the national statistical agency but should ideally be at least every five to ten years in order to allow for the tracking of trends.

Consultation with stakeholders

117. Consultations with survey sponsors, stakeholders and data users must be initiated in the early planning phases of the survey and undertaken periodically at specific stages. These consultations are essential for formulating the objectives and scope of the survey and for identifying the uses to which the data will be put, which then determines many other aspects of the project, such as design and content of the questionnaire, sample size and sampling frame and mode of interviewing and, later on, data analysis, interpretation of results and formulation of recommendations.

118. The pool of stakeholders that will be invited to provide input into a statistical sample survey on violence against women will depend on national circumstances. It should always include government agencies that will use the results of the survey for policy formulation, programme development and research. In most settings, stakeholders will also include health and social service agencies, counsellors for abused women, legislators, researchers in governmental and non-governmental organizations, police and other criminal justice officials, non-governmental groups advocating on behalf of female victims of violence and others as local circumstances dictate.

119. These consultations are also important in terms of providing a forum for developing consensus on the range of concepts and detail required, setting priorities, making stakeholders aware of the constraints of the project, arriving at compromises, maintaining realistic expectations and determining the form in which the data will be produced, including levels of disaggregation and dissemination strategies (UNODC and UNECE, 2010). Engaging stakeholders throughout all phases of the project also ensures that there will be knowledgeable experts who are prepared to speak about the results once the findings are disseminated.

120. The scope of the survey and level of precision of the data collected will also be determined through consultations with stakeholders, balanced with the resources available for the survey. At the very minimum, the data collected should allow for the production of the core indicators as per the guidelines presented in chapter II, i.e., the core indicators identified by the Friends of the Chair of the United Nations Statistical Commission on indicators on violence against women (see box II.1). Depending on the requirements of stakeholders, the level of disaggregation of statistics by major civil divisions and subgroups of the population must be decided, as this has a direct impact on the sample size and, therefore, on the cost of the survey.

Table III.1
Essential steps in planning a survey on violence against women

Step	Main tasks
Establishing the legal basis	• Ensure there is a legal provision for surveys on violence against women • Ensure that the survey is incorporated into the national statistical system's programme as a regular, periodic data collection activity
Consultation with stakeholders	• Establish survey objectives, parameters, data requirements and outputs
Specifying the objectives of the survey	• Set out the objectives, scope, purpose and goals of the survey • Balance objectives with available budget and other resources
Choosing the mode(s) of data collection	• Establish how interviews will be conducted (face to face, by telephone or by another method) and how computer technology will be integrated into interviewing and data capture
Budget and timelines	• Establish timelines for all phases of the project • Identify all budget items, including staffing requirements, testing requirements, sample size, mode of interviewing, data collection system development, training of interviewers, fieldwork (including safety and support measures), data analysis and dissemination (see table III.3) • Identify available technology and equipment purchasing needs
Establishing the organizational structure	• Identify all tasks and the expertise required to carry out all aspects of the work (see table III.4) • Clarify the roles, responsibilities and reporting structures of all managers, supervisors, field staff and other project staff

Step	Main tasks
Questionnaire design and testing	• Identify data requirements through consultation with stakeholders • Conduct research to identify questionnaires that have been successfully used in similar settings for similar objectives • Conduct focus group discussions and other qualitative research • Draft questions and test them with small samples of the target population • Prepare a test questionnaire and modify and finalize it following the pilot test
Sample design	• Identify the sampling frame • Establish the sample size on the basis of survey objectives, expected prevalence of key phenomena, level of precision required and ethical and safety considerations • Identify the most appropriate sampling method
Selection of interviewers	• Develop selection criteria (including selecting more interviewers than needed) • Recruit interviewers from outside the national statistical agency if needed
Training	• Identify the training needs of interviewers, supervisors and other project staff • Develop training manuals and other materials • Conduct basic training as well as training on specific aspects of interviewing on this topic in order to ensure compliance with ethical and safety guidelines • Assess the competencies of field staff following the pilot test and provide remedial training if needed
Data collection	• Establish the time period for fieldwork • Establish the number of interviewers and field supervisors required for the planned sample size and mode of interviewing
Data capture, editing and verification	• Identify the technology, processes, staff and time required • Plan the logistics for these processes
Data analysis	• Determine analytical requirements through consultations with stakeholders and data users • Plan the format of analytical outputs
Dissemination	• Identify the methods to be used to disseminate the results of the survey • Identify the requirements for a communication strategy
Evaluation	• Establish an evaluation strategy • Determine data requirements for evaluation early in the planning of the survey so that necessary data can be collected throughout all survey processes

Specifying the objectives of the survey

121. In general, the objective of a survey on violence against women is to quantify the prevalence of specified forms of violence experienced by women in a country within a specific time period, such as in the recent past (past 12 months) and/or during their lifetime. The purpose of such a survey is to provide comprehensive and reliable statistics in order to guide the development of policies that aim ultimately to eradicate violence against women.

122. A clear statement of objectives should be developed in consultation with stakeholders, funders and data users. Clarifying these objectives will help to keep the project focused throughout all phases of development, implementation, data analysis and dissemination. Within the broad survey objectives, specific goals should be identified, for example, timely production of statistics on various forms of violence against women for specific subpopulations or geographical subdivisions, analytical reports focusing on intimate partner violence and other outputs.

Choosing the mode of data collection

123. Decisions involving the mode of data collection should be made early in the planning phase of a survey on violence against women. The mode of data collection has implications for

the cost of the survey, the efficacy of data collection and capture and ultimately the quality of the data collected. Thus, the various options, including the use of electronic technology at any specific stage of data collection and capture, should be thoroughly and carefully considered. Additionally, in a survey on violence against women, the choice of the mode of data collection must consider the need to ensure the safety of the respondent and to safeguard the privacy of the respondent and the confidentiality of the data.

124. In principle, all modes of data collection are able to capture the required data if questionnaires are constructed appropriately, thoroughly tested with the target population and implemented with due consideration for the sensitivity of the topic. In practice, the mode of data collection varies across countries and generally depends on the budget available and on context-specific logistical considerations. Besides the available resources and the objectives of the survey, factors to be considered when determining the mode of data collection include the literacy level of the target population, telephone coverage in the study area, available sampling frames, the physical characteristics of the targeted geographical areas, the availability of computer technology and expertise in using this technology.

125. Several modes of data collection have been used successfully in surveys on violence against women. A combination of methods may be employed within a country, if the logistical situations so dictate; for example, in some countries, telephone interviews may be used in major cities and face-to-face interviews in rural settings.

126. The most common modes of data collection may be categorized as follows:

   (a) Interviewer-assisted methods
      (i) Face-to-face interviewing
         - Computer-assisted personal interviewing (CAPI)
         - Paper questionnaires
      (ii) Telephone interviewing
         - Computer-assisted telephone interviewing (CATI)
   (b) Self-administered methods
      (i) Self-administered paper questionnaires (postal survey)
      (ii) Self-administered questionnaires on disk (disk-by-mail) or other storage device (CD-Rom or USB flash drive) and web-based questionnaires
   (c) Combination of methods
      (i) Computer-assisted self-interviewing (CASI) incorporated into CAPI.

Each method will be elaborated in the sections that follow.

Interviewer-assisted methods

127. The personal contact entailed in a survey where interviewers are managing the questionnaire provides several advantages for a survey on violence against women. These include the ability of interviewers in terms of persuading or motivating selected respondents to participate, explaining the objectives of the survey, clarifying question wording, probing for deeper responses, assessing respondent safety and reducing potential harm to respondents. Interviewer-assisted surveys can be conducted face to face or by telephone. The precise techniques vary depending on how technology is integrated into the interview situation.

128. Whether conducted face to face or by telephone, the interview can be completed using paper and pencil alone or with the aid of a computer. Owing to advances in technology,

however, telephone surveys are at present conducted almost entirely with the aid of computer technology. In all cases, data should be collected in electronic format wherever possible, as this facilitates data capture and editing.

Face-to-face interviewing

129. Face-to-face interviewing is the most common method of conducting surveys on violence against women in developing and transitional countries, where incomplete telephone coverage rules out the possibility of telephone interviewing.

130. Face-to-face interviewing has many advantages. The personal contact between interviewers and respondents helps to build rapport, which leads to a greater willingness to participate, lower drop-out rates and higher disclosures of sensitive experiences.[14] This is particularly important in surveys on violence against women, where rapport is critical for developing the trust required to disclose very personal experiences. Interviewers are able to use non-verbal cues and prompts as well as visual aids such as showcards to explain specific concepts and to allow respondents to point to the responses to sensitive questions without responding verbally. Respondents may therefore be more willing to disclose personal information if this method is available to them.

131. Respondents in face-to-face interviews also tend to provide greater detail and to be more tolerant of longer interviews. They are also less likely than respondents in telephone interviews to exhibit response set bias, such as responding "no" to each question about physical or sexual violence, which can occur out of boredom or a wish to speed up the interview.

132. Face-to-face interviews may instil higher confidence in the legitimacy of the survey as interviewers can provide their official credentials. Interviewer presence also makes it easier to identify the selected respondents, which can have a positive impact on participation rates.

133. With face-to-face interviews, interviewers have greater control over the interview environment. They can more easily determine whether other persons are present during the interview and whether it would be safer for the respondent if the interview were rescheduled (Holbrook, Green and Krosnick, 2003; Statistics Canada, 2003; UNODC and UNECE, 2010). Also, interviewers will be able to refer respondents as needed and to give them information on potential sources of support.

Computer-assisted personal interviews (CAPI)

134. Surveys conducted through face-to-face interviews can incorporate computer technology in the form of computer-assisted personal interviewing (CAPI), utilizing what is called an electronic questionnaire. In this method, the questionnaire is programmed into the interviewer's computer in advance of the fieldwork. Survey questions are read out by the interviewer as they appear on the computer screen, while responses are entered into the database in real time. This automated technology allows survey designers to formulate a complex questionnaire with skip patterns or filter questions which automatically skip sections of the questionnaire that are not relevant to the respondent (e.g., skipping sections about partner violence for women who have not had an intimate partner or blocking questions about a specific form of violence for women who did not experience it). Compared to paper questionnaires, the CAPI method allows a greater number of open-ended questions to be included, since interviewers can more easily capture detailed narrative responses.

---

14 In an empirical study of disclosure of rape, sexual assault and intimate partner violence in the National Crime Victimization Survey in the United States, rape/sexual assault was reported more than twice as frequently and intimate partner violence was reported three times more frequently when interviews were conducted face to face rather than by telephone (Coker and Stasny, 1995).

135. Preprogramming ensures that the interview can progress smoothly. Interviewers cannot make errors by skipping questions or sections since filters and skips are automated. Checks for missing or invalid entries are also built into the program, so that interviewers are alerted when the value entered falls outside a valid range of responses. These immediate feedback mechanisms improve the quality of the data collected.

136. Capturing data electronically has the further advantage of eliminating an additional data entry step, thus reducing not only the costs and time involved in preparing a data file for analysis, but also coding and transcription errors that can occur when responses are copied from paper forms to an electronic database.

137. The need to securely store completed paper questionnaires is also eliminated with the CAPI method, thus helping to protect the privacy of respondents and the confidentiality of data. Tabulations on results and on interviewer and disclosure rates can be produced quickly on an ad hoc basis throughout the fieldwork in order to keep track of response rates and other performance indicators.

138. When considering the CAPI method, the cost of providing all interviewers with a laptop computer or similar equipment must be incorporated into the project budget. Less expensive tablets and notebooks are becoming widely available, meaning that computer costs may be offset by savings derived from eliminating the printing, editing and transport of the questionnaires and the transfer of data from paper forms to an electronic database.

Paper questionnaires

139. If, for budgetary or resource reasons, it is not feasible to incorporate computer technology into the data collection process, the layout of paper questionnaires must be kept relatively simple so that interviewers can easily follow the skip patterns and routing errors are avoided. Respondents will be less motivated to continue an interview that seems disorganized or in which there are large delays while interviewers navigate through pages.

140. One advantage that paper questionnaires have over CAPI is that they can be developed more quickly and easily. The "front end" development of paper questionnaires is quicker and therefore less costly than that of electronic questionnaires. However, the "back end" tasks associated with processing paper questionnaires are more time-consuming and costly than those associated with questionnaires that rely on computer technology (de Leeuw, Hox and Kef, 2003). In addition, inconsistent and missing data are more often a problem with paper questionnaires, since data cannot be verified with respondents once the interview is over.

Telephone interviewing

141. Telephone interviewing is commonly used in locations where telephone coverage is complete or almost complete and an up-to-date sampling frame that does not rely solely on telephone number listings is available. In areas where these requirements can be met, telephone interviewing can result in substantial cost savings, especially where the target population is dispersed over a large geographical area. Several attempts can be made to reach selected households at very little additional cost and interviewers can be flexible about arranging interviewing times or continuing interviews that are interrupted by family members or respondent fatigue.

142. Telephone surveys have many additional advantages that make this mode of interviewing a useful and popular choice for surveys on violence against women in some countries. Telephone interviews are less susceptible to interviewer effects and provide the anonymity that can encourage disclosure of stigmatized behaviours and sensitive or embarrassing experiences. Respondents are also provided with privacy, as others in the household are unable to hear the questions being posed, thus ensuring that confidentiality and safety are managed

more effectively. However, if other household members are present during the interview the interviewer may not be aware of this. Interviewer safety is not a factor.

143.   In telephone surveys, computer-assisted telephone interviewing (CATI) has become a common practice in industrialized countries. With this method, telephone numbers are usually generated by random digit dialling or other methods of random number generation, thereby circumventing the problem of unlisted telephone numbers. Interviewers read questions from a laptop computer screen and enter respondents' answers on the computer. Answers are then transferred directly into a database. The CATI method operates in much the same way as the CAPI method and the same advantages exist, such as ability to devise a complex questionnaire with elaborate skip patterns, immediate data editing, reduction of data entry errors and rapid production of a data file for analysis at the end of the interviewing period.

144.   Before a final decision is made to use telephone interviewing, project managers must identify potential disadvantages and put in place plans to reduce any negative impacts. For example, respondents are less tolerant of long telephone interviews and a questionnaire on violence against women can be very long. With telephone interviewing, establishing rapport and putting respondents at ease can also be challenging. Visual aids cannot be used. Data confidentiality and respondent safety are more difficult to ensure, as interviewers cannot ascertain that respondents are alone at the time of the interview. Interviewers cannot establish the identity and availability of selected respondents as easily as they can in face-to-face interviews and respondents cannot as easily establish the authenticity of the survey, both of which may affect participation rates.[15] Technological advances in caller identification and call blocking that screen out unknown callers and toll-free numbers have also begun to affect response rates.

145.   In addition, women living in violent situations may be prevented from using the telephone or may not want to take the risk of undergoing detailed questioning over the telephone if their movements are monitored by a violent partner. It is therefore critical that interviewers are trained to recognize this possibility and are able to provide options to respondents as to how they may participate.

146.   Owing to the rising use of mobile phones, the number of households without landlines is increasing. This poses a significant challenge to telephone surveys. A sample that excludes households without landlines can be biased, as these households may be disproportionately lower-income or transient or living in unstable housing situations, all of which are important correlates of violence against women. Households with mobile phones and no landlines also tend to be younger and younger women are at higher risk of violence both by intimate partners and other perpetrators.

147.   Random digit dialling can include mobile phone numbers in the event that a working bank of mobile phone numbers can be obtained from telephone service providers; however, this is not usually done because of the higher costs of calling mobile phones. Problems have also been encountered in securing the participation of mobile phone owners, as they frequently receive the invitation to participate while they are in public places or "on the move", situations that are not conducive to participating in a survey on violence against women.

---

[15] Controlled experiments comparing response rates of telephone and face-to-face surveys are in short supply; however, among the nine countries included in the International Violence against Women Survey, where other aspects of the methodology were the same, countries where interviews were conducted by telephone had lower response rates than countries where interviews were conducted face to face (Johnson, Ollus and Nevala, 2008). It may be easier to refuse to participate over the telephone than when faced with an interviewer.

148. However, there may be situations in which it is feasible to include mobile phone numbers in the sample frame for the survey. In such cases, survey managers must ensure that mobile phone users are represented in the sample as appropriate, taking into consideration their characteristics and their proportion in the population of telephone users. The survey questionnaire and all protocols will need to be thoroughly tested among mobile phone users; safety and confidentiality requirements must be met. A number of factors—for example, the time of day to call and flexibility regarding the need to reschedule interviews—need to be taken into consideration.

149. A comparison of the main features of face-to-face and telephone interviewing is presented in table III.2.

Table III.2
Comparison of face-to-face and telephone interviewing

Feature	Face-to-face interviewing	Telephone interviewing
Budget	Costs are higher owing to the need to travel to households, to return when selected respondents are not available and to travel in pairs, the higher supervisor-to-interviewer ratio and the possible use of paper questionnaires.	Costs are lower owing to the centralizations of fieldwork, the lower supervisor-to-interviewer ratio and, in most cases, the absence of paper questionnaires.
Use of computer technology	CAPI and CASI applications are advisable but face-to-face surveys are often conducted using paper questionnaires.	CATI applications are typically used.
Questionnaire content and design	Paper questionnaires must be easy to follow, with few skips or filters, and clearly formatted. CAPI questionnaires can be more complex. Show cards and other visual aids can be used.	With CATI, questionnaires can be more complex with many skips and filters. Confidentiality is easier to ensure. Visual aids cannot be used.
Sample design	Cluster sampling may be needed. It may not be possible to reach all geographical areas. The sample may have to be reduced to stay within budget. The participation rate is higher.	Sample design is more flexible. Random samples are easier to achieve. The sample can be larger and more geographically dispersed. Sample bias can result from incomplete telephone coverage.
Training of interviewers	Interviewers require training on sample selection and on the handling of CAPI/CASI or paper questionnaires. Interviewers require training on ensuring interviewer and respondent safety, responding to emotional reactions and offering community-based support in a safe way.	Interviewers require training on CATI. Interviewers require training on ensuring respondent safety, responding to emotional reactions and offering support in the community.
Field work	Because fieldwork is less centralized, it is more difficult to supervise and support interviewers. A higher supervisor-to-interviewer ratio is required. Paper questionnaires require special handling to guard against breaches of confidentiality. Interviews tend to be longer. Participation rates are higher.	Because fieldwork is highly centralized, interviewers can be directly supervised and supported. A lower supervisor-to-interviewer ratio is required. Confidentiality is easier to ensure. Refusal rates are higher.
Data entry	Data entry in surveys using paper questionnaires is time-consuming and costly. Paper questionnaires have higher rates of data entry and coding errors, first by interviewers then by data entry clerks. Data entry steps are reduced with CAPI.	With CATI, data edits built into computer programming help to reduce data entry errors.

Feature	Face-to-face interviewing	Telephone interviewing
Quality control	With paper questionnaires, data capture requires several extra steps. Interviewers' work cannot therefore always be overseen in real time. This is particularly true when it is not possible to perform questionnaire editing in the field, immediately after each interview. CAPI and CASI applications capture data in real time with built-in error checks but require an extra step to submit data to field supervisors.	With CATI, data are captured and a data file is created in real time. Errors can be detected and remedial action can be taken more quickly.

Self-administered methods

150. The self-administered mode of data collection, whereby respondents complete the questionnaire themselves without the assistance of an interviewer, is less often used in surveys on violence against women. This method requires respondents either to enter their responses into a database by answering questions on a computer or to complete a questionnaire on paper (or data storage device) and then to return it by mail to the agency conducting the survey.

Self-administered paper questionnaires (postal survey)

151. The self-administered paper questionnaire, sometimes called a postal survey, has the advantage of offering respondents privacy and anonymity, which can result in a greater willingness to disclose sensitive or embarrassing information. As sexual assault and partner violence are highly stigmatizing, the removal of an interviewer may encourage more honest victimization reports. Self-administration also provides respondents with flexibility and control over the pace of responding, which allows them time to reflect on the question and to respond more accurately (de Leeuw, Hox and Kef, 2003). Finally, the flexibility of a self-administered questionnaire allows a respondent to complete the survey at a time when their spouse or other family members are not present or to pause the survey should they be interrupted unexpectedly.

152. A self-administered paper questionnaire is typically less expensive than any method requiring the assistance of an interviewer. It has the added advantage of eliminating potential negative impacts or biases that interviewers may introduce to an interviewing situation by way of their tone of voice or interview manner, as well as by their personal characteristics such as race, ethnicity or age.

153. However, the use of self-administered paper questionnaires for a survey on violence against women should be approached with caution. They typically have the lowest response rates of all methods and result in high item non-response. They are also subject to illogical responses, since there is no opportunity for interviewers to clarify or probe and there are no built-in checks for errors or missing data. Thus, paper questionnaires must be as short and as straightforward as possible, avoiding complex skip sequences and filter questions, to reduce the possibility of error. With postal surveys, it is not possible to know whether the respondent answered the questions without input from others; this may affect the truthfulness and accuracy of responses. This method also requires a high degree of literacy in the study population, which makes it impractical in many contexts.

Self-administered questionnaires on disk (disk-by-mail) or other storage device (CD-ROM or USB flash drive) and web-based questionnaires

154. A variant of the self-administered paper questionnaire is the computer-assisted equivalent, in which a data storage device—disk, CD-ROM or USB flash drive—containing the

questionnaire and computer program is mailed to selected participants. Respondents install the program, complete the survey and return the data storage device containing the completed questionnaire (de Leeuw, Hox and Kef, 2003). An alternative form of this approach is the Internet- or web-based survey where respondents are invited electronically (either through a website or by e-mail) to participate in the survey through a dedicated web address or as an electronic document sent as an e-mail attachment. The software includes built-in checks for missing, invalid or inconsistent data along with help menus and prompts to guide the user and thereby to encourage completion of the survey.

155. These approaches have the advantage of eliminating interviewer effects, providing privacy and allowing flexibility regarding the time and place of participant response. They are also very low-cost and may help to improve participation rates among younger people, who are often difficult to reach using more conventional methods such as by telephone.

156. At present, however, the possibility of applying these methods to surveys on violence against women is limited. These methods require widespread computer ownership and Internet access, as well as literacy in the survey language. Internet access is presently not sufficiently widespread in any country to enable a sampling frame of Internet users to be designed. Web-based procedures may be used in combination with other methods to ensure that women without computer ownership or Internet access are able to participate (UNODC and UNECE, 2010).

Combination of methods

Computer-assisted self-interviewing (CASI) incorporated into computer-assisted personal interviewing (CAPI)

157. With rising computer literacy, some surveys on violence against women have elected to incorporate computer-assisted self-interviewing (CASI) into the CAPI method.[16] In this method, interviews are conducted by interviewers, who ask questions in face-to-face mode and enter responses into a computer. When they reach the section with sensitive questions, such as those relating to intimate partner violence, interviewers hand the computer to respondents so that they can complete this section on their own by reading the questions and entering their responses themselves. This gives respondents complete privacy when disclosing sensitive experiences.

158. The CASI method eliminates interviewer effects and reduces anxiety and social desirability effects as well as the third-party effects of a spouse or other family member being present during the interview. It is recommended that all face-to-face interviews should consider developing a CAPI application if the cost of laptops, tablets or notebooks can be accommodated in the project budget and that CAPI applications should incorporate a CASI component for sensitive sections, such as violence experienced. The CASI method will not be feasible, however, in contexts where literacy rates are low or respondents are not familiar with computer technology.

Budget and timeline

159. The cost of implementing a statistical sample survey on violence against women will depend on what decisions are made with respect to many aspects, including but not limited

---

16 One example of a survey where CASI has been added to a CAPI application is the British Crime Survey, which has included a CASI component with modules measuring domestic violence, sexual assault and stalking (Mirrlees-Black, 1999; Walby and Allen, 2004).

to the scope of the survey, the sample size and design, the mode of data collection and data capture, the use of computer technology at various stages of the survey and the outputs to be delivered. There are usually also costs attached to the special ethical and safety measures that need to be in place, such as overrecruiting interviewers and hiring counsellors. The need to balance these choices with available resources is critical. Cost considerations and decisions are required at the very early stages of survey planning, as they will impact on the survey processes.

160. Resources required for the conduct of the survey include not only financial resources, but also personnel resources. Technological resources are also required for data collection, capture, processing and dissemination. Setting clear parameters, at an early stage, about the maximum resources that can be expended on each phase of the survey will guide the development and design of each phase of the survey and overall help to ensure that the project objectives are met within the prescribed budget (UNODC and UNECE, 2010).

161. A realistic appraisal of cost must take account of the cost of using existing staff, infrastructure and facilities. For example, the impact of adding responsibilities for the survey on violence against women to the regular workload of staff must be recognized and planned for, so as not to compromise the quality of the survey or disrupt the regular work programme.

162. Related to the budget is the need to establish timetables for all phases of the project and to ensure that they correspond to available resources. Shorter timelines will mean that more personnel may have to be assigned to certain phases of the work. Timelines must be realistic in terms of available resources so that the quality of the data and outputs are not compromised by time pressures.

163. The cost of the survey will depend to a large extent on the size and design of the sample. Working within the available budget, the sample size determination will have to take into consideration the survey objectives, the expected prevalence of violence against women in the target population, the planned level of disaggregation of the data and the level of precision required for the estimates. Low expected prevalence, high levels of precision and a need to conduct analysis for subgroups in the population all point to the requirement for larger samples.

164. The resources required for the development and testing of the survey instruments and protocols could represent a considerable part of the survey budget. This will be the case especially if a survey on violence against women is to be conducted in the country for the first time. Resources should be allocated to the following areas:

- Organizing and conducting of focus groups or discussions with panels of stakeholders and experts in order to adapt international guidelines on key concepts and definitions to national circumstances

- Design and testing of questionnaires, including cognitive and other forms of testing (and translation if an existing questionnaire is being adapted and translated)

- Printing, translation and programming of questionnaires (as appropriate to the mode of data collection)

- Preparation and testing of data capture systems.

165. The mode of interviewing will also have an impact on the budget. Postal and Internet-based surveys have lower costs associated with data collection, telephone surveys are more costly and face-to-face interviews are the most costly, especially in large geographical areas with sparse populations living in remote areas. If there is a need to interview subgroups such as minority populations, interviews may have to be conducted in different languages; this also adds to the cost of the survey. Depending on the mode of interviewing, budgets may

have to incorporate new computer equipment. Additional related costs may include network, telephone and Internet charges.

166. The quality of interviewing is crucial to the success of a survey on violence against women. It is imperative that the budget allocates an adequate amount towards the recruitment and specialized training of the interviewers and staff overseeing various aspects of the survey. The sensitivity and difficulty of broaching the topic of violence against women, coupled with the need to satisfy safety and ethical requirements, dictate that interviewers and supervisors need to be extremely well-trained and prepared for all possible situations that they are apt to encounter. Resources should also be allocated for the preparation and reproduction of instructional, training and administrative materials for field use.

167. Field operations take up the bulk of the survey budget and there is a high risk of loss of control over monitoring the disbursement of funds once the fieldwork starts. Effective cost control systems must therefore be established from the start by the organization conducting the survey in order to monitor actual expenditures in relation to estimated costs (United Nations, 2008).

168. If the national statistical agency does not have the infrastructure or capability required to undertake portions of the violence against women survey, some activities may have be to be outsourced to consultants or outside agencies that have the required expertise. For example, subject matter expertise on violence against women is often not available from within national statistical agencies, making it necessary to engage consultants to assist in the development of questionnaire content, to train interviewers or to participate in data analysis. Expertise may be found within other Government departments, universities, research organizations and community agencies. The costs associated with engaging consultants and external agencies must be incorporated into the budget.

169. In certain circumstances, outsourcing may reduce project costs. However, overseeing the work of an external agency can present challenges in terms of ensuring the quality of the data, response rates or the privacy and confidentiality of respondents' personal information. Outsourcing should be used only if potential negative impacts are thoroughly investigated and considered to be minimal. There are advantages to developing and maintaining in-house capability if these do not already exist so that similar surveys can be more easily implemented and budgets reduced in future cycles of the survey (UNODC and UNECE, 2010).

170. Finally, the budget will have to take account of data processing and the dissemination of survey outputs.

171. Examples of budget items and how they factor into a survey on violence against women are listed in table III.3.

Table III.3

Examples of budget items for a survey on violence against women

Budget item	Considerations
I. Planning and preparatory activities	
Initial planning and subsequent monitoring	The personnel infrastructure required to adequately manage the various stages of the survey will involve senior staff; at the very minimum, it should include a project manager and unit manager(s).

Budget item	Considerations
Development of survey design	Initial design planning includes survey structure, population coverage, sampling procedures and data collection method. This will involve professional staff and extensive consultations with stakeholders. Consultants may be engaged to advise on various aspects of the survey design, development and implementation if expertise does not exist in-house.
Sample design, selection and preparation	Advanced statistical expertise is required to ensure that the sampling design is sound and will yield the data required to meet the project objectives. Sampling statisticians may be in-house or external.
Questionnaire design and printing	Time and resources are required for the development and testing of the questionnaire. This can be substantial if it is the first survey on violence against women to be conducted in the country or if new topics are being introduced. Face-to-face interviewing will require printed questionnaires and other forms. The sample size will determine the number of questionnaires required for the fieldwork. There may be costs associated with translating questionnaires.
Pretesting of the questionnaire	Various forms of testing are required. First-time applications of the survey will require several stages of testing.
Manuals and other instruments for field operations	Field supervisors and interviewers require printed manuals. Printed information on sources of support/referral for respondents is an important budget item.

II. Field operations

Budget item	Considerations
Selection and training of interviewers	There may be a need to recruit interviewers from outside the national statistical agency for a survey on violence against women. Training will cover basic field operations and interviewing techniques with particular attention to the sensitivity of the topic of violence against women and all associated ethical and safety considerations. The size of the sample will determine the number of interviewers and field supervisors required to manage the fieldwork.
Training of field supervisors	Field supervisors will need basic training as well as training specific to violence against women to ensure that they have the competencies required to oversee all aspects of the fieldwork.
Pretesting of field operations	Careful testing of all aspects of the field operations requires time and resources. These include safety measures for respondents and interviewers as well as methods of providing support to respondents and debriefings with interviewers.
Data collection and field administration	The costs associated with interviewing will depend on the sample size, the mode of interviewing and the length of the questionnaire. Cost of travel, lodging, supplies, quality control and other logistics, such as callbacks to reduce non-response needs, must be factored into the budget. Costs associated with the time required for implementing safety measures and responding to emotional reactions on the part of respondents and interviewers must also be calculated in the budget.
Data capture and data editing	The purchasing and programming of data capture systems requires specialized expertise, time and resources. Face-to-face interviews are resource-intensive in the data capture phase. All survey modes require resources for data editing proportionate to the size of the sample.

III. Data processing and dissemination

Budget item	Considerations
Data processing	Systems planners and analysts, computer programmers, survey statisticians and analysts are required to produce tabulations with indicators of the precision of the estimates and analytical reports in a policy-relevant format. Technical and support staff are needed for coding and related clerical work in this phase.
Dissemination and communication of results	Personnel with communications expertise are required to advise on the dissemination of survey results. There will also be costs associated with survey outputs disseminated in printed format.

172. Once the expected costs of the various components of the survey operation have been calculated, the survey manager is in a good position to determine whether the goals and objectives of the survey can be met with the available resources. If not, it may be necessary to consider changes to scope, sample size, complexity, outputs or time frames (UNODC and UNECE, 2010).

Establishing the organizational structure

173. Planning for a survey on violence against women also entails clearly defining the organizational structure within the national statistical agency. The personnel and expertise for each task must be properly identified and assigned. This entails identifying discrete tasks that need to be fulfilled, linking each task to the responsible personnel or office and specifying relationships. Table III.4 provides examples of personnel or office requirements and associated tasks for a survey on violence against women. An organizational structure for such a survey will have to be devised by the national statistical agency. The hierarchical relationships and reporting lines specified therein must be consistent with its existing organizational structure.

Table III.4

Examples of personnel or office requirements and associated tasks for a survey on violence against women

Personnel requirement	Tasks
Project manager	The project manager is responsible for overseeing all aspects of project management, including budgeting, resource allocation, consultation with stakeholders, hiring, training, sample design, quality control, data analysis, dissemination and evaluation (including final debriefing of field staff).
Questionnaire design experts	Questionnaire design experts are responsible for consulting with stakeholders to determine data requirements, operationalizing key concepts, conducting research to identify questionnaires on similar topics in other settings, overseeing cognitive and other forms of testing, drafting survey questions, incorporating results of testing into drafts of the questionnaire and finalizing the questionnaire.
Sampling experts	Sampling experts are responsible for determining sample size, appropriate sampling frame and sample design required to meet the survey objectives and constructing appropriate survey weights.
Field supervisors	Field supervisors are responsible for overseeing field operations, selecting and training interviewers, supervising interviewers in the field, ensuring quality control and ensuring adherence to ethical and safety guidelines.
Interviewers	Interviewers are responsible for conducting interviews with household and survey respondents in a professional and thorough manner, thereby minimizing item and survey non-response and ensuring data quality, ensuring secure management of completed questionnaires and respondent identity and ensuring adherence to ethical and safety guidelines.
Data entry and editing clerks	Data clerks are responsible for entering and/or editing data. Data collected via paper-and-pencil method will need to be entered manually into a data capture system. Regardless of the method of data collection, data will need to be edited to ensure logic and internal consistency.
Data analysts	Data analysts are responsible for preparing a data analysis plan in consultation with stakeholders, providing advice to stakeholders regarding requirements for minimum statistical power, conducting exploratory and in-depth analysis according to analytical requirements, ensuring inclusion of standard errors and other indicators of the precision of the estimates and preparing analytical reports for publication.
Communications experts	Communication experts are responsible for preparing a communications strategy for the release of analytical reports in consultation with stakeholders and data analysts, including identification of optimal methods for release of data.
Evaluation experts	Evaluation experts are responsible for developing an evaluation plan and identifying data requirements and conducting an evaluation of all survey processes and making recommendations for the improvement of processes and the efficient use of resources in future iterations of the survey.

Sample design

174. Sample design is the process of selecting a portion of the population to be included in the survey. As with any survey, a survey on violence against women must have a sample

design that satisfies the survey objectives, takes into account the mode of data collection and the constraints associated with fieldwork in the specific country context and is cost-efficient.

175. Designing the sample for a statistical survey on violence against women, as for any large statistical sample survey, requires comprehensive knowledge of the principles and techniques of sampling. Such knowledge is impossible to convey in a few pages. This expertise must be sought by the survey manager in the person of a highly specialized statistician, who must be involved early in the planning stage. The present section provides only an overview of sample design considerations as they relate to a survey on violence against women. It focuses on sample size determination, structure of the sample and the sampling frame and mentions special considerations stemming from the sensitivity of the topic.

Sample size determination

176. Factors that must be considered when determining the appropriate sample size for a survey on violence against women are similar to those that must be considered for any statistical sample survey. They include the following:

- Level of precision required for the key estimates to be obtained from the survey (of which there are usually several or many)
- Number of planned subgroups of the population for which estimates will be produced (are estimates needed separately for urban and rural areas, geographical regions and population subgroups such as age groups and minority groups?)
- Prevalence in the population of the key characteristics to be measured.

177. The level of precision is a major consideration when determining the size of the survey sample. As a general rule, the more precise or reliable the survey estimates must be, the larger the sample must be. It must be noted that, in estimating precision, sampling error needs to be estimated in a manner that takes into account the complex sample design that is planned.

178. The need for estimates for subgroups of the population significantly increases the sample size required. The subgroups are generally defined as analytical subgroups for which equally reliable data are wanted. A subgroup can be a stratum, a combination of strata, an administrative region or an urban, rural or other subdivision of these regions. The subgroups can also be subpopulations defined by age, education or other characteristics. For violence against women, data are often required for a number of subgroups in order to enable appropriate policy interventions to be targeted to subgroups on the basis of their experience of violence. While it is desirable to have data for many domains, it is important to keep the number in check. The number of subgroups has to be carefully considered because the sample size required to produce reliable estimates for all domains would necessarily be large when the number of domains is large (United Nations, 2008).

179. When a key characteristic to be measured in a survey occurs rarely in the study population, a large sample is generally needed to obtain a reliable estimate of it. For example, if the prevalence of stranger rape within a given age group or geographical area is less than 5 per cent, a larger sample will be needed to produce a reliable estimate of the prevalence, compared to a situation where prevalence is nearer to 50 per cent. When planning a statistical sample survey on violence against women, the expected size of critical estimates may not be known in advance, for instance if it is the first time that a survey on this topic is being conducted. In such cases a rough estimate may be calculated on the basis of statistical sample surveys conducted in similar contexts. It is recommended to err on the side of a larger sample when critical estimates are not known.

180. An additional factor that must be considered when calculating sample size is anticipated non-response. This will take account of the actual number of household contacts and partial and completed interviews that will take place. Non-response is likely to vary by country and should be calculated on the basis of national survey experience. Owing to the sensitivity of the topic, surveys on violence against women, in particular, can be prone to high rates of non-response or partial response unless strong measures have been put in place to reach and obtain complete interviews with the sampled women.

181. Sample size is a major budget item for a survey on violence against women. The size of the sample will determine the number of interviewers, field supervisors and data entry and processing staff required for the project. The sample size needed to produce key estimates at a specified level of precision may, however, be larger than can be accommodated by the available resources. In this case, a balance will have to be reached between the ideal sample size and the available budget. Additional funds will need to be secured or the objectives of the survey scaled back. For instance, the list of key estimates may be trimmed or precision requirements adjusted down.

182. Sample size also has important implications for the time frame and operations involved in the conduct of the survey. When it is determined that a relatively large sample is required to meet the survey objectives, survey managers must take the steps necessary to ensure that neither the quality of the data nor the safety and well-being of respondents and interviewers are compromised. Larger samples present particular challenges in terms of selecting and training interviewers, effectively monitoring all aspects of field operations and verifying and editing the data. Efforts to minimize non-response by recontacting households will be difficult to sustain with large samples, particularly in settings where interviews are conducted face to face and large or remote geographical areas must be covered. This can have a negative impact on data quality (Yansaneh, 2005).

Structure of the sample

183. The structure of the sample for a survey on violence against women will be broadly similar to that of other national household surveys within a country but may differ in some details. In most countries, a stratified multistage sample design has been used in surveys on violence against women that used face-to-face interviewing. For surveys on violence against women that relied on telephone interviewing or postal surveys, the sample design is typically simpler, as the logistics of a physical visit by an interviewer is omitted; in many of these cases, simple random sampling or systematic sampling with a random start has been used, some with stratification (see annex V for examples of sample designs used in previous violence against women surveys).

184. In a stratified multistage sample design, sampling efficiencies are achieved by techniques such as stratification, sampling in stages and cluster sampling. Each of these techniques figure prominently in national household surveys that employ the face-to-face interview method, including those on violence against women.

<u>Stratification</u>

185. Stratification of the population to be surveyed prior to sample selection is a commonly used technique in household survey design. It can be applied at any stage of sampling (see sampling in stages below). Stratification partitions the units to be sampled into mutually exclusive and collectively exhaustive subgroups or strata based on auxiliary information that is known about the full population. Sample elements are selected from each stratum independently.

186. One purpose of stratification is to improve the precision of the survey estimates. The gains in precision are greatest when strata sample sizes are proportional to the strata population size and the strata formed are as different as possible from each other and when the units within the same stratum are as homogeneous as possible, with respect to the characteristics of interest in the survey.

187. Another important reason for stratifying the population is to provide survey estimates with the required level of precision at the level of stratification. Survey estimates are often desired not only at the national level but also for administrative regions or urban/rural areas, making these a natural basis for stratification. Stratification by administrative regions and by urban and rural areas within administrative regions is done in many surveys, because sharp differences exist between urban and rural areas and (in many cases) across administrative regions with respect to population characteristics. These considerations apply to surveys on violence against women, where it is expected that prevalence rates and characteristics related to violence against women will vary considerably across administrative regions and/or between urban and rural areas.

188. An important rule in stratification is that each stratum must be sampled in order for an unbiased estimate of the population mean to be calculated. However, this is not always possible in practice, especially in face-to-face interviewing, where decisions are often made to omit certain areas because they are too remote, dangerous or costly to include. In such cases, documentation accompanying the data release must clearly identify any areas or population subgroups that were omitted.

<u>Sampling in stages</u>

189. In a multistage sample design, sampling units or elements are selected in several (usually two) stages. In the first stage, primary sampling units (PSUs), usually geographical units, are selected. In low- or middle-income countries, the PSUs are often the enumeration areas (EAs) from the most recent national population and housing census. EAs could be districts, subdivisions, villages or other geographical units. From the list of PSUs, a sample is selected; if stratification has been applied at this stage, a sample of PSUs is selected within each stratum. Once the sample selection of PSUs is complete, a sample of secondary sampling units (SSUs) is selected from each sampled PSU. In most cases, SSUs are households or dwellings. In surveys on violence against women, the unit of study is an individual woman; this necessitates an additional process of selection whereby one eligible woman from each sampled household is selected to participate in the survey.[17]

190. There are two main reasons for using multistage samples. The first is the absence or poor quality of household listings for the country, a situation not uncommon in developing countries. In a multistage sample design, a listing of households or addresses needs to be constructed only for the PSUs (typically EAs) that have been selected, thereby circumventing the disadvantage of missing or deficient frames. The second reason for using multistage designs is that it controls the cost of data collection when PSUs consist of sets of households that are geographically clustered (Yansaneh, 2005).

191. At each stage of sampling, all sampling units to be chosen—geographical units, households, individual women—must have a known and non-zero probability of being selected. It is important to note that the chance of each sampling unit being chosen need not be equal but can vary in accordance with the objectives of the survey. A commonly used technique, for example, is to allow larger PSUs to have a greater chance of selection, in what is termed sampling with probability proportionate to size.

---

[17] The possible risks if more than one woman from the household is selected for an interview are elaborated in chapter V.

192. The techniques for determining the optimum combination of the number of PSUs and SSUs to be selected are complex. For example, a sample of 5,000 households could be produced by taking a sample of 100 PSUs and 50 SSUs within each PSU or a sample of 200 PSUs and 25 SSUs within each PSU. Decisions involving the allocation of PSUs and SSUs have to be made very carefully and with the help of a sampling statistician, as they have critical implications for the precision of the estimates and the survey cost. In general, a large number of PSUs relative to SSUs will increase precision of the survey estimates; however, it will also increase costs in a face-to-face survey because of the increased travel costs associated with visiting selected households across a more widely dispersed area. The challenge for the survey designer is to find the right balance between precision and cost.

Cluster sampling

193. Cluster sampling is a multistage random sampling technique whereby the study population is divided into clusters and a sample of those clusters is chosen. These clusters are often naturally occurring units or groups, such as neighbourhoods, villages, enumeration areas or city blocks. The final sample is then drawn from these clusters.

194. In household surveys, the sampling design will invariably and of necessity utilize some form of cluster sampling if survey costs are to be contained (United Nations, 2008). Cluster sampling is particularly cost-effective in face-to-face interview situations with widely dispersed populations where clustering interviews in specific geographic areas can significantly reduce travel costs and, hence, the overall costs of the survey. The disadvantage of cluster sampling is that it decreases the reliability of the estimates because people living in the same cluster tend to be relatively alike in the characteristics under study. The high correlation among units within the same cluster inflates the variance (lowers the precision) of the survey estimates.

195. Whereas stratification tends to decrease the sampling variance to a small degree, clustering increases it considerably, thus affecting the precision of the estimates. The effects of clustering are measured by the design effect, which expresses how much larger the sampling variance for the cluster sample is compared to a simple random sample of the same size.[18] The design effect cannot be known in advance of the survey and should therefore be kept as low as possible by maximizing the number of clusters, keeping the size of clusters small and uniform and selecting a geographically dispersed (rather than contiguous) sample of households at the last stage (United Nations, 2008). However, all of these aims should be balanced with the way in which the number and size of clusters affect overall costing and survey logistics. It should be borne in mind that cluster sampling is generally used in order to reduce costs and increasing the number of clusters will increase costs.

196. Particular caution must be exercised with respect to the use of cluster sampling in a survey on violence against women. The sample design should ensure that selected households are not so close together that news of the survey's topic gets out in the community. This is needed to protect the safety of respondents, as well as their privacy and the confidentiality of their responses. It is recommended that the size of the sample in a single cluster should be kept small enough so that interviewing can be completed in one day. Another rule of thumb commonly used is that in urban areas sampling density should preferably not be higher than 1 in 10 households. This is to avoid a situation whereby the survey topic becomes known and households or respondents contacted on subsequent days either refuse to, or are not permitted to, participate.

---

[18] For a detailed discussion of design effect and weighting, see United Nations (2008) or Yansaneh (2005).

The sampling frame

197. Another crucial aspect of sample design is the sampling frame. The quality of the sampling frame has significant implications for the quality of a household survey. Inaccurate sampling frames, particularly undercoverage of important population groups, are a common source of non-sampling error (United Nations, 2008).

198. The sampling frame may be defined as the set of source materials from which particular members of the target population are chosen. More than one set of materials may be necessary when choosing the sampling frame for a given household survey. In a multistage sample design, for example, the sampling frame is different for each stage. Surveys on violence against women will likely require an area sampling frame comprised of geographical units for the first stage of sampling and a list frame for the second stage (United Nations, 2008).

199. An area sampling frame consists of geographical units arranged hierarchically. It is important that an area frame for a national survey covers the totality of the country's geographical areas. An area frame may include province, district, tract, ward and village (rural areas) or block (urban areas). For census purposes, these administrative subdivisions are further divided into EAs. The EA is typically the smallest geographical unit that is defined and delineated in a country, making it a natural and convenient choice for the PSU in household sample surveys where clustering is desired. A recent population census is the usual starting point when developing an area sampling frame for a household survey.

200. A list frame is a frame made up of a list of the target population units. The most recent population census is an ideal sampling frame for a household survey as it provides a list of every household in the country arranged geographically. Sometimes, the most recent census will be out of date; in this event, if cluster sampling is being used, clusters can be sampled using the census as the sampling frame, but the list of households within selected clusters should be updated in order to provide a more accurate sampling frame at that level. Population registers are viable alternatives to population censuses when creating a list frame provided they are complete and accurate, but this is unlikely to be the case in many countries.

201. The list frame most often used in surveys conducted by telephone is a register of telephone subscribers. Sampling is done through random digit dialling in order to ensure that unlisted and new telephone numbers have a chance of being selected. Random digit dialling entails obtaining a listing of working telephone numbers from telephone service providers and randomizing the last few digits. This ensures that the area codes and prefixes of the numbers dialled belong to working telephone numbers so that fewer calls are made to non-existent numbers. Some telephone numbers selected using this method will be out of scope because they represent businesses, fax numbers or numbers not in use, but this method is superior to using completely randomly generated numbers or telephone directories. However, there may be problems with this method if landlines are not the norm or are unevenly distributed. For example, in the United States of America, the National Health Interview Survey found that 32 per cent of households did not have a landline; it also found that the probability of not having a landline was highest for young adults, renters and lower-income groups (Blumberg and Luke, 2011). The probability of women living in these groups experiencing violence is likely to be different from that of other women and a telephone survey would therefore be subject to bias. In many developing countries, ownership of a landline is rare and concentrated heavily in richer urban areas. If mobile or cellular phones are universal, it may be possible to utilize that network in addition to the landline network, but obtaining a valid sampling frame could be problematic.

202. Whether an area frame or a list frame is used, the sampling frame from which survey samples are drawn must be as complete, accurate and current as possible. If the sampling

frame fails to achieve these ideal properties, the survey results will be biased. Often, the general result is an underestimation of the target population.

203. Non-coverage of the target population can occur at the geographical, household and individual levels. Geographical non-coverage occurs when a specific geographical area is excluded from the survey, typically as a result of inaccessibility owing to extreme remoteness, a natural disaster or political instability. Non-coverage of PSUs is a less serious problem than non-coverage of households or eligible women within households (Yansaneh, 2005). The latter occurs when households or women are excluded from the survey as a result of complex definitional or conceptual issues regarding household structure and composition. Strict operational instructions are needed to guide interviewers as to which women in the household are eligible for interview.

204. A good example is whether domestic helpers, lodgers, visiting relatives or renters are eligible for interview. Depending on the survey objectives, it may be appropriate to include visitors staying for at least four weeks in the household, as well as caregivers and domestic helpers staying five or more nights per week, as these women have a low probability of being selected to participate in their own households. The disadvantage of this approach is that the information collected about the economic status and make-up of the household will not reflect these women's own situation if they are domestic helpers, visitors or lodgers. Another disadvantage is that domestic helpers may not be allowed by their employers to take time away from work to be interviewed. Again depending on the survey objectives, it may be useful to ensure that domestic helpers are included as being eligible in their own households if they are not eligible in their place of work. Although this is logistically challenging, if populations such as domestic workers are systematically undercounted, a group that is at higher risk of violence may be overlooked.

205. Like all household surveys, dedicated surveys on violence against women will be faced with the problem of sampling frames that exclude some groups of women, resulting in non-coverage of those groups and hence a biased sample. Telephone surveys exclude women without telephones, while household surveys exclude women living in shelters, refuges or temporary housing owing to partner violence. Countries will have to deal with these issues in light of their survey objectives.

206. In sum, each country will have to make decisions about the most appropriate sample design for a survey on violence against women according to the social, demographic and economic conditions at the local level, available resources and sampling frames, and the specific objectives of the survey.

Selection of interviewers

207. The interviewer is the interface between the statistical agency and the respondent. They are the person in direct contact with the respondent, the provider of data. Given their crucial role in the survey, interviewers should be selected with great care. An interviewer must have the qualities needed to obtain the required information with accuracy and within a reasonable time. A higher than primary level of education is necessary in order to be able to manage the complexity of the topic. An interviewer should demonstrate a working knowledge of interviewing techniques, knowledge and experience of technology such as personal computer or telephone, strong communication skills, interest in the work, alertness and a willingness to receive feedback on their performance.

208. Personal characteristics of interviewers should also be given great consideration, as they affect the willingness of women to participate in surveys on violence against women

and to disclose very personal information. The most important personal characteristic to be considered when choosing interviewers for a survey on violence against women is their sex: the interviewer must be female. Utilizing female interviewers increases the disclosure of sensitive information, particularly that relating to experiences involving sexual victimization and violence perpetrated by male partners (UNODC and UNECE, 2010).

209. Age is another factor to consider when selecting interviewers. Interviewers who are seen as too young may elicit the distrust of respondents, leading to an outright refusal to participate in the survey or a reluctance to disclose personal or sensitive information. In some contexts, it would be considered inappropriate for a young woman to pose questions about violence to an older woman. While it is not possible to recommend an age limit or age range applicable across all settings, many respondents perceive older female interviewers as instilling more warmth and reassurance than younger women (UNODC and UNECE, 2010). Other personal characteristics that can affect participation and disclosure rates are marital status, attitudes and interpersonal skills (Jansen and others, 2004).

210. It should not be assumed that the regular interviewers used for other surveys are necessarily appropriate for surveys on this special topic. Even very experienced interviewers who have demonstrated competence in surveys on other topics may not feel equipped to manage the potential stresses that participation in this survey may bring. Selection of interviewers should ensure they are well briefed on the subject matter and have considered their ability to perform effectively over the duration of the fieldwork. It may be necessary to recruit interviewers from outside the national statistical agency for the purpose of a survey on this topic.

211. In forming teams of fieldworkers in face-to-face interviewing situations, project managers must take into account local norms that may prohibit women from working in public spaces and other barriers that female interviewers may face when approaching households in order to obtain interview. In these situations, teams of male and female interviewers working in tandem have been shown to improve household contact and to lower refusal rates; they may also be necessary to ensure the safety of female interviewers (UNODC and UNECE, 2010). Additional logistical considerations concerning interviewing in face-to-face contexts are discussed in chapter VI (see paragraphs 419 to 421 and 449).

212. In settings where minority groups will be interviewed, interviewers may require multilingual communication abilities. In these cases, consideration should also be given to including interviewers from targeted ethnic groups on the team.

213. In addition, interviewers also must be screened for their maturity, their motivation to work on the topic of violence against women and their experience doing similar work on other sensitive topics and for any judgements, stereotypes or prejudices towards women who have experienced violence.

214. Interviewers must also have the ability to establish and maintain an appropriate level of professionalism while at the same time expressing warmth and reassurance. Interviewers in possession of personal strategies for self-care and stress reduction will be better able to perform their duties for the duration of the interviewing period.

215. It is recommended to always recruit more fieldworkers/trainees than are required, since some may not be adequate and others may want to withdraw from the job. Experience with surveys using face-to-face interviews has shown that it is practical to have selection moments at fixed points during the training with the final selection after the field pilot and that it is important to clarify and agree on the selection process from the beginning (Jansen, 2010). The rigorous processes required for selecting interviewers for violence against women surveys are evident in the examples of Kiribati and Namibia (see box III.1).

> **Box III.1**
>
> **Selection of interviewers for violence against women surveys in Kiribati and Namibia**
>
> The research team for the Kiribati Family Health and Support Study began the interviewer selection process with an initial pool of 60 potential interviewers. All were required to sign an oath of confidentiality witnessed by a magistrate prior to entering the field. Given the sensitivity and complexity of the survey topic, an in-depth three-week training programme was provided for the candidates. After the candidates had been trained and the survey had been piloted, the pool of interviewers was reduced to 34 on the basis of demonstrated competence and participation during the evaluation period. The most important factors for interviewer success were identified as empathy, the ability to listen, the ability to instil confidence that responses would be kept confidential and higher level of education. Many of the older women in the initial pool of candidates lacked the literacy skills necessary to navigate the complexity of the questionnaire (Secretariat of the Pacific Community, 2010).
>
> Namibia was part of the WHO Multi-country Study on Women's Health and Domestic Violence against Women. The criteria for selecting interviewers in Namibia included language proficiency (in English), a grade 12 certificate and interviewing experience. Of the 300 women who applied, 100 were interviewed and 40 were selected for training. About half of those selected had interviewing experience with the Demographic and Health Surveys. Multicultural sensitivity was an important component of the training. The final selection of interviewers took place following three weeks of training; selection criteria were based on technical and personal criteria (Jansen and others, 2004).

216. In some cases, field supervisors are selected early in the planning phase before interviewers have been selected. However, in many surveys using face-to-face interviews, field supervisors are selected from among the participants in the interviewer/fieldworker training, either during the training or after the training has ended (Jansen, 2010). It cannot be assumed that field supervisors who perform well on other surveys will be suited to or willing to work on a survey on violence against women because of the added stressors that such a survey contains. Field supervisors must be selected carefully on the basis of the following personal characteristics:

- In face-to-face interviewing situations, field supervisors must be female, since they must travel with interviewers periodically to oversee their work. In telephone interviewing situations, it is possible to use male field supervisors, provided they do not have any contact with respondents and provided they have the training and sensitivity required to train interviewers and to support them through regular debriefings.

- Field supervisors must be screened for their maturity, their motivation to work on the topic and their experience working on surveys on similar sensitive topics, in addition to all other screening criteria specified above.

217. Like interviewers, field supervisors must go through extensive training before working on a survey on violence against women, including specific training on their tasks and responsibilities as supervisors. The topic of training is resumed in chapter V.

Study protocol

218. The study protocol is a document that outlines background, aims, design, methodology, data collection procedures and other important considerations that provide the basis of the survey. It provides an overall plan on which the project is based and will need to include many of the factors discussed in this chapter. Interviewers and field supervisors often will receive their own interviewer or supervisor manual clarifying all aspects related to their specific tasks. Additionally, they can refer to the study protocol in order to respond to questions

from respondents regarding the purpose of the survey and to persuade selected respondents of the importance of their participation. The study protocol has the additional function of outlining appropriate safeguards and policies for reacting to unusual or challenging situations that may arise. Box III.2 outlines a sample template for a study protocol.

> **Box III.2**
> **Study protocol template**
> Protocol title:
> Protocol date:
> *Abstract*
> - Brief summary of the study background, aims and design
>
> *Background and significance*
> - Presentation of the problem
> - Contribution of the proposed project to current knowledge
>
> *Study objectives, research questions and outcomes*
> - Purpose of the study
> - Primary and secondary objectives and project goals
> - Research questions to be answered
> - Proposed outcomes of the project
>
> *Project structure*
> - Project structure
> - Principal agency responsible for the survey and funders
> - Participating units, data management centre and coordinating centre as applicable
>
> *Operationalization*
> - Working definitions for all relevant terms
>
> *Formative research*
> - Aims and objectives of the formative research
> - Findings of any preliminary or pilot research that contribute to the current project
>
> *Study design*
> - Design of the study
> - Study population
> - Geographical locations
> - Sampling strategy, including inclusion/exclusion criteria
> - Sample size determination
> - Study outcomes
>
> *Study procedures*
> - Study procedures, assessments and activities
> - Composition of the survey team and field staff
> - Selection and training procedures for supervisors and interviewers
> - Quality control procedures
> - Procedures for stopping interviews, rescheduling interviews and managing attrition
>
> *Questionnaire development*
> - Development process
> - Pretest procedures
> - Translation of the questionnaire
>
> *Outline of questionnaire content*
> - Sections of the questionnaire
>
> *Ethical and safety considerations*
> - What constitutes adverse events and serious adverse events?
> - Who is responsible for identifying, documenting and reporting adverse events?
> - Procedures for monitoring and ensuring respondent safety
> - Procedures for monitoring and ensuring interviewer safety
> - Procedures for rescheduling interviews
> - Procedures for responding to emotional trauma on the part of respondents
> - Procedures for responding to emotional trauma on the part of interviewers

Source: Watts and others, (2007b) and University of Iowa (2003) (modified).

Chapter IV
Questionnaire design

219. Questionnaire design is instrumental, since the questionnaire is the conduit through which the information requirements of data users and stakeholders are operationalized and transferred into concrete questions. Questionnaires are comprised primarily of highly structured closed-ended sequences of questions designed to obtain accurate information from survey respondents. Development of the questionnaire can begin once the survey objectives and specifications have been determined through consultations with stakeholders and general principles on the sampling design, such as sample size, sampling frame and sampling method, have been established. Survey managers should continue to involve stakeholders throughout the questionnaire design phase of the project in order to ensure that the survey outputs will meet the policy development needs of data users and that realistic expectations are maintained.

220. The design and quality of the questionnaire has a major impact on the quality of the data obtained and the final outputs of the survey. It is therefore essential to consider several general elements that pertain to all questionnaires, including the household screening section, where the composition of the household is recorded and the selected respondent is identified, introductions to particular sections, the number of questions and specific question wording and the flow or sequence of the questions. While guidelines for designing questionnaires can be found in numerous examples of literature, one particularly useful resource is the Manual on victimization surveys (UNODC and UNECE, 2010) which contains generic advice on questionnaire design for population surveys on the topic of crime victimization, a topic closely related to that of violence against women.

221. For surveys specific to interviewing women about violence, these general elements take on particular importance with respect to encouraging participation in the survey while ensuring that respondents are able to participate safely and that confidentiality and privacy are assured. There is also the need to incorporate into the questionnaire opportunities for interviewers to develop rapport and to put respondents at ease. Careful attention must therefore be paid to both general and specific elements of the questionnaire, as they can have an impact on respondents' willingness to participate and to disclose sensitive information and, ultimately, on the quality of the data collected.

222. The content of the questionnaire should be developed in accordance with the goals, objectives and required final outputs of the survey. The design of the questionnaire comprises listing the topics to be addressed, agreeing on the principle concepts to be measured and examining how this can be translated into specific series of questions. Important considerations when developing a questionnaire on violence against women include the length of the completed interview, the mode of interviewing, the need for skip and filter questions, the importance of establishing a rapport with respondents, the wording and order of questions, including multiple opportunities to disclose, the need to ensure respondent safety and the importance of minimizing emotional trauma. The survey module on violence against women developed for the United Nations Economic Commission for Europe (see annex VII) pro-

vides a full set of questions aimed at producing data on the core indicators identified by the Friends of the Chair of the United Nations Statistical Commission on indicators on violence against women. This questionnaire can be expanded and/or adapted for individual country contexts and used as a dedicated survey.

Background qualitative research

223. Questionnaire development begins with qualitative research, in which survey managers review the relevant studies on violence against women in order to assess the primary policy and research issues that a survey on violence against women could help to address. Workshops, meetings and focus group discussions are also very useful at this early stage of the survey design. Holding discussions with stakeholders and small non-random samples of the target population can help to establish priorities, to explore strategies for encouraging participation in the survey and to refine question wording and response categories.

224. Qualitative research is particularly important when surveys on violence against women are conducted for the first time. Through qualitative research, inputs for the development of the questionnaire can be obtained from experts such as researchers and community groups and other agencies that provide services to female victims of violence, as well as from stakeholders and others who will use the analytical outputs for policy formation.[19]

225. Focus group discussions constitute an exploratory method of qualitative research that is frequently used in the initial stages of a project, when researchers meet with small groups of individuals representing the target population of the survey in order to discuss various aspects of the project, such as operationalization of key concepts or development of response categories. Focus group participants should include women who have been identified as experiencing partner violence and sexual violence who can be recruited from shelters and counselling groups, as well as women in minority groups, in order to ensure that the survey will be suitable for all target groups. Focus group discussions are also an effective forum for obtaining feedback on the proposed survey protocols.

226. In the case of violence against women surveys, it is critical from the outset to plan how all aspects of the project will incorporate methods of meeting the ethical requirements to ensure the safety of respondents and research teams, to protect the confidentiality of respondents, to minimize emotional distress, to provide information on sources of support and to refer respondents to sources of support in the community if needed. All of the above touch on aspects of designing and administering the questionnaire and will also be incorporated into the training of interviewers and survey implementation, which are discussed in chapter V.

227. One of the fundamental challenges for surveys on violence against women is that of obtaining accurate estimates of the prevalence of violence, especially in contexts where there are strong taboos on speaking to outsiders about family relationships, violence in the family or sexual relations. Focus group discussions and other qualitative research methods that engage local women in discussions about the feasibility of the survey and about ways to surmount these taboos and to adapt the questionnaire and protocols to the local context will be critical to the success of the survey.

---

[19] The WHO Multi-country Study on Women's Health and Domestic Violence against Women incorporated formative research into each of the study sites, which included interviews with key informants, in-depth interviews with survivors of violence and focus groups with women and men in different age groups. The purpose of these discussions was to develop the questionnaire in the early stages of the project and to interpret the survey findings at the end stage (Garcia-Moreno and other, 2005).

Important aspects of questionnaire development

228. There are several key elements to be considered when developing questionnaires. For example, the time required to complete an interview is an important factor to consider for the success of the survey, since respondents will be less likely to complete interviews that are lengthy or complex. Attention to the length of individual questions is also important, especially when a survey is conducted over the telephone.

229. Data requirements will therefore need to be balanced with the need to minimize respondent burden and to reduce drop-off rates and item non-response. (Strategies for minimizing unit non-response are outlined in paragraphs 383-399 and strategies for minimizing item non-response are outlined in paragraphs 400-406.) The calculation of the average length of an interview should incorporate the total time required, from contacting the selected household, selecting the respondent and following up with respondents who are not immediately available, to completing the questionnaire and ending the interview. This calculation factors in the expected participation rate, efforts to reduce non-response, such as follow-up visits to households or additional phone calls, measures to ensure the safety of respondents and interviewers, efforts to respond to emotional reactions on the part of both respondents and interviewers and other related factors that may extend the time required to complete an interview.

230. The estimated average length of an interview will determine the allowable content for the questionnaire as determined by the available budget. If a more detailed questionnaire is required to meet the survey objectives but the budget cannot support such a questionnaire within the targeted sample, project managers will need to reduce the sample size, modify the survey objectives or seek additional funding. It is therefore imperative that the budget established at the outset of the project is sufficient to meet the project objectives.

231. The mode of interviewing is a principle determinant of the structure and layout of the questionnaire. For example, face-to-face interviews or postal surveys conducted without the aid of a computer will require a simple format that allows interviewers to move smoothly through the questions, while interviews conducted using CAPI or by telephone using CATI can accommodate complex skip patterns that are incorporated into the computer programming. Although the mode of interviewing will determine the complexity of the questionnaire, all good questionnaires should be designed to balance clear, understandable, easily answered questions for respondents in a format that is easily followed by interviewers and suitable for subsequent analysis by data analysts (Statistics Canada, 2003).

232. Questionnaires that are overly complex or contain design flaws may require additional probes on the part of interviewers which can be time-consuming. Long or complex questionnaires may also decrease the willingness of respondents to cooperate or result in coding errors. Certain specific principles must be followed to ensure that the topic is reliably measured, although country-specific adaptation may be required to ensure that question wording is culturally acceptable and easily recognizable. Accuracy of translation is particularly important if the questionnaire is translated from English or another language into local languages.[20]

233. Whether interviews are conducted face to face or by telephone, in order to yield high quality information a good questionnaire should contain clear instructions to interviewers

---

[20] An example of how easily translation can affect survey results is the Swiss component of the International Violence against Women Survey. The French word ami is a term that can refer to both a platonic friendship and an intimate relationship and in the translation from English to French this word was used to refer to both boyfriends and friends. None of the women identified rape perpetrators to be boyfriends, which was interpreted by the survey analysts as an indication of a lack of clarity that resulted from the translation (Jaquier, Fisher and Killias, 2006).

and respondents in order to ensure that interpretation of questions is consistent and clear. Additional detail about the purpose of each question and instructions about coding should be included in the interviewer's manual. (Details about the contents of the interviewer's manual are presented in paragraphs 355 to 358).

234. In addition to these important general principles of questionnaire design, a number of other principles are pertinent to surveys on violence against women. For example, the wording of introductory sections is essential in terms of setting the context and providing interviewers with an opportunity to establish rapport and trust. Artificially low disclosures of experiences of intimate partner violence and sexual violence can be associated with the way in which the introduction to the survey is framed, as well as the framing of specific modules of questions concerning experiences of violence. Surveys that ask respondents in the early stages to think about crime in the neighbourhood, for example, may orient respondents away from thinking about intimate partners when asked to divulge experiences of violence. Introductions also provide essential instructions to respondents concerning measures that have been put in place to ensure their safety while they respond to sensitive questions, such as rescheduling to another time or switching to a neutral questionnaire if a family member comes on the scene.

235. The sequence of questions that lead gradually to sensitive questions about violence and the specific question wording are also critical for eliciting honest and complete disclosure of violence. The potential for these questions to elicit emotional trauma must also be considered and efforts built into the questionnaire and interviewer training to reduce this possibility.

236. Immediately prior to reaching modules of questions concerning experiences of violence, respondents should be informed more specifically about the nature of the questions to follow and reminded of the voluntary nature of their participation so that free and informed consent to proceed with those questions is obtained.

Questionnaire content

Questions aimed at measuring experiences of violence

237. In order to produce a reliable and valid measurement of women's experiences of violence, specific acts of violence must be explicitly operationalized and clear definitions provided. Over the years, researchers have come to agree that single questions such as "Have you ever been attacked?" yield much lower estimates and are therefore less reliable than multiple behaviourally based questions such as "Have you been slapped?" and "Have you been choked?". Respondents who are given multiple opportunities to assess whether their experiences fit within the objectives of the survey and the specific questions being asked provide more detailed accounts of their experiences. This requires the necessary space on the questionnaire and time during the interview to be allocated to comprehensive modules of clearly worded questions.

238. As a general principle, value-laden and stigmatizing terms such as "rape" and "violence" must be avoided, as they lead to underreporting on statistical surveys compared to detailed behaviourally specific terms, which yield much higher disclosures of identical experiences. For example, only one-third of the women who disclosed forced sex on the British Crime Survey described the incident as rape in a follow-up question (Percy and Mayhew, 1997). In a study in the United States of America, less than half of the women who reported experiences matching the legal definition of rape described the incident as rape (Fisher, Cullen and Turner, 2000).

239. National and international experience with dedicated surveys on violence against women indicates that the occurrence, nature and severity of violence vary significantly depending on the characteristics of the woman, her partner and her family situation, such as age, education, employment status, marital status, place of residence and ethnicity. Consequently, the content and structure of the questionnaire must be developed in such a way as to allow for an assessment of the type and severity of violence and the relationship to the perpetrator(s) according to the different characteristics of women in the population.

240. Survey questions should also cue respondents to consider a variety of different settings (e.g., home, work, school, outside locations, etc.) and specific categories of perpetrators (e.g., current partners, former partners, other male relatives, males in positions of authority, etc.). Special consideration should be given to the difficulty that many women may have talking about experiences of violence, especially if they continue to live with a violent man or if their culture discourages them from discussing family problems with outsiders. In the violence against women survey conducted in Pakistan, the survey managers were concerned about low levels of disclosure of violent experiences early in the field practice and instructed interviewers to say to respondents "I know how hard this is to talk about. I myself know of someone who has experienced abuse". Using this lead-in, interviewers felt more comfortable asking women about their experiences and respondents disclosed violence at a higher rate (Andersson and others, 2009).

241. In addition to questions aimed at measuring women's experiences of different types of violence, it is important to be able to assess the details of these events, such as severity and frequency, impacts and consequences, and actions taken by victims. The severity of the violence can encompass the nature of the specific acts, the frequency of assaults and the immediate and long-term impacts on victims.

Questions aimed at producing statistics on the core indicators identified by the Friend of the Chair of the United Nations Statistical Commission on indicators on violence against women

242. The principles governing, and the recommended framing of, survey questions addressing the core indicators identified by the Friend of the Chair of the United Nations Statistical Commission on indicators on violence against women are specified in chapter II. It should always be kept in mind that intimate partner violence and non-partner violence are essentially different in nature and violence by these two different types of perpetrator should always be asked about separately. The topics necessary to obtain data on the core indictors are as follows:

(a) Types of violence against women

    (i) Physical violence

    (ii) Sexual violence

    (iii) Psychological violence

    (iv) Economic violence

(b) Classification and characteristics of violence against women

    (i) Relationship of victim to perpetrator

    (ii) Severity of violence

    (iii) Frequency of violence

(c) Personal characteristics of all respondents

   (i) Marital/relationship status

   (ii) Age.

Types of violence against women

243. The decision to collect information about type of violence must be made with great care and with careful consideration of how ethical and safety requirements can be met. Furthermore, the nature of abusive behaviour, especially that of physical and psychological violence, varies greatly among countries and regions. Survey questions should be formulated in such a way as to capture commonly occurring acts in a local sociocultural context. It is recommended that questions on psychological and economic violence should apply only to intimate partners.

Physical violence

244. As discussed in chapter II (see paragraphs 57 to 59), women may experience a wide range of physically abusive acts. Below are some examples of questions that might be used to enquire about the experience of such acts in a survey (see model questionnaire contained in annex VII). The first three questions are aimed at capturing data on non-partner violence, while the others would be used to capture data on intimate partner violence.

- Has anyone ever hit, beaten, kicked or done anything else to hurt you physically?
- Has anyone ever pushed you or pulled your hair?
- Has anyone ever threatened you with or actually used a gun, knife or other weapon against you?
- Has he ever slapped you or thrown something at you that could hurt you?
- Has he ever pushed you or shoved you or pulled your hair?
- Has he ever hit you with his fist or with anything else that could hurt you?
- Has he ever kicked you, dragged you or beat you up?
- Has he ever choked or burned you on purpose?
- Has he ever threatened with or actually used a gun, knife or other weapon against you?

Sexual violence

245. Sexual violence refers to harmful or unwanted behaviour aimed at forcing or coercing a woman to engage in sexual acts against her will or without her consent. It encompasses rape, attempted rape and other sexual acts. Below are some examples of questions that might be used to ask about sexual violence in a survey (see model questionnaire contained in annex VII). The first question applies to non-partner violence, while the others apply to intimate partner violence.

- Since the age of 15, has anyone ever forced you into sexual intercourse when you did not want to, for example by threatening you, holding you down, or putting you in a situation where you could not say no. Remember to include people you have known as well as strangers.
- Did he ever force you to have sexual intercourse when you did not want to?
- Did you ever have sexual intercourse you did not want to because you were afraid of what he might do?

- Did he ever force you to do something else sexual that you did not want or that you found degrading or humiliating?

Psychological violence

246. While psychological violence against women can take a variety of forms, it can be largely grouped into emotional abuse and controlling behaviour. Below are some examples of questions that might be used to capture data on psychological violence (see model questionnaire contained in annex VII). It should be remembered that these questions may need to be adapted to an individual country's context and that only psychological abuse by an intimate partner is included in the core indicators.

   (a) Emotional abuse:

   - Has he ever insulted you or made you feel bad about yourself?
   - Has he ever belittled or humiliated you in front of other people?
   - Has he ever done things to scare or intimidate you on purpose (e.g., by the way he looked at you, by yelling and smashing things)?
   - Has he ever verbally threatened to hurt you or someone you care about?

   (b) Controlling behaviour:

   - Has he ever tried to keep you from seeing your friends?
   - Has he ever tried to restrict contact with your family of birth?
   - Has he ever insisted on knowing where you are at all times?
   - Has he ever ignored you and treated you indifferently?
   - Has he ever got angry if you speak with another man?
   - Is he often suspicious that you are unfaithful?
   - Does he expect you to ask his permission before seeking health care for yourself?

Economic violence

247. There are no generally accepted questions for capturing data on economically abusive behaviour that work across all settings. There are a wide range of acts that could be considered economically harmful, some of which might be considered to be an aspect of psychologically controlling behaviour. Again, it is important to remember that the core indicators specifically call for data on economic violence inflicted by an intimate partner. It must be emphasized that capturing data on economic violence will require individual countries to create questions that truly capture data on economic abuse in their specific context. Below are some examples of questions that might be used to capture data on economically abusive behaviour (see model questionnaire contained in annex VII).

- Has he ever refused to give you enough money for household expenses, even when he has money for other things?
- Has he ever prevented you from knowing about or having access to family income?
- Are you able to spend money without his permission?
- Has he ever stopped you or prevented you from working?

> **Box IV.1**
>
> **Measuring female genital mutilation**
>
> The Friends of the Chair of the UN Statistical Commission on indicators on violence against women recommend that the topic of female genital mutilation should be included in surveys on demographic and health topics in countries where it is relevant. The Demographic and Health Surveys incorporate the following set of questions (with appropriate skip patterns):
>
> Women's circumcision
> - Have you ever heard of female circumcision?
> - In some countries, there is a practice in which a girl may have part of her genitals cut. Have you ever heard about this practice?
> - Have you yourself ever been circumcised?
> - Now I would like to ask you what was done to you at that time. Was any flesh removed from the genital area?
> - Was the genital area just nicked without removing any flesh?
> - Was your genital area sewn closed?
> - How old were you when you were circumcised?
> - Who performed the circumcision?
>
> Daughters' circumcision
> - Have any of your daughters been circumcised?
> - Which of your daughters was circumcised most recently?
> - Now I would like to ask you what was done to her at that time. Was any flesh removed from her genital area?
> - Was her genital area just nicked without removing any flesh?
> - Was her genital area sewn closed?
> - How old was she when this was done?
> - Who performed the circumcision?
> - Do you have any daughter who is not circumcised?
> - Do you intend to have any of your daughters circumcised in the future?
> - What benefits do girls themselves get if they are circumcised?
> - Do you believe that this practice is required by your religion?
> - Do you think that this practice should be continued or should it be stopped?
>
> For more information, see www.childinfo.org/fgmc_methodology.html.

Classification and characteristics of violence against women

Relationship of victim to perpetrator

248. Relationship of victim to perpetrator is a key element of any survey on violence against women. It is important to offer responses containing sufficiently detailed categories. Violence perpetrated by an intimate partner should be asked about separately from violence perpetrated by a non-partner. This question is therefore important in the context of non-intimate partner violence. The following question can be used to identify the relationship of victim to perpetrator:

- Could you please tell me about the type of relationship you have with the person who committed the violence against you?

    1. Relative
    2. Acquaintance or friend from the community

3. Supervisor, co-worker
4. Teacher, school official, schoolmate
5. Civil or military authority
6. Stranger
7. Other
8. No answer.

Severity of violence

249. Severity of violence is one of the key dimensions necessary for producing data on the core indicators on violence against women. Severity of violence can be measured by the impacts or consequences of the assault as well as by the nature of the acts of violence themselves. For instance, severe physical violence refers to acts that resulted in bruises, cuts, broken bones, miscarriages and/or a need for medical treatment or hospitalization, acts that caused the woman to be afraid of her partner and/or to fear for her life and acts that occurred at a specific time in the woman's life, such as when she was pregnant. Questions used to assess the consequences of violent acts are likely to differ depending on whether or not the perpetrator was an intimate partner. The following questions can be used to assess the impact of intimate partner violence (see model questionnaire contained in annex VII):

- Did the following ever happen as a result of what your (current or most recent) husband/partner did to you?
    1. You had cuts, scratches, bruises or aches.
    2. You had injuries to eye or ear, sprains, dislocations or burns.
    3. You had deep wounds, broken bones, broken teeth, internal injuries, or any other similar injury.
    4. You had a miscarriage.
- Are you ever afraid of your (current or most recent) husband or partner? Would you say never, sometimes, many times, most/all of the time?

The following question can be used to assess the impact of non-partner violence (see model questionnaire contained in annex VII):

- Did the following ever happen as a result of what .... (USE SAME WORDS TO REFER TO THE PERPETRATOR AS RESPONDENT) did to you?
    1. You had cuts, scratches, bruises or aches.
    2. You had injuries to eye or ear, sprains, dislocations or burns.
    3. You had deep wounds, broken bones, broken teeth, internal injuries or any other similar injury.

250. Acts of beating, choking, threatening with or using a knife, gun or other weapon are considered acts of severe physical violence, regardless of the consequences. It should be noted that one case of victimization can include several acts and that, in the case of repeated victimizations, one severe incident raises the overall severity of all victimizations.

Frequency of violence

251. Frequency of violence can be measured by directly asking the woman how many incidents of violence she has experienced in the past 12 months (or during her lifetime or

since the age of 15, as appropriate). However, when the frequency of violence is high, as is often the case with partner violence, the woman is unlikely to be able to recall the actual number of incidents precisely. In such cases, frequency can be classified into different groups of intensity. By way of example, three different approaches to collecting detailed information on the frequency of violent acts are shown below. It should be remembered, however, that the appropriate way to ask this question will vary according to country context. The question should always therefore be carefully piloted.

- Can you tell me how many times it happened in the past 12 months? (Note that the same question should also be asked for during her lifetime or since the age of 15).
- Can you tell me how often it happened in the past 12 months (or during your lifetime/since the age of 15)?
    1. Every day or nearly every day, all the time
    2. Once or twice a week
    3. Once or twice a month
    4. Less than once a month
- In the past 12 months (or during your lifetime/since the age of 15), did it happen once, a few times or many (5 or more) times? (Note that this question is most often used for partner violence.)

Personal characteristics of respondents

Marital/relationship status

252. Marital/relationship status is a critical component of a survey on violence against women and one of the most difficult questions to measure with accuracy. It can also be one of the most sensitive.

253. It is important to be as inclusive as possible when identifying marital/relationship status because this forms the basis for routing respondents to relevant questions about violence in relationships and, therefore, for establishing prevalence rates for violence in current and previous relationships. The questions and the response categories should extend beyond relationships that are socially or legally sanctioned. It is important to note that intimate relationships do not need to be sexual.

254. The way in which questions about marital/relationship status are framed will depend on the country context. For example, in countries where divorce and intimate relationships outside the context of formal marriage are socially acceptable, a broad range of relationships should be included. In some countries, women do not have relationships before marriage and it is not therefore appropriate to include questions about boyfriends; however, previous relationships should be included in order to capture respondents who are widowed. In some contexts, there is a need to include situations in which a woman has a relationship with a man who has another legal wife. In some countries, de facto relationships are officially recognized only after a certain time period; a survey on violence against women should not have this restriction. In countries where women are officially engaged but will not see their betrothed until the wedding, they should not be considered to have a partner because they are not at risk of partner violence. In some contexts, it will be important for married women to indicate whether or not they are living with their husbands.

Age

255. Every effort should be made to ascertain the exact age of all women respondents in terms of age in completed years or year of birth. Where age cannot be reported with precision, age groups (e.g., 25 to 29 years of age) can be used.

Questions aimed at producing statistics on additional variables

256. The core indicators identified by the Friends of the Chair of the United Nations Statistical Commission on indicators on violence against women form only the minimum required for improving available data on the prevalence and nature of violence against women. The inclusion of additional variables will significantly enrich the overall results of the survey and increase their relevance for policymaking. The range and depth of additional variables considered necessary for policy development will depend on the country context, the objectives of the survey and the heterogeneity of the population. Through consultations with stakeholders, survey managers should identify the additional variables that need to be included in the questionnaire in order for the objectives of the project to be met in that particular setting.

257. The additional variables that are recommended for inclusion in surveys on violence against women are listed below. Examples of questions aimed at capturing data on these variables are provided in annex VIII.

   (a) Personal characteristics of respondents

       (i) Age at first marriage (see para. 259)

       (ii) Educational attainment and literacy (see paras. 260 to 261)

       (iii) Economic activity status (see paras. 262 to 263)

       (iv) Place of residence (see paras. 264 to 265)

       (v) Ethnicity, religion and language (see paras. 266 to 271)

   (b) Experience of violence

       (i) Attitude towards violence against women (see paras. 272 to 273)

       (ii) Reporting to authorities/seeking help (see para. 274)

       (iii) Location of violence (see para. 275)

   (c) Personal characteristics of intimate partners

       (i) Age of partner (see para. 259)

       (ii) Educational attainment and literacy (see paras. 260 to 261)

       (iii) Economic activity status (see paras. 262 to 263)

       (iv) Substance abuse (see paras. 280 to 281)

       (v) Witnessing partner violence in the family of origin (see para. 282)

   (d) Personal characteristics of non-partner perpetrators

       (i) Relationship to victim/Sex (see para. 283).

a. Personal characteristics of respondents

258. Additional details about the characteristics of all women respondents are needed to identify groups of women who are at higher risk. This information is critical for developing appropriate responses and interventions. Selected topics for understanding how different

subgroups of women experience violence are elaborated in this section and include age at first marriage, educational attainment and literacy, economic activity status, place of residence, and ethnicity, religion and language.

a.i.   Age at first marriage

259.   Depending on national circumstances, it may be appropriate to remind respondents that this question refers to her age at the time of the wedding ceremony, not the age at which she became engaged or was committed to be married.

a.ii.   Educational attainment and literacy

260.   The measurement of educational attainment and literacy is specific to the national context owing to the great variation among countries in education systems, structures, terminology and accessibility. Questions must be devised in such a way at to be relevant to the educational system in each country, while at the same time consulting international standards. Educational attainment of respondents is defined as the highest grade or number of years of education that respondents have achieved. This can be measured in open-ended format, i.e., number of years of formal education, or in a structured question with specific response categories such as partial or completed primary education, partial or completed secondary education, and partial or completed post-secondary education. Categories should reflect the unique education system within each country or region. Categories should also be as detailed as possible in order to allow for the flexible regrouping of the data according to different analytical objectives. For international comparisons, survey questions could include categories such as no schooling, primary education, secondary education and post-secondary education in addition to a generic variable on total number of years of schooling.

261.   If relevant, data on the literacy level of respondents should also be captured. Literacy cannot simply be assumed owing to school attendance or educational attainment. There are instances where people leave school without strong literacy skills or lose those skills through lack of practice. It is therefore important to enquire about the literacy level of respondents irrespective of educational attainment. A literate person is one who can read and write a short, simple statement about his or her everyday life. An illiterate person is one who cannot, with understanding, both read and write such a statement. Hence, a person capable of reading and writing only figures and his or her own name should be considered illiterate, as should a person who can read but not write as well as one who can read and write only a ritual phrase that has been memorized.

a.iii.   Economic activity status

262.   Economic activity refers to working for pay or profit, for example for a business or enterprise, on a family farm or service undertaking or in self-employment. It also includes the respondent's temporary absence from a job or self-employment activity in which she had worked and maintained a formal attachment. Possible formats of questions aimed at measuring economic activity include: (i) One question to determine whether the respondent was employed during a specific reference period; (ii) Two questions, one to determine whether the respondent did any work during the reference period and the other to determine whether, if not, she had a job or business to which she would return; (iii) One composite question that includes elements aimed at determining two or more economic characteristics of the respondent; and (iv) Two or more questions, one basic question on economic activity status and additional questions to cover specific categories of workers who are not easy to enumerate. While the single question format is included as an option, two or more questions are generally required.

263.   In surveys where the objective is to derive rates of employment and unemployment, economic activity is measured in greater complexity by including in the calculation such

concepts as actively looking for work and able to start work immediately if a job is offered. In most cases, this level of detail is not needed for a survey on violence against women, where the objective of measuring economic activity is to examine availability of and access to economic resources rather than official unemployment rates.

a.iv. Place of residence

264. The respondent's place of usual residence is the place where she has lived continuously for most of the past 12 months or the place where she intends to live for at least the next six months (if she has recently moved). Place of residence may be categorized as urban or rural. Owing to national differences in the characteristics that distinguish urban and rural areas, there is no single definition that would apply to all countries. Countries must therefore establish their own definition depending on their analytical needs, the objectives of the survey and the national context.

265. Some countries have developed a classification of localities based not only on population size but also on the socioeconomic structure of the population in the localities and contiguous areas. Locality may coincide with a cluster in cluster sampling designs.

a.v. Ethnicity, religion and language

266. Owing to the great variation among countries, questions aimed at measuring ethnicity, religion and language must be developed at the country level. The most recent census of the population may be useful as a starting point for developing these questions. Depending on the country context, ethnicity, religion and language may reflect equivalent characteristics and may not therefore all be needed.

267. Ethnicity can be measured using a variety of concepts, including ethnic ancestry or origin, ethnic identity, cultural origins, nationality, race, colour, minority status, tribe, caste, language and religion, or a combination of these concepts. Because of interpretative difficulties that can occur, it is important that the basic criteria used to measure concepts are clearly explained to interviewers and respondents. The method and the format of the questions used to measure ethnicity can influence the choices that respondents make regarding their ethnic background and ethnic identification.

268. Because of the subjective nature of concepts and increasing intermarriage among groups in some countries, information on ethnicity must be acquired directly from respondents (as opposed to interviewers making that assessment based on personal appearance) and respondents must have the option of indicating multiple ethnic affiliations. Care must be taken to identify indigenous people, as they are an important subgroup in surveys on violence against women. The indigenous population can be identified by ethnic origin (ancestry) and/or by indigenous identity. The number of respondents who specify that they have indigenous ancestry may be much larger than the number who hold an indigenous identity.

269. Data on ethnicity should not be derived from information on country of citizenship or country of birth. The classification of ethnic groups also requires the inclusion of the finest levels of ethnic groups, self-perceived groups, regional and local groups, as well as groups that are not usually considered to be ethnic groups, such as religious groups and those based on nationality. Pre-coding or pre-classification of ethnic groups in closed-ended survey questions may result in a loss of detailed information on the diversity of a population. Since countries collect data on ethnicity in different ways and for different purposes and since the ethnocultural composition of a country could vary widely from country to country, no internationally relevant criteria or classification can be recommended.

270. Religion can be defined as either religious or spiritual belief of preference, regardless of whether or not this belief is represented by membership of or affiliation with an organized group having specific religious or spiritual tenets. Each country that investigates religion as

part of a survey on violence against women should use the definition most appropriate to the national and local contexts and clearly specify in all survey documentation, interviewer training and analytical reports the definition that has been used. For the purposes of international comparisons, each sect should be shown as a subcategory of the religion to which it belongs.

271. Language can be defined as mother tongue (the language usually spoken in early childhood), the usual language most often spoken at home at the current time, or the ability to speak one or more designated languages. Each of these definitions of language serves a different analytical purpose and the decision as to which one to adopt in a survey on violence against women will depend on the local population and on the survey objectives. With respect to data on mother tongue or usual language, it is recommended that each language that is numerically important in country, not just the dominant language, should be shown.

b. Experiences of violence

b.i. Attitude towards violence against women

272. Violence against women is largely hidden and in some contexts there is a high level of tolerance for such acts. Individuals' acceptance of certain social norms concerning gender roles and the use of violence to uphold these norms can serve as a proxy for acceptance of violence against women in the broader society. The Demographic and Health Surveys (DHS) and Multiple Indicator Cluster Surveys (MICS) have developed a standardized module for measuring attitudes towards domestic violence[21]. Some countries have adapted these questions to their local context by including different circumstances, such as if she spends too much money, if she disobeys, if she is unfaithful, if she insults him, if she neglects household chores, if she shows disrespect for her in-laws and if she speaks about the need to protect herself against HIV/AIDS.

273. The WHO Multi-country Survey on Women's Health and Domestic Violence measured women's attitudes towards domestic violence by asking them about the situations in which they believe that a man has a good reason to beat his wife, including situations in which she does not complete the housework, disobeys her husband or refuses to have sex with him. A second set of questions addressed the situations in which women believe that a woman has the right to refuse to have sex with her husband, including situations in which she does not want to, he is drunk, she is sick or he is mistreating her (Garcia-Moreno and others, 2005).

b.ii. Reporting to authorities/seeking help

274. A set of questions on help seeking is generally included in order to identify the proportion of women who have never disclosed what has happened to them as well as the proportion who report crimes of violence to the police or make use of health or social services or informal sources of support, such as family members or others in the local community. These questions are particularly important for partner violence. Taken together, they can shed light on the hidden nature of these crimes. The International Violence against Women Survey (Johnson, Ollus and Nevala, 2008) included a set of questions aimed at assessing the extent to which victims of violence report incidents to the police or other judicial authorities or seek help from health or social services or informal sources of support. As acknowledged in the International Violence against Women Surveys, questions designed to assess the extent to which women seek help from health or social services will need to be modified according to the national context, as the availability of such services varies greatly from country to country.

---

21 See www.childinfo.org/attitudes-methodology.html.

b.iii. Location of violence

275. Examples of locations where non-partner violence can occur include schools, public transport, the workplace, bars and cafes, and public and private spaces. The International Violence against Women Survey included a question on this (Johnson, Ollus and Navala, 2008). It may need to be modified to suit national circumstances.

c. Personal characteristics of intimate partners

276. Knowledge of the characteristics of intimate partners will provide essential information for early intervention and prevention initiatives. The range of relevant characteristics depends to some extent on the national and local contexts, as well as on the survey objectives and sample size. The recommended list includes age, educational attainment and literacy, economic activity status, substance abuse and witnessing partner violence in the family of origin. Given the potential complexity of gathering this information for multiple partners and the burden this implied for respondents, it is recommended that the collection of data on intimate partner characteristics should be restricted to the current or most recent partner.

c.i. Age

277. Age of intimate partners will be determined in the same manner as age of respondent (see para. 259).

c.ii. Educational attainment and literacy

278. The questions on educational attainment and literacy of intimate partners should be consistent with the question on educational attainment and literacy developed for respondents (see paras. 260 to 261).

c.iii. Economic activity status

279. The question on economic activity status of intimate partners should be consistent with the question on economic activity status developed for respondents (see paras. 262 to 263).

c.iv. Substance abuse

280. Measuring substance abuse is a complex undertaking which, for diagnostic and screening purposes, can involve several lengthy test items. For a survey on violence against women, where the purpose is to identify frequency of intoxication, one or two questions that can be easily understood by respondents and for which they have accurate knowledge are sufficient. Depending on the national context, substance abuse can include excessive consumption of alcohol (including commercial or home-brewed), consumption of illegal drugs, misuse of prescription medications and misuse of consumer products in order to achieve an altered state (e.g., sniffing petrol).

281. It is important that measures of substance abuse include frequency of consumption or intoxication and amount consumed within a typical consumption period. This could be defined as drinking to get drunk or drinking a set amount, such as five or more drinks on one occasion.

c.v. Witnessing partner violence in the family of origin

282. Respondents can be asked about their husband's or partner's experience of witnessing domestic violence in their family of origin. If this topic is positioned towards the end of the questionnaire, it can be approached in an abbreviated form. There is no need for the level of detail used to measure intimate partner violence; rather, interviewers can define what is meant by such terms as "violence" or "assault" by referring back to earlier sections of the questionnaire.

d. **Personal characteristics of non-intimate partners**

d.i.   Relationship to victim/sex

283.   The set of characteristics for which data can realistically be captured for non-intimate partner perpetrators of sexual and physical violence is limited to their relationship to the victim and their sex. In some instances, the sex of the perpetrator will be evident from the relationship category selected (e.g., mother or sister), but in others it will be necessary to include a specific question to ascertain this.

Sequence of questions

284.   Aside from the wording of questions, the sequence of questions also requires particular attention when designing the questionnaire, as it can encourage or discourage completion of the survey and affect responses to individual items. Questions in surveys on violence against women must be ordered in such a way as to encourage and facilitate the recall of pertinent information.

285.   The interview should resemble as much as possible, a conversation that flows logically from one set of questions to another and in which questions are linked by brief connecting statements that orient respondents towards a specific topic. Introductory questions should be easy and pleasant to answer, spark the respondent's interest in participating and begin to open communication between the interviewer and the respondent. These principles are particularly important for surveys on violence against women, since they contain topics that can cause embarrassment, shame and fear and which respondents would often prefer to keep private. The sequence of questions is therefore critical in terms of preparing respondents for the questions to come and ensuring that respondents are oriented towards thinking about and disclosing their experiences.

286.   While the questionnaire must contain sufficient non-threatening introductory questions to encourage honest disclosures of violence, care must also be taken to ensure that the opposite problem does not occur, i.e., that the structure of the questionnaire creates the possibility that incidents of violence are double counted, thus leading to confusion among respondents and a possible inflation of estimates of violence.

287.   Following the introduction, individual questions should be grouped in modules/sections according to themes wherever possible and be ordered in a logical sequence. Transitioning statements that signal a change of topic help to add a conversational tone and help respondents to begin to shift their thinking towards the new topic.

288.   Owing to the extremely sensitive nature of the topics to be included in a survey on violence against women, it is important that the question design provides ample opportunity for interviewers to develop a rapport with the respondent. This can be facilitated by situating questions about family composition, health, social networks, personal characteristics and partner characteristics before questions about experiences of violence. This allows interviewers to approach the more sensitive topics gradually, once they have been able to develop a degree of trust with respondents.

289.   If very sensitive questions are placed too close to the beginning of the interview, before interviewers have had an opportunity to develop familiarity with respondents, there is a risk that some respondents will either terminate the interview prematurely or be reticent to respond; this would result in a great deal of important data being lost. Survey developers should not assume that they can predict which questions will be considered sensitive by respondents. For example, in the WHO Multi-country Study on Women's Health and

Domestic Violence against Women, the questions considered most sensitive varied by country: in Bangladesh, questions about family planning are routine and were therefore seen as a good way of building rapport, whereas in Japan such questions are considered highly sensitive and were therefore situated later in the questionnaire (Garcia-Moreno and others, 2005).

290.   With respect to introducing sensitive questions on intimate partner violence, it is good practice to introduce this module of questions by assuring respondents that relationships have both good and bad moments in order to avoid the risk that only socially desirable responses, i.e., those that portray the relationship in positive terms, are given. Situating questions about psychological and economic abuse before questions about physical and sexual violence is important in terms of providing a gradual lead-up to these more sensitive questions. Ordering questions in this way is likely to lead to higher quality data as respondents will be more prepared to answer the questions truthfully. The WHO Multi-country Study provides a good example in this area: the section of the questionnaire dealing with partner violence follows detailed questions about the respondent's personal characteristics, general health, reproductive health and children, the characteristics of her partner and her attitudes towards gender roles. This sequence helps to establish the context for questions about violence.

291.   It is also good practice to place questions about forced sexual acts after questions about physical assaults, since many respondents will have difficulty disclosing these very personal experiences to an interviewer owing to such factors as shame and embarrassment.

292.   There is no clear preference as to whether the module of questions on partner violence should precede the module of questions on non-partner violence or vice versa. Situating questions about violence perpetrated by individuals other than intimate partners before questions about intimate partner violence can help to introduce the topic and to provide a more gradual lead-up to the more sensitive questions concerning intimate relationships. The ordering of these modules should be thoroughly tested prior to implementation of the survey in order to ensure the best situation of questions for disclosures of experiences of violence. This may vary according to particular country contexts.

> **Box IV.2**
>
> **Introductions to sensitive questions**
>
> Introductions to sensitive questions are critical tools for helping interviewers to orient respondents towards thinking about acts of violence occurring within particular contexts and situations that they might be reluctant to disclose. The recommended introduction set out below is designed to orient respondents towards thinking about relationships as having both good and bad times (and therefore to help them to understand that they are not alone if they experience some bad times), to reassure respondents that their answers will remain confidential and to remind respondents of the voluntary nature of their participation. This introduction was used effectively in the WHO Multi-country Study on Women's Health and Domestic Violence against Women. It is worded in such a way as to ensure both that estimates are reliable and that the ethical requirement regarding safety and confidentiality is met.
>
> > *When two people marry or live together, they usually share both good and bad moments. I would now like to ask you some questions about your current and past relationships and how your husband/partner treats (treated) you. If anyone interrupts us I will change the topic of conversation. I would again like to assure you that your answers will be kept secret and that you do not have to answer any questions that you do not want to. May I continue?*
>
> It is equally important to include an introduction to questions about violence involving individuals other than intimate partners in order to ensure that respondents consider a wide range of acts and actors, including acts committed by men and women and acts committed by relatives, friends and acquaintances, and strangers. The following introduction from the UN Economic Commission for Europe survey module on violence against women (see annex VII) is recommended:
>
> > *In their lives, many women have unwanted experiences and experience different forms of maltreatment and violence from all kinds of people, men or women. These may be relatives, other people that they know and/or strangers. If you don't mind, I would like to briefly ask you about some of these situations. Everything that you say will be kept private. I will first ask about what has happened since you were 15 years old and thereafter during the past 12 months.*

Use of skips and filters

293. In a statistical survey on violence against women, not every respondent will be asked every question on the questionnaire. Depending on the answers to some questions, other questions will be skipped. For example, if a respondent replies that she did not have any experiences of victimization, then the questions asking how often these acts occurred and what level of injury was caused can be skipped. Skip patterns make the interview flow smoothly and reduce frustration on the part of respondents owing to the appearance of questions that are irrelevant and time-wasting questions. Such frustration may lead to early termination of the interview.

294. Care must be taken to ensure that skips are correctly placed so that respondents are not excluded from important questions. This requires thorough field-testing of the questionnaire, because once errors are made they are difficult or impossible to correct. An example of an erroneous skip pattern is when only women with children living in the household at the time of the interview are asked if their children ever witnessed their male partners being violent towards them. This will undercount the prevalence of cases where children witnessed violence because some women will have older children who no longer live in the household but were nonetheless exposed to the violence at an earlier time.

295. Often there are occasions where it is necessary to ask one question in order to determine whether or not the respondent has the knowledge or the appropriate characteristics to

respond to a subsequent question or module of questions. These are known as filter questions. For example, in order for respondents to be asked questions about intimate partner violence that are relevant to their particular situation, they must first be asked whether they currently have an intimate partner and whether in the past they have had an intimate partners with whom they are no longer involved. Thus, the question on relationship status is a filter question.

296. The format and design of the questionnaire will also depend on the mode of interviewing and method of data capture. In paper questionnaires, skip instructions and filter questions must be simple enough for interviewers to follow them without error and without causing long delays in the interview. In computer-assisted questionnaires, there is no limit to the number of skip instructions or filter questions that can be included because they are programmed into the computer program in advance and therefore allow interviewers to move through the questionnaire smoothly and accurately. However, excessive use of filter questions nested within other filter questions can cause confusion to data analysts when they attempt to convey the survey results in clear, straightforward messages and may yield results that are unusable owing to the fact that multiple filters have resulted in very small sample counts. Filter questions should therefore be used only as necessary.

297. Since violence by a partner can occur in any type of intimate relationship, a series of questions are required to accurately identify current and previous relationship types so as to screen respondents for modules of questions that address, for example, violence by current or most recent partner, and violence by all other previous partners (as is the case in the UNECE survey module on violence against women). The definition of "intimate partner" is subject to national circumstances; some of the questions listed below, such as those referring to living with a man without being married and being involved in a relationship with a man, may not be appropriate for all country contexts.

- Are you currently married, living together or involved in a relationship with a man without living together?
    1. Currently married
    2. Currently living with a man, not married
    3. Currently having a regular partner (involved in a relationship) without living together
    4. Not currently married or living with a man, not involved in a relationship with a man
    5. Refused/No answer.
- Previously were you married, living together or involved in a relationship with a man without living together? Mark all that apply.
    1. Previously married
    2. Previously living with a man, not married
    3. Previously having a regular partner (involved in a relationship) without living together
    4. Never married or living with a man and never involved in a relationship with a man
    5. Refused/No answer.

These questions can be succeeded by follow-up questions on how the most recent relationship ended and on the total number of relationships.

298. In the examples shown above, respondents who reply that they are currently married, living with a man without being married to him or involved with a man without living together (regular or steady dating) will be filtered into modules of questions concerning violence by current partner. The marital status variable can then be used by analysts to determine whether the relationship entails a married partner, a de facto partner or a dating partner. By including different types of relationships in the marital status question, analysts are able to examine violence prevalence rates by relationship status.

299. All respondents who report ever having had a partner should be filtered into the module of questions concerning psychological, economic, physical and sexual violence by current or most recent partner. Those who report having had at least one other intimate partner in the past can be filtered into the module of questions concerning psychological, economic, physical and sexual violence by previous partners. Some respondents will therefore be asked the same modules of questions twice: once concerning current or most recent partner and a second time concerning previous partners. It should be remembered that questions concerning psychological and economic violence should always be positioned before those concerning physical and sexual violence so that respondents are eased into the more sensitive questions gradually.

300. In the UNECE survey module on violence against women respondents who have a current partner will first respond to questions about violence in the current relationship and will then be filtered into the module of questions pertaining to violence perpetrated by previous partners. Respondents who do not have a current partner should be asked to refer to their most recent previous partner followed by any other previous partner. This ensures that intimate partner violence is not restricted to current relationships and that relationships that have ended are also counted. Questions about violence by any other previous intimate partner (before the current or most recent partner) should be asked only once in order to avoid placing an excessive burden on respondents who have had more than two partners.

301. All respondents, regardless of their marital status or the presence of previous partners, are filtered into modules of questions concerning physical and sexual violence by perpetrators other than intimate partners, followed by questions about the relationship with the perpetrator.

Other aspects of questionnaire design

302. In addition to the content and structure of the questionnaire, consideration should also be given to the format of the questionnaire in order to improve the flow of questions. For example, in the case of paper questionnaires, it is known that the use of graphics, such as arrows, or coloured or bold text, aids in the accurate flow of questions, particularly where skip and filter questions are used. Using different graphic characters and colour variation can help interviewers to navigate the questionnaire more easily, to follow skip patterns accurately, to reduce data entry errors and to reduce the chance that respondents will end the interview prematurely.

303. All responses associated with a particular question should appear on the same page in order to ensure that none are missing and questions associated with the same theme or topic should be grouped closely together. This should be done without crowding the questions, which might cause some to be overlooked.

304. The layout of questions and answers on the questionnaire should be uniform in order to assist with the flow of questions and responses. Uniformity refers to applying a particular layout consistently to all questions and another consistently to all responses. It is advisable to

use bold text for all questions and responses that are to be read out loud by the interviewer and to clearly identify questions for which there can be more than one response by using uniform notation.

305. Different coloured paper can be used to differentiate components of the questionnaire so that interviewers can easily move through sections and omit those that are not applicable. For example, sections concerning the impacts of partner violence will apply only to respondents who report experiencing partner violence. If this section is a different colour from the main part of the questionnaire, it will be easy for interviewers to flip to it without wasting time and appearing to be disorganized.

Testing a questionnaire

306. It is imperative that, once developed, a questionnaire be tested to determine whether it serves the purpose for which it was designed or whether further revision is necessary. Different methods for testing a questionnaire will be covered in this section, including informal testing or pretesting, split samples test or alternatives test, expert revision, cognitive testing and behavioural coding of interview or respondent interactions.

Informal testing/pretesting

307. Informal testing, also called pretesting, is an essential component of the preparatory phase for statistical surveys. Informal testing allows researchers to test their operational concepts and definitions, individual questions and the questionnaire as a whole, the method of interviewing, the data collection protocols and procedures, and (sometimes) the quality and completeness of interviewer training (UNODC and UNECE, 2010). Informal testing is also useful for ensuring that the system developed to capture the data functions efficiently and detects errors.

308. Hence, informal testing should capture the following issues:

- The completeness of individual questions and the questionnaire as a whole in terms of project objectives, clarity and relevance
- The ease of comprehension of survey instructions for interviewers and respondents
- The ease of use of the questionnaire in terms of time requirements, instructions and sequence and flow of questions
- Problems using filter questions and skip patterns
- The completeness and appropriateness of response categories and coding instructions given to interviewers
- The way in which the questionnaire is perceived by respondents in terms of feelings experienced, level of comprehension, response burden and sensitivity to the topics discussed
- Respondent reactions to specific questions, including willingness to disclose sensitive information
- Potential sources of respondent error in terms of recall difficulty or telescoping.

309. Informal testing is particularly important in cases where no pre-existing questionnaire or topic-specific survey exists and new survey tools have been developed. Informal testing

may also be necessary if a pre-existing questionnaire has been adapted for a new culture and/or language. The structure and suitability of the questionnaire needs to be evaluated from wide perspectives, not only from the point of view of respondents, but also in terms of the manageability for interviewers, supervisors and data analysts. The testing of the questionnaire, including the operationalization of major concepts, specific wording of questions and sequencing, is critical for ensuring that outputs will meet expectations.

310. Informal testing is the most basic and the absolute minimum form of testing that should be conducted. This type of testing involves conducting the interview or parts of the interview with a small sample of test respondents. Testing can be undertaken by interviewing respondents using open-ended questions and identifying appropriate closed-ended response categories from the results. When used for this purpose, it is considered that a minimum of 50 respondents is needed to determine appropriate response options from open-ended questions (Statistics Canada, 2003).

311. Informal testing should be conducted in as broad and diverse an environment as possible and should take place across all targeted subgroups in order to ensure that the questionnaire and protocols are appropriate across groups and that there are no differences in terms of understanding of questions or willingness to participate.

312. It can be expected that informal testing will result in revisions to the survey questionnaire and possibly the training materials. Once the instrument is finalized, the entire survey processes should undergo pilot testing (see paragraphs 407 to 410).

Split samples or alternatives test

313. When two or more versions of a questionnaire or survey instrument exist, the split samples test can be used to determine the optimal version of the two. Researchers can assess the relative benefits of differences at the level of question wording, interviewing technique or question sequence (UNODC and UNECE, 2010). This method incorporates an experimental data collection component into the survey project if researchers are unsure about and wish to test the relative merits of different approaches. In its most basic form, half of respondents receive version A and the other half receive version B and the results are then compared. Adequate sample sizes, unbiased samples and a probability sample design are required for valid results to be obtained. This method can be used to test alternative questionnaires, methods of interviewing or other aspects of the methodology. Box IV.3 provides an example of this method as applied to the Swiss component of the International Violence against Women Survey (Johnson, Ollus and Nevala, 2008).

> **Box IV.3**
>
> **Example of split samples or alternatives test: The Swiss component of the International Violence against Women Survey**
>
> While the International Violence against Women Survey (IVAWS) was conducted with a standard methodology and protocols across participating countries, the Swiss study also included a split samples test. The objective of the experimental component was to assess whether differing approaches in the initial screening questions had an impact on disclosure of violence later in the questionnaire. Two versions of the questionnaire were produced: 1,352 interviews were conducted in German and 623 in French. The German questionnaire was almost identical to the one used in the other IVAWS countries, in that it included seven acts of physical violence and five acts of sexual violence. However, it omitted two measures: a residual category asking about "other" types of violence and one type of sexual violence that was considered to be extremely rare. The French questionnaire utilized only three screening questions: two related to physical violence and one related to sexual violence. The researchers were testing whether the selection of respondents with victimization experiences could be completed as effectively with a shorter version of the questionnaire, thereby reducing the time required to complete an interview, response burden, and cost. When the lifetime prevalence rates obtained by the two methods were compared, the shorter (French) version was found to have obtained lower overall prevalence rates (Killias, Simonin and de Puy, 2005).

Expert revision

314. Expert revision involves sharing the draft survey questionnaire and supporting documents with topic experts for review and comment. In addition to the draft survey instrument, experts should also be provided with information regarding the objectives of the study, the resources allocated to the study and the methodology of the project. Experts should then provide a written critique of the draft and identify sections of concern as well as suggestions for possible modification and improvement. The survey developers can then use the expert feedback to adjust and improve the questionnaire and project protocols. Expert revision is an inexpensive form of pretesting and can be repeated multiple times throughout the development of the project (UNODC and UNECE, 2010). Bringing these experts together to discuss their suggested revisions in a group setting can be very beneficial in terms of developing consensus on the survey's content and approach to measurement.

Cognitive testing

315. Cognitive testing provides an insight into respondents' thought process related to how they perceive and respond to the survey questions. Cognitive tests thus provide a measure of the reliability and validity of questions and can help identify potential sources of measurement error. Cognitive testing assesses respondents' comprehension of the survey questions and their reactions to the survey instrument by:

- Evaluating whether questions are understood as they were intended by survey developers
- Evaluating the clarity, ease and completeness of question response codes
- Identifying sensitive topics that can lead to refusals or early termination of the interview
- Assessing the effectiveness of filtering questions
- Assessing the reliability of recall associated with specific reference periods.

316. Cognitive testing can also help identify whether other aspects of the survey, such as the time required to complete the interview and safety measures that have been put in place, are feasible and acceptable to respondents.

317. Typically, cognitive testing occurs in a laboratory setting with specially trained cognitive interviewers testing a small pool of participants; the number of participants can, however, be expanded according to available resources (UNODC and UNECE, 2010). In-person interviews allow for the inclusion of visual or behavioural cues and a natural exchange between interviewer and respondents. That said, it is possible to conduct cognitive testing over the telephone in locations with sufficiently wide telephone coverage. This can be particularly useful for contacting hard-to-reach populations, such as people living in remote communities, or those with limited mobility, such as elderly or disabled people. If the questionnaire was designed to be administered using telephone interviewing, at least some testing should be conducted by telephone in order to evaluate this aspect of the survey method (UNODC and UNECE, 2010).

318. Cognitive testing can include direct observation and thinking aloud exercises. In the direct observation method, researchers simply observe respondents completing the questionnaire or interview and collect information regarding the following (Statistics Canada, 2003):

- Sections that cause confusion to respondents
- Instructions that are read and followed
- Sequences of questions that are completed
- The time that is required to complete each question
- Corrections or revisions that are made to responses.

319. The thinking aloud method requires respondents to think aloud and narrate their thought process as they answer each question (UNODC and UNECE, 2010). Respondents are asked to explain how each of their final responses was chosen. Respondents can provide the rationale behind their selections either in real time, as they complete the survey, or retrospectively in a debriefing session. These exercises help to identify potential sources of error resulting from misunderstandings, unclear questioning or word choice and problems with the sequence or flow of questions or with skip or filter questions (Statistics Canada, 2003). An example of the think aloud method used to construct survey questions on violence against women by Statistics Canada and the insights provided by this testing is presented in box IV.4.

> **Box IV.4**
>
> **Cognitive testing of questions to measure spousal violence**
>
> Statistics Canada includes a module on spousal violence as part of the General Social Survey on Victimization. Ten behaviourally based questions on physical and sexual violence and ten questions designed to measure emotionally abusive and controlling behaviour were included in cognitive testing. The goal of the testing was to ensure that the final questionnaire would appropriately capture a range of experiences and be comprehensive and clearly understood by respondents and that respondents would be willing to disclose sensitive information to interviewers.
>
> Cognitive interviews were conducted with individuals who were recruited through emergency shelters, refugees and support groups. The goal of the face-to-face think aloud interviews was to assess how well the survey and its concepts reflected the lived experiences of these individuals and to ensure that the questions were appropriate for a large scale victimization survey. In addition, respondents completed the survey over the telephone and were then invited to participate in a focus group. During the focus group, participants were asked about their impressions of the survey and its delivery.
>
> The findings from this study provided valuable insights and led to changes in the questionnaire. It also produced the following findings relevant to the study of intimate partner victimization:
>
> - Interviewer training and sensitivity were crucial for identifying respondents in crisis.
> - Many respondents were prepared to disclose sensitive information; for some, it was the first time they had disclosed this information.
> - Many respondents also indicated a level of confidence in the national statistical agency as being the appropriate entity to be collecting this information.
> - Personal suitability and ability to manage stress were among the most important interviewer traits.
> - Establishing rapport and trust with respondents were particularly important for surveys dealing with sensitive topics.
> - Providing a toll-free number for respondents to confirm the legitimacy of the survey was helpful in terms of establishing respondent trust.
> - Introductory statements before modules of questions about violence were key to obtaining disclosures of information about sensitive topics.
> - Behaviourally specific acts were important in terms of facilitating disclosure of violent incidents and helping to reduce personal interpretations of these acts.

Source: Paletta and Mihorean (1998).

320. Interviewers can acquire further information in thinking aloud exercises by utilizing additional techniques such as probing, paraphrasing and confidence ratings. With probing, the interviewer asks the respondent a series of questions in order to delve deeper into the rationale and motivation of the respondent. With paraphrasing, the interviewer asks the respondent to repeat instructions in their own words in order to ensure that they comprehend the questions in the way they were intended. Confidence rating is a subjective measure of how confident a respondent is in the accuracy of their response. This helps to identify decisive answers compared to guesses or less certain answers (Statistics Canada, 2003).

Behavioural coding of interviews

321. Behavioural coding of interviews involves a third person observing. The interviewer and the respondent are observed completing the questionnaire. The observer is looking for specific behaviours and codes the exchange between the pair in a set fashion. Rather than cognitive explanations, this method focuses on behavioural cues exchanged between the pair. The focus is on how the interviewer asks the questions and what responses those questions

elicit from the respondent. This method is useful for identifying problems related to interviewers misreading questions, respondents requesting clarification and topics that appear to be sensitive (Statistics Canada, 2003).

Chapter V
Survey implementation

322. Survey implementation pertains to all steps involved in data collection and data processing. The complexity of the survey operations will vary depending on a variety of factors, such as the mode of interviewing and the social and demographic characteristics of the population, as well as the geographical features of the study area and transportation and communication networks in the case of face-to-face surveys. This chapter expands on important factors to be considered when implementing a survey on violence against women and focuses specifically on interviewer training, ethical and safety issues specific to fieldwork on this particular topic, quality control and pilot testing.

Training of interviewers

323. Specialized training for all project team members is essential to the success of dedicated surveys on violence against women. The team of interviewers, in particular, must receive specialized training on how to conduct the interview owing to the sensitivities involved in interviewing women about experiences of violence. As the public face of the survey and the primary collectors of the statistical data, interviewers and field supervisors must be trained to conduct their work with sensitivity and professionalism.

324. Training should ensure that interviewers are able to perform their duties across a variety of scenarios and possible outcomes. Interviewers should also be trained on the possible dangers that women face when responding to questions concerning their experiences of violence and on ways to help ensure the safety and emotional well-being of respondents and to protect the confidentiality of the information collected.

325. Field supervisors will need to understand all aspects of the interviewing and data collection processes, including safety and other ethical issues, and must therefore receive extensive training so that they are prepared to respond to and support interviewers during data collection. This training may precede interviewer training. However, in many surveys field supervisors will be trained at the same time as interviewers but will also need to attend specific sessions for field supervisors. This knowledge is also essential for questionnaire designers and other team members, as the survey instruments and all protocols must provide the basis necessary for conducting the survey ethically and with all due regard for the safety of respondents and interviewers.

Basic training

326. Some of the basic training for interviewers working on a survey on violence against women will be the same as that used in other household surveys. The goals of the basic training are to ensure that, at its conclusion, interviewers fully understand the purpose and structure of the survey, understand how to effectively and correctly conduct an interview, are able to develop a rapport with respondents and to manage the relationship, are motivated and

understand the importance of their role and are able to accurately record the data according to participants' responses. An effective training programme for interviewers will outline the various goals and phases of the training. It is also recommended to develop manuals and learning materials incorporating everything that will be covered in the training.

327. The elements to be included in a basic training programme for interviewers are as follows (UNODC and UNECE, 2010):

- Understanding the purpose, goals and background of the project so as to be able to respond to participants' questions and thereby to instil confidence and legitimacy to the survey

- Understanding the purpose of each question in the questionnaire and its possible responses, as well as the overall structure of the questionnaire, including skip patterns, filter questions and specific components

- Understanding concepts and terminology, such as how physical, sexual, psychological and economic violence are defined

- Understanding the methodology behind the survey, including sampling and respondent selection (it is common for respondents to enquire how their household was selected)

- Understanding how to probe without prompting, how to avoid errors while recording responses and the importance of accurately identifying certain subgroups, such as those based on marital and relationship status, which are critical for deriving accurate estimates of current and previous partner violence

- Managing relationships with respondents and learning how to effectively develop and maintain rapport, create a climate that encourages participation and disclosure, and respond to questions

- General interviewing techniques

- Being comfortable and confident with the survey technology and other technical aspects (e.g., procedures for properly completing a paper questionnaire)

- Managing difficult situations while remaining calm and professional.

Specialized training for surveys on violence against women

328. In addition to the basic training required for conducting statistical sample surveys, interviewers who are selected to work on surveys on violence against women must receive training specific to carrying out their role, taking into consideration the sensitivity of the subject matter and all measures required to protect the safety and confidentiality of respondents. The primary objectives of specialized interviewer training on this topic are to provide an understanding of the following:

- The extreme sensitivity of the topic

- Violence against women and its impacts on victims

- Societal myths about violence against women and how they affect victims and interviewers

- Gender issues at the personal and community levels

- The goals of the survey or module of questions on violence against women

- The ethical requirements of surveys on violence against women, including the importance of strategies for addressing the confidentiality and safety of and support for respondents

- The skills needed to interview on this topic, including encouraging participation in the survey and creating a climate that promotes disclosures of sensitive information

- Interviewing techniques for building a rapport with respondents

- The skills needed to detect when respondents are at risk of being overheard and to reschedule interviews accordingly

- How to identify and respond appropriately to emotional trauma by referring respondents to resources in the local community and by avoiding emotional involvement or counselling

- How to identify emotional reactions in themselves that result from working on this topic (such as traumatization due to reliving their own experiences or hearing traumatic stories day after day) and how to develop the skills needed to manage and reduce stress.

329. At the end of the training, interviewers must fully understand the importance of their role and the legitimacy of the survey, as this will send a message to respondents that their participation is important. They must also have confidence in their own personal skills and in their ability to manage the interview in a competent manner in order to prevent doubts and insecurities surfacing during an interview as this could have a negative effect on participation and disclosure rates and on the quality of the data collected. Interviewers who do not seem suitable for the job will need to be released without prejudice.

330. The interviewer selection process should include screening for basic knowledge and for sensitivity to the topic of violence against women (as outlined in paragraphs 207 to 217). To ensure consistency among interviewers, it is recommended that training should be designed around a model in which interviewers are assumed to have little pre-existing knowledge of the particular sensitivities of this topic.

331. Surveys on violence against women entail a wide range of ethical issues that need to be clearly elaborated during the planning phase and throughout the training and consistently monitored during data collection. All interviewer training should follow the ethical and safety recommendations for research on domestic and violence against women established by WHO (see box V.6).

332. Below are some elements of sensitivity training that are essential in terms of creating effective protocols to ensure that interviewers and supervisors are adequately trained to undertake this work and to produce reliable data in an ethical manner, taking into account the sensitivities of the research topic and the fact that many participants will find it difficult or be reluctant to respond to questions.

333. Sensitivity training is an important component of interviewers' training. Sensitivity refers to interviewers' ability to pose very delicate questions about experiences of violence in a respectful manner, to accurately assess the feelings or reactions of respondents in a variety of situations and to respond appropriately.

334. Sensitivity training must also incorporate sensitization to gender issues, the dynamics and causes of violence against women and the impacts of violence on women's health and well-being. Listening to and discussing in-depth testimonies of abused women and advocates for abused women can be helpful in this regard. During the training, interviewers should

be encouraged to discuss any bias or stereotypical views they may have concerning women who are experiencing violence or their decisions to leave or stay with their violent partner or to access help. This is necessary in order to reduce the chances that interviewers will respond with judgemental comments when interacting with respondents. Models of sensitivity training are available for adaptation to specific country contexts (e.g., Jansen and others, 2004).

335. The sensitivity training that was done as part of the International Violence against Women Survey included the following (Johnson, Ollus and Nevala, 2008; Ellsberg and others, 2007):

- An understanding of how violence against women is defined by law or custom in the country and how it is measured in the survey
- Common societal myths concerning women's experiences of sexual violence, intimate partner violence and other forms of violence
- How these myths may affect respondents and their willingness to report their experiences to a survey interviewer
- How these myths may affect interviewers in the course of their work
- The appropriate attitude and tone for speaking with respondents and posing sensitive questions without appearing to be judging or blaming them
- Using non-judgemental language and attitude
- How to engage in active listening
- How to ensure respondents' safety during the course of the interview (this will vary depending on the mode of interviewing)
- How to ensure their own safety when interviewing in face-to-face contexts
- How to recognize and respond to emotional distress on the part of respondents by referring women to resources available locally
- Establishing limits on the types of support and assistance that an interviewer is able to provide
- Barriers and factors that contribute to non-disclosure of sensitive information
- How to develop the rapport needed to encourage honest disclosures of violence, recognizing that the survey interview may be the first disclosure
- How to identify potential crisis situations and respond appropriately
- How to identify personal stressors and strategies for self-care.

336. One objective of sensitivity training is to stimulate a discussion about stereotypes, prejudices and myths about female victims of violence that may be widespread in the general population. A variety of different formats can be used to raise important issues during the training, such as films, documentaries, newspaper articles, statistical data, theories about the causes of violence, testimonials, guest speakers and brainstorming. Holding discussions among interviewers about their own bias during the training is important in order to prevent such bias from surfacing during an interview, as if it did, the interviewer could come across as blaming or judging the respondent.

337. Given the personal and delicate nature of the information requested in surveys on violence against women, participants can be expected to react in a wide range of ways. Some respondents may be open to disclosing their experiences and may view the survey as an opportunity to make their experiences known. Others may be fearful that a violent partner

might learn of their participation in the survey, feel disturbed by the content of the interview, be traumatized by recent experiences of violence or feel embarrassed or stigmatized when disclosing their experiences. Some women may be very reluctant to discuss family matters with an outsider. Therefore, interviewer training should be designed to include a multitude of possible reactions by respondents, including crisis situations and pleas for assistance, and should include opportunities for interviewers to develop the skills necessary to effectively respond in an empathetic and supportive manner (UNODC and UNECE, 2010).

338. It is important that interviewers are trained to react to emotional distress in a warm, empathetic but neutral manner, to provide information on potential sources of support to every respondent without putting them at risk of (more) violence and to refer respondents to a pre-prepared list of agencies in the local community that can provide assistance. For some interviewers, the natural reaction to someone in distress is to offer help and advice. However, interviewers must be instructed not to counsel respondents themselves. The list of agencies in the local community is provided in order to absolve the interviewers from this responsibility, while at the same time meeting the ethical requirement to provide support to respondents who are distressed by the survey questions.

339. Interviewers must also be prepared to respond to additional situations that come into play in a survey on violence against women. For example, interviewers should receive training on possible situations in which respondents may find themselves when presented with the survey questions, including situations where their safety may be at risk, and be prepared, if necessary, to find a more convenient time or a safer place for the interview. The project budget must incorporate the costs associated with rescheduling a portion of interviews.

340. Interviewers should also be trained to ensure that interviews are conducted with privacy and to detect whether respondents actually have the privacy necessary to respond to sensitive questions. All efforts must be made to interview respondents at a time when other household members, particularly male partners, are not present. In some countries, it is unacceptable or even dangerous for a woman to speak about family matters to outsiders. In other cases, there may be great reluctance to discuss these matters candidly if other people are present. When presented with assurances of confidentiality and a well-trained and skilled interviewer, most respondents will disclose very personal and sensitive information.

341. Ensuring that respondents have privacy will require different training in face-to-face and telephone interviewing situations. For example, in face-to-face interviews, interviewers should be trained to terminate the interview or to change the subject to a "dummy" questionnaire if interrupted. In telephone interviews, interviewers should be trained to detect when a respondent is at risk of being overheard, either by hearing other people in the background, by hearing the respondent speaking to others or by noticing pauses in the respondent's replies. It is good practice to confirm with respondents that they have the privacy to continue before beginning modules of questions on sensitive topics.

342. A number of interactive methods for training interviewers in the necessary skills are recommended, such as role playing and group discussion. Role playing is an effective technique for developing the skills needed to recognize and react effectively and professionally to challenging situations. It provides opportunities to rehearse a variety of scenarios and to discuss strategies for meeting challenges. It also allows interviewers to observe effective strategies in others and to analyse their own reactions and behaviours. Examples of role play scenarios include the following:

- A threatening husband interrupts the interview
- A respondent has an emotional reaction to a disclosure of rape

- A respondent reacts negatively to questions about intimate partner violence and wants to end the interview
- A child or teenager interrupts the interview
- A selected respondent refuses to participate in the survey citing a lack of time or interest.

343. Other interactive methods such as group discussions and debriefings can be effective in terms of identifying concerns that interviewers may have about survey content, strategies for interacting with respondents and ways to manage their own reactions to the survey content as well as those of respondents.

344. Given the nature of the work, which involves hearing numerous personal disclosures of violence and the possibility of observing the effects of violence on respondents directly, recognizing and reducing emotional trauma among interviewers during fieldwork is an essential component of interviewer and supervisor training. Additionally, given the prevalence of many forms of violence against women, it is probable that some interviewers will have personal experience of the types of violence included in the survey. Such interviewers may experience distress or be reminded of painful experiences during training or data collection.

345. The Pan American Health Organization/World Health Organization manual "Helping ourselves to help others: Self-care guide for those who work in the field of family violence" (Claramunt, 1999) has been incorporated into the training and survey protocols of various surveys on violence against women.[22] This manual is designed to help people who work directly or indirectly with victims or perpetrators of sexual or domestic violence to manage and minimize the emotional distress that they suffer as a result of being exposed to stories of violence and abuse. It contains useful suggestions for avoiding burnout and promoting self-care that apply equally to survey interviewers, who must listen to personal stories of violence as part of their everyday work.

346. It is common in violence against women surveys to include a counsellor or psychologist in the project team. This person must be skilled in stress management as he/she will be required to train interviewers to recognize a build-up of stress in themselves and to identify the impact it is having on them. He/she will also teach interviewers self-care techniques that help to minimize the negative effects of stress over the immediate and long terms. Interviewers should also be offered opportunities for regular debriefings as well as a final debriefing with, for example, a psychologist or counsellor and to receive trauma counselling as a group or on an individual basis as needed (see box V.1 for a description of the trauma debriefings that were provided for interviewers working on the International Violence against Women Survey). Field supervisors will also need to be trained to respond to interviewer stress and to provide debriefings. This is particularly important in face-to-face settings, where field operations tend to be less centralized.

---

[22] An example is the National Survey on the Dynamics of Relationships in Homes conducted in Mexico in 2006.

> **Box V.1**
>
> **Trauma debriefings provided for interviewers in the International Violence against Women Survey**
>
> It was recommended to national coordinators in all countries that interviewers in the field should have access to the following three levels of support for dealing with emotional distress:
>
> - The option of contacting the project coordinator at any time during the fieldwork to ask for assistance or to talk about distressing interview experiences. At least once a week, a counsellor should be available; on the other days, a qualified member of the research staff should be available. The counsellor should be on call during the survey period to provide emergency assistance to interviewers when necessary.
> - Group meetings once a week during the fieldwork and required afterwards.
> - Individual meetings with a counsellor as required.

347. Together with the careful selection and thorough training of interviewers (including training more than actually needed so as to have a pool of reserves), the provision of emotional support throughout the fieldwork will help to ensure that interviewers are able to conduct their work effectively and will eliminate the need to recruit and train additional interviewers while the survey is in the field, something which can be disruptive and have unanticipated cost implications. Interviewers who feel unable to continue with the project despite extensive training and emotional support must be permitted to leave the interviewing team and be supported in their decision to do so.

348. Maintaining participant confidentiality in a survey on violence against women is of paramount importance and can be challenging in certain locations. Interviewers must be trained not to jeopardize or compromise the confidentiality of the data collected. They must be given clear instructions not to comment on any of the survey work and be made acutely aware of the consequences of a breach of confidentiality. They are also responsible for the protection and safekeeping of questionnaires until they are submitted to field supervisors.

349. Considering the sensitivity of the survey topic, it may be beneficial to extend some of the interviewer training beyond the actual training course and into the field implementation phase in order to allow the contents of the training and skill development to be assimilated over time. Shorter training sessions accompanied by readings and exercises to be completed at home are just two suggestions for alternating the format of the training. By way of example, an outline three-week training programme developed for fieldworkers and supervisors in the WHO Multi-country Study on Women's Health and Domestic Violence against Women can be found in box V.2. Evidence of the value of the specialized training programme developed for interviewers in the same study is given in box V.3.

Box V.2

Three-week training programme developed for fieldworkers and supervisors in the WHO Multi-country Study on Women's Health and Domestic Violence against Women

Training day	Topics covered

Day 1	Introduction to training
	Group introductions
	Exploring concepts of sex/gender
	Overview of gender-based violence
	  - Definitions
	  - Prevalence
	  - Characteristics

Day 2	Causes and consequences of gender-based violence
	  - Ecological framework
	  - Health effects
	Dynamics of abuse
	Strategies and local services available to abused women

Day 3	Overview of the project
	  - Goals of the study
	  - Major areas to be covered
	  - Organization of fieldwork
	  - Dates
	  - Expectations
	Overview of the questionnaire
	Basic interviewing techniques
	  - Introducing the study to respondents
	  - Field procedures
	  - Conducting the interview
	  - Safety measures

Day 4	Household questionnaire and selection of respondents Review of sections 1 and 2 of the questionnaire
Day 5 - 7	Review of the remaining sections of the questionnaire and role plays for each section
Day 8 - 9	Practice interviews (preferably in the field)
Day 10	Discussion and debriefing and revision of protocols or questionnaire, as needed
Day 11 - 12	Pilot test
Day 13	Discussion and debriefing and final revision of protocols or questionnaire, as needed

Source: Ellsberg and others, (2007)/modified.

> **Box V.3**
>
> **Evidence of the value of the training programme developed for interviewers in the WHO Multi-country Study on Women's Health and Violence against Women**
>
> Additional evidence of the value of the training approach comes from the survey conducted in Belgrade in 2003. With technical support provided by WHO, 13 previously inexperienced interviewers were fully trained over 2.5 weeks. However, because of pressure to finish the fieldwork, 6 weeks after the start of the fieldwork, an additional group of 21 professional interviewers from a survey company were recruited to assist with the interviews. This new batch of experienced interviewers received less than a day's training, which included orientation on gender and violence issues and a brief review of the questionnaire and field procedures. In total, 1,445 complete interviews were conducted in Belgrade, with 47 per cent of the households being visited by the study-trained interviewers and 53 per cent by the professional interviewers. This provided a unique opportunity to see how levels of participation and disclosure differed between the two groups.
>
> The previously inexperienced but carefully selected and trained interviewers obtained a significantly higher response rate (93 per cent versus 86 per cent; $p < .0001$) and a significantly higher disclosure rate (26 per cent versus 21 per cent; $p < .05$) for physical and/or sexual partner violence than the professional interviewers. The interviews that were conducted by the study-trained interviewers were shorter than those conducted by the professional interviewers: The median duration was between 5 and 7 minutes less for every type of partner violence. Respondent satisfaction at the end of the interview was significantly higher for women, both with (46 per cent versus 29 per cent; $p < .01$) and without violence (46 per cent versus 38 per cent; $p < .05$), interviewed by the study-trained interviewers.
>
> These findings highlight the degree to which interviewer selection and training can affect levels of participation, disclosure, and satisfaction with the interview and illustrate the inadvisability of assuming that less training is needed when using professional interviewers.

Source: Jansen and others, (2004).

Training manuals

350. Time and resources must be dedicated, in the planning phase, to the development and preparation of instructional and training materials that cover all aspects of the fieldwork. These manuals are needed to provide unambiguous guidance to interviewers in terms of handling all foreseeable situations that might affect the nature or quality of the collection of reliable data. A basic list of essential components of manuals to be developed for dedicated surveys on violence against women includes the study protocol (see paragraph 218 and box III.2), interviewer's manual and field supervisor's manual.

Interviewer's manual

351. The interviewer's manual is designed primarily to assist interviewers in maintaining consistency in their day-to-day responsibilities, including that of responding to participants' questions about the survey. The interviewer's manual will include information on the background of the project, interviewing techniques, field operations and procedures, complying with data collection requirements and addressing the ethical and safety issues associated with conducting interviews on violence against women.

352. In addition to outlining expectations and providing information regarding interviewer-respondent interactions, these manuals should also outline solutions for handling problematic situations that can occur during any phase of the interview. The manuals should offer tools and strategies for addressing various situations that may arise during the performance of an interviewer's duties. All of these situations should have been discussed during the training. Providing a frequently asked questions section can help to prepare interviewers for many of the common questions that respondents will ask. In general, this section can be used

to help interviewers to be better prepared and to respond to difficult situations (UNODC and UNECE, 2010).

353. The interviewer's training manual and accompanying training process are the main tools used to familiarize interviewers with the questionnaire in terms of content and procedure. Many of the topics covered in the training will be included in the interviewer's manual. The interviewer's manual is typically presented in a modular format and includes sections on the following (UNODC and UNECE, 2010):

- Interviewing techniques, including instructions on establishing rapport, preventing telescoping,[23] encouraging disclosure and managing safety and ethical considerations
- Topics related to the timing of interviews and beginning and ending the interview
- Method of questionnaire administration and managing the use of data collection tools or software
- A question-by-question explanation of the questionnaire to enable interviewers to respond to queries from participants and to understand how responses should be coded.

354. Box V.4 provides a list of items to be included in the interviewer's manual.

Box V.4

Essential items for the interviewer's manual

I. Background on violence against women
   A. Extent of violence against women
   B. Consequences of violence against women
   C. Understanding the causes of domestic violence
   D. Women's responses to violence: Coping and retaliation

II. Overview of the study
   A. You and the study
   B. Survey objectives
   C. The sample
   D. Survey questionnaire
   E. Role of the interviewer
   F. Training of interviewers
   G. Supervision of interviewers

III. Conducting an interview
   A. Dress
   B. Building a rapport with the respondent
   C. Finding somewhere safe to conduct the interview
   D. Tips for conducting the interview
   E. Language of the interview (for multilingual surveys)

IV. Field procedures
   A. Preparatory activities
   B. Contacting households
   C. Introducing the study
   D. Contacting selected female respondents
   E. Revisiting households
   F. Consent form
   G. Interviews
   H. Checking completed questionnaires

---

[23] Telescoping refers to a respondent's incorrect specification of when an event occurred in relation to the reference period.

        I. Returning completed questionnaires
        J. Data quality
        K. Supplies required for fieldwork
  V. General procedures for completing the violence against women module
        A. General format of the violence against women module
        B. Asking the questions
        C. Recording the responses
        D. Correcting mistakes
        E. Following instructions
  VI. Ethical and safety issues
        A. Sensitivity of research topic
        B. Individual consent and voluntary participation
        C. Confidentiality
        D. Physical safety of respondents
        E. Handling interruptions
        F. Being non-judgemental and respecting women's decisions
        G. Reporting child abuse
        H. Provision of crisis intervention
  VII. Supporting women who report experiencing violence
        A. Your role as an interviewer
        B. Responding to women who become distressed
        C. Identifying whether to terminate or reschedule an interview
  VIII. Interviewer well-being
        A. Support for interviewers
        B. Safety of interviewers
        C. Working as a team
  IX. Employment conditions and expectations
        A. Expectations of interviewers
        B. Mechanisms for quality control
        C. Conditions of employment
        D. Payment and working conditions

Source: Jansen (2011).

Field supervisor's manual

355. The field supervisor's manual is the complementary volume to the interviewer's manual and is written expressly to meet the needs of field supervisors and site managers and to address the foreseeable challenges that they may encounter during the course of the study. Field supervisors should also be experts in the interviewer's manual and fully understand the expectations and requirements of the interviewer's role in order to provide interviewers with guidance, coaching and intervention, when necessary.

356. Generally, field supervisors can expect to receive from interviewers queries related to scheduling and following up on interviews, dealing with difficult or challenging situations involving respondents or other household members, appropriate coding of ambiguous responses and responding to questions from participants or household or community members about the legitimacy and focus of the survey. The field supervisor's manual must contain clear instructions on how to handle each foreseeable situation in a consistent and professional manner that will not put at risk the safety of respondents or interviewers, response rates, the success of the survey or the credibility of the national statistical agency or the agency sponsoring the project.

357. In addition, field supervisor training and the field supervisor's manual must cover all aspects of the management of field operations, logistics and procedures, procedures for monitoring the performance of interviewers in terms of refusals and disclosure, as well as the

requirements designed to ensure the safe and ethical conduct of the survey. Box V.5 outlines the essential components of the field supervisor's manual.

Box V.5

Essential items for the field supervisor's manual

I. Study protocols
II. Responsibilities of the field supervisor
III. Expectations of interviewers
IV. Conducting an interview
    A. Building rapport
        i. Identifying safe interview locations
        ii. Interviewing tips
V. Field procedures
    A. Preparation
    B. Arranging transportation and accommodation
    C. Contacting households
    D. Introducing the study
    E. Contacting selected respondents
    F. Revisiting households
    G. Consent forms
    H. Supplies required for fieldwork
VI. Quality control procedures
    A. Completing quality control checklists
    B. Observing or monitoring interviewers' performance
    C. Providing feedback to interviewers
VII. Providing feedback to project managers on quality control indicators
VIII. General procedures for completing the questionnaire
    A. General format of the questionnaire
    B. Asking questions
    C. Recording responses
    D. Correcting errors
    E. Follow-up with refusals to participate
IX. Ethical and safety issues
    A. Sensitivity training
    B. Consent and voluntary participation
    C. Confidentiality
    D. Physical safety of respondents
    E. Physical safety of interviewers
    F. Handling interruptions
    G. Non-judgemental and respectful attitude
    H. Provision of crisis intervention
    I. Responding to women who become distressed
    J. Responding to interviewers who become distressed or experience emotional trauma

---

Source: Jansen and others (2007)/(modified).

Ethical issues in the implementation of violence against women surveys

358. This section will elaborate on the specific ethical issues related to survey implementation, including safety of respondents and interviewers, confidentiality and anonymity of respondents and minimizing and responding to emotional trauma on the part of respondents and interviewers. An additional requirement is the ethical conduct of statisticians in releasing the survey data. A comprehensive list of the ethical principles to be followed when implementing a survey on violence against women is set out in box V.6.

> **Box V.6**
>
> **Ethical and safety recommendations for research on domestic violence against women**
>
> The World Health Organization recommends that all statistical surveys on violence against women should adhere to the following ethical principles in order to ensure that they are conducted in an ethical manner that minimizes harm to participants and interviewers. These are widely accepted as an essential component of planning and undertaking surveys on this topic.
>
> - The safety of respondents and the research team is paramount and should guide all project decisions.
> - Prevalence studies need to be methodologically sound and to build upon current research experience about how to minimize the underreporting of violence.
> - Protecting confidentiality is essential in order to ensure women's safety and data quality.
> - All research team members should be carefully selected and receive specialized training and ongoing support.
> - The study design must include actions aimed at reducing any possible distress caused to the participants by the research.
> - Fieldworkers should be trained to refer women requesting assistance to available sources of support. Where few resources exist, it may be necessary to create short-term support mechanisms.
> - Researchers and donors have an ethical obligation to help ensure that their findings are properly interpreted and used to advance policy and interventions.
> - Violence questions should be incorporated into surveys designed for other purposes only when ethical and methodological requirements can be met.

Source: World Health Organization (2001).

Safety of respondents

359. The potential for putting women at risk of violence by inviting them to participate in a survey cannot be underestimated. In order to achieve reliable results, it is essential that women who are experiencing violence from intimate partners or other family members at the time that they are contacted to participate in an interview are able to respond in a manner that will not jeopardize their safety. It is therefore critical that survey designers put in place mechanisms that will help to ensure that respondents are in a position to answer freely and without fear of repercussions. Safety must be a guiding principle for ethical conduct throughout all stages of the survey, including during the early stages of drafting the questionnaire and training interviewers, but most particularly while conducting interviews and collecting data.

360. Field supervisors may be required to contact households that have refused outright to participate in the survey in order to attempt to engage the women concerned, thus improving response rates and the representativeness of the sample. Great care must be taken, however, to ensure that attempts to "convert" reluctant households do not jeopardize the safety of women who may be living with violence or the safety of field staff.

361. An important aspect of reducing the risks to respondents' safety is to apply a "safe" name to the survey, i.e., one that does not identify the survey topic by using a term such as violence against women or domestic violence or any other similarly revealing term. For example, to ensure that community and family members did not know the focus of the WHO Multi-country Study on Women's Health and Domestic Violence against Women, the survey was introduced at all stages during the field implementation as a survey on women's health and life events (Garcia-Moreno and others, 2005). The International Violence against Women

Survey, meanwhile, was introduced as a survey on women's personal safety (Johnson, Ollus and Nevala, 2008).

362. Being aware of the possible risks to safety requires different strategies depending on the mode of interviewing. In telephone surveys, interviewers must be trained to detect the presence of others during the interview. For instance, interviewers in a Canadian survey, which was conducted by telephone, were trained to detect whether another household member was present and to offer respondents a toll-free telephone number that they could use if they had to hang up suddenly or wanted to continue the interview at another time. Over 1,000 women out of a total sample of 12,300 called this number either to verify the legitimacy of the survey, to continue a disrupted interview or to add additional information (Johnson, 1996). Also, interviewers on the National Intimate Partner and Sexual Violence Survey in the United States were trained to establish a safety plan with respondents whereby respondents could stop an interview by saying "goodbye" if at any time they felt unsafe. Interviewers also checked in with respondents periodically during the interview to confirm they were able to proceed (Black and others, 2011).

363. It is difficult to anticipate specific safety features that will be appropriate in all contexts. However, successful experience gained in past surveys on violence against women can be used to guide future surveys on the topic. For instance, in a survey of violence against women conducted in Pakistan, where many women live in multigenerational households and have their movements controlled by male household members and senior women (the mother or mother-in-law), survey designers prepared two questionnaires: one for interviewing one eligible woman in the household, which focused on violence against women, and another to administer to the senior woman and male household members, which covered household demographics and the family's customs and traditions, factors that might be related to female family members' experiences of violence (Andersson and others, 2009). This helped to ensure that women responding to the main questionnaire had privacy to speak while others in the household would assume that she was given the same questionnaire as they were. (In households with just a senior woman, she was given both questionnaires.) This required at least two female interviewers and one male to travel as a team to each household. The role of the male team member was also to obtain permission to conduct the interviews from community leaders and to ensure the safety of female team members.

Safety and well-being of interviewers

364. An important component of overseeing interviewers' work and performance in a survey on violence against women is that of anticipating, detecting and responding to the emotional impacts of this work. Regardless of the mode of interviewing, interviewers will be engaged in emotionally draining work. Attention must be paid to strategies for preventing burnout, for example, by offering interviewers regular debriefings by supervisors or counsellors specially engaged as part of the project team and by giving interviewers time between interviews to participate in less taxing administrative tasks. If they do not take these precautions, and if they did not over recruit sufficiently to have extra interviewers to begin with, field managers may need to undertake additional recruitment and training in the midst of the fieldwork, something which can be disruptive and costly to the overall project. It is preferable to carefully select interviewers with the requisite skills, to train them thoroughly and to aim to retain them for the duration of the project by ensuring that they receive adequate supervision and are given sufficient opportunity for regular debriefings by qualified members of the project team.

365. In contexts where the mode of interviewing is face to face, the safety of interviewers is of paramount concern. Interviewers' personal safety may be threatened if they are required to

enter unsafe neighbourhoods or travel alone or if they are in a household with an aggressive household member. The safety of female interviewers may be threatened in locations where it is not customary for a woman to work outside the home or to travel with a man who is not her husband (Andersson and others, 2009). Field managers must assess each situation and provide male escorts, emergency telephone numbers and other security mechanisms as required to ensure the safety of the interviewers at all times.

Confidentiality and anonymity

366. While confidentiality and anonymity are requirements for all statistical data collection exercises, they are particularly important for surveys on violence against women, owing to the sensitivity of the topic and the potential harm that could come to respondents if their participation in the survey or particular responses are made public. All interviewers and field supervisors and anyone else working on the survey in any capacity must complete a pledge of confidentiality and all violations of confidentiality must be met with swift action to minimize harm to respondents or field staff. Provisions for legal action against breaches of confidentiality should be put in place and action taken in response to violations. In order to ensure respondent confidentiality and anonymity, the following principles must be observed, depending on whether interviews are conducted face to face or by telephone:

- No interviewers should conduct interviews in their own community.

- Participants should be informed of confidentiality and anonymity procedures as part of the process of obtaining informed consent.

- No names or other identifying information, such as telephone numbers or addresses of respondents, should be written on questionnaires. Unique codes should be used for each respondent instead. Any personal identifiers should be kept separately from the questionnaires and destroyed upon completion of the interviews.

- Questionnaires must be kept in a secure location with limited access. Paper questionnaires should ultimately be destroyed, but only after data entry and data checks have been carried out. It may also be possible to create electronic versions of paper questionnaires, which should then be kept under the same rigorous protection as other data; this would allow paper questionnaires to be destroyed more quickly. Before the destruction of any paper questionnaires, it must be ascertained that either they will never need to be checked again or electronic copies have been made.

- Access to and control of data files must be rigorously protected. Data files should be shared with researchers only when it has been determined that individuals cannot be identified. Some variables may have to be suppressed or aggregated if they contain identifying information, for example, small geographical areas or unique personal characteristics.

- Particular care should be taken during the analysis of the data and presentation of the research findings to ensure that data are aggregated and no one community or individual can be identified.

367. Informed consent is extremely important for any survey but, given the sensitive nature of the topic, informed consent should be considered very carefully in a survey on violence against women. Informed consent for this type of survey should not just be considered at one moment, but reiterated throughout the process. It should also be noted that consent forms

signed by the respondent may cause problems in this type of survey. The reasons for this are as follows:

- Any document of consent that uses a signature may allow a breach of confidentiality and/or privacy that could pose a risk to subjects. This does not need, however, to breach the data protection rules that have been established for the survey; the consent forms should be marked with a code and the identification data of the individual kept elsewhere.

- The mere act of signing a consent form may affect a respondent's willingness to disclose violence and may bias the results from women most at risk of violence at home. For example, women who experience domestic violence often have very controlling partners requiring women living in such situations to sign any piece of paper resembling a "contract" may cause them high levels of distress and ultimately result in their refusal to participate in the survey or to disclose violence. The act of signing may make the woman afraid that her partner will find out about the survey and she will not therefore mention anything about his behaviour. In some countries, women are even afraid to put a cross on a piece of paper, because for every action involving a pen they require permission from their husband.

368. Of course consent must always be obtained, but the obligation for the respondent to sign a consent form could be waived. Again, consent is not waived, only the signature. Written consent and the reasons the subject may choose to consent without signing should be discussed; the study must always be discussed and the subject's questions answered. Most ethical committees (whether national committees or those of research institutes) have lists of circumstances in which signing can be waived. These include telephone surveys and situations in which signing poses a risk.

369. Researchers have devised many creative strategies for ensuring privacy and protecting the confidentiality of respondents during the data collection phase. For example, in Nicaragua and Zimbabwe, interviewers often accompanied women to the river as they washed clothes (Ellsberg and Heise, 2005). Members of the research team can distract household members by interviewing them simultaneously or by engaging them in conversation. Numerous strategies can be used to keep children busy, such as offering candy and colouring books (Ellsberg and Heise, 2005). In addition, ensuring privacy affects the final results. For instance, the British Crime Survey found that someone else was present during questions about intimate partner violence in 35 per cent of interviews and that, women whose male partners were involved in the completion of the questionnaire, disclosed incidents of violence at less than half the rate of women who responded in private (Mirrlees-Black, 1999).

Minimizing and responding to emotional distress

370. Research shows that sexual violence and intimate partner violence result in negative emotional and psychological consequences for victims. It can therefore be expected that survey questions may elicit negative emotional reactions among both respondents and interviewers.

371. The ethical requirement to respond to emotional distress should always be integrated into national and international surveys on violence against women. However, interviewers must be explicitly advised about their responsibilities and the limits of their role. While it is well within the purview of an interviewer's role to be empathetic towards emotional distress, it is not appropriate for an interviewer to assume a counselling role. In-depth training must ensure that interviewers are equipped to refer respondents to sources of support in the local

community, for example, in the form of referral information to local community resources. These might include sexual assault/rape crisis centres, crisis hotlines, refuges and other emergency shelters for abused women, women's groups, community centres, religious groups, hospitals and health services, and other community-based services. Such information should be given to all respondents and in a way that would not put them at risk.

372. In face-to-face interviewing situations, referral information could, for example, be contained on a card small enough to be easily concealed or disguised and should be offered only if it is safe for the woman to accept it. In contexts with very low literacy, written referrals have limited utility and leaving such material behind may actually increase safety risks (Andersson and others, 2009). Decisions regarding how to effectively respond to the need to minimize emotional trauma must be carefully thought out with all due regard for the particular local context. Examples of discrete referrals for care and support in surveys on violence against women in a variety of contexts are listed in box V.7.

Box V.7

Discrete referrals for care and support

Strategies for referrals to local services in diverse countries have included the following:

Brazil - Interviewers carried a service guide with them listing local services that work with women and violence, as well as small pocket-sized leaflets to leave with women who requested them (Ellsberg and Heise, 2005).

Zimbabwe - Contact information for resources and services were disguised on a physician's referral pad to avoid attracting suspicion (Ellsberg and Heise, 2005).

Ethical conduct of statisticians

373. In addition to the ethical responsibilities of interviewers and supervisors, national statistical agencies must also consider ethical issues associated with the results that are produced and disseminated. Poor quality data that provide inaccurate estimates of the prevalence of violence can mislead the public and policymakers and harm the efforts of community groups to respond to this issue. This is an important concern given the high levels of confidence that national statistical agencies enjoy in many countries and internationally. There will be an assumption that data produced by national statistical agencies will be valid and reliable. While there are many benefits when a highly respected agency produces carefully designed and executed research, if this work fails to incorporate certain fundamental principles to ensure reliable results, that reputation can work to diminish the perceived need for policy action and women who suffer the effects of violence will be deprived of the potential benefits.

374. National statistical agencies also have a responsibility to ensure that benefits are widely distributed. This includes reporting and explaining results accurately and in the detail needed to formulate policy. Policymakers, service providers, advocates and other stakeholders must be engaged in stakeholder consultations at all stages in order to ensure that research reports will be relevant to their needs. National statistical agencies must take all precautions necessary to ensure that results are interpreted correctly and to publicly correct misinterpretations.

Quality control during the data collection phase

375. Large-scale statistical sample surveys are complex operations that require effective and efficient management of activities at all levels. Quality control entails identifying all possible non-sampling errors and making efforts to reduce them as much as possible. This includes minimizing non-response, data processing errors and coding errors. This section focuses on

quality control during the data collection phase and covers the following topics: (a) overseeing interviewers' work and performance; (b) reducing unit non-response; and (c) reducing item non-response. Unit non-response occurs when selected women refuse to participate. Item non-response results when the answer to selected survey questions are not provided.

Overseeing interviewers' work and performance

376. The job of overseeing interviewers' work and performance is a central aspect of field supervisors' responsibilities; it takes on particular importance in surveys on violence against women. In the case of face-to-face interviews, without effective supervision by highly trained field supervisors the expected results may not be achieved. A fairly high ratio of supervisory staff to interviewers is recommended: one supervisor for every four or five interviewers is considered highly advantageous (United Nations, 2008). Field supervisors' duties involve determining field assignments, reviewing completed work and continually monitoring interviewers' ability to consistently achieve satisfactory response rates and disclosures of sensitive information. In view of the sensitivity of the topic and the impact that this may have on interviewers personally, their duties also involve conducting regular debriefings with interviewers. Interviewers who encounter difficulties either with the technical aspects of the survey or with its subject matter may require additional training or need to leave the survey.

377. Debriefings should be considered ongoing training for interviewers while they are conducting fieldwork. One important aspect of debriefings with interviewers is that of detecting and responding to any emotional impacts of working on a survey on this sensitive topic. Interviewers may experience emotional impacts as a result of hearing one distressing account of violence or numerous accounts over the course of weeks or months. Hearing such accounts may also force them to relive their own past experiences of violence. During training and fieldwork, supervisors must work to develop among the interviewing team an atmosphere in which it is permissible to express such difficulties so that they can be dealt with. Debriefings are particularly important in the early stages of fieldwork when interviewers are becoming comfortable with the questionnaire and developing confidence in their role. Over the course of the survey, debriefings may become less frequent. During debriefings, supervisors should encourage interviewers to share any difficulties that they may have encountered in the field in terms of both the technical aspects of the survey and interacting with respondents. Debriefings can generally take place in a group so that interviewers can learn from the experiences of others; however, given the sensitivity of the subject matter, supervisors should make themselves available to meet with interviewers individually, as requested.

378. Field supervisors need to monitor all aspects of the data collection process on a daily basis in order to ensure that errors are detected and corrected early in the process and ultimately minimized as much as possible. In surveys conducted by telephone, supervisors can monitor interviewers' performance by listening in on the conversations between interviewers and respondents. Supervisors are able to assess all aspects of interviewers' behaviour and skills in securing participation, establishing rapport, obtaining disclosures of violence and responses to other sensitive questions, handling difficult questions, observing ethical conduct, and reading questions and coding responses accurately. This is an advantage of telephone surveys over face-to-face surveys, where it is more difficult to monitor interviewers' interactions with respondents directly. In these contexts, supervisors must occasionally travel with interviewers to observe their work in order to ensure that they are following established procedures. Regardless of the mode of interviewing, field supervisors have a responsibility to monitor, anticipate, manage and respond to all aspects of field operations and any problems encountered during the data collection phase and to provide quality control indicators to the survey managers at various stages throughout the fieldwork.

Reducing unit non-response

379. The quality of the sample selected for a survey on violence against women depends to a large degree on the completeness of the sampling frame from which it is drawn as well as the response rate. Low response rates or low rates of participation by particular subgroups will jeopardize the representativeness of the sample, while large item non-response (missing information for certain questions) affects the overall quality of the data.

380. Unit non-response is a source of non-sampling error that occurs when sampled women refuse to participate. Non-response can occur for a variety of reasons, including outright refusal to participate, inability to participate owing to language difficulties, illness or impairment and inability to contact selected respondents.

381. Unit non-response will affect the representativeness of the sample because those who are not immediately available for an interview or who refuse to participate generally differ from those who agree to participate on characteristics that are relevant to the topic of the survey. For example, in many societies younger women are more likely than older women to engage in social, educational and employment-related activities that take them outside the household and are consequently less likely to be immediately available for an interview. Younger women in certain societies that are living independently of their families, such as students, are more likely to have mobile phones and not landlines. Underrepresentation of young women systematically biases the sample.

382. Various strategies have been shown to be successful in raising response rates on surveys on violence against women. These include sending advance letters, making free phones available, offering incentives, ensuring proper training of interviewers and making return visits or callbacks.

383. Sending letters to households before they are contacted by an interviewer can help to prepare respondents for being contacted and to reduce suspicion about the legitimacy of the survey. Advance letters should be professional in appearance and bear the letterhead of the national statistical agency. They should include a general description of the survey, using the "safe" name (see paragraph 365), explain how the household was selected and set out why the respondent's cooperation is important. They should also emphasize the steps that will be taken to ensure the confidentiality of their responses and clarify the nature of their participation. It is recommended that letters should reach selected households no more than 10 days before contact is made by the interviewer so that the content of the letter is not forgotten. Therefore, the mailing of letters should be staggered over time to correspond with the interviewing schedule.

384. Using advance letters in telephone surveys poses some challenges. If the random digit dialling method of selecting households is used, there must be a way to link the selected telephone numbers to addresses (a list-assisted frame). In the Australian component of the International Violence against Women Survey, the "White Pages plus one" method of contacting households was used and letters sent to households in advance.[24] Because of unlisted numbers, not all households in the "plus one" sample received letters. However, it was possible to electronically match the "White Pages" and "plus one" samples and, where names and addresses were available for the "plus one" sample, letters were sent. All letters were addressed to a woman in the household (Ms. Surname) to minimize the possibility that a male family member would open the letter (Mouzos and Makkai, 2004). The National Intimate Partner

---

[24] The "White Pages plus one" method is an adaptation of the random digit dialing method. Residential telephone numbers are selected from the telephone directory (called the White Pages in some countries) at random and the last digit of the number is increased by one. This should provide a sample of numbers that are not or are not yet listed.

and Sexual Violence Survey in the United States used reverse address matching to link available addresses to approximately half the telephone numbers in the landline sample (this survey also incorporated a mobile phone sample which could not be matched) (Black and others, 2011).

385. The decision to send advance letters must take into consideration all efforts to protect the safety of respondents. For example, the survey must be described not as a survey on violence against women, but as a survey focusing on women's safety or health concerns. If the letter invites sampled households to contact the survey sponsor or national statistical agency to confirm the legitimacy of the survey or to have questions concerning their participation answered, strict rules must once again be followed in terms of not disclosing the nature of the survey to either the respondent or other household members. Sending advance notices will, however, not be effective in contexts with low levels of literacy.

386. A joint strategy of using an advance letter and a free (or toll-free) phone number to allow respondents to contact the national statistical agency before, during or after the interview if they have questions about the survey or want to confirm the legitimacy of the survey can substantially improve response rates (UNODC and UNECE, 2010). If staff responding to the calls are very skilled and highly trained about the aims and content of the survey and are effective communicators, they can influence the willingness of callers to participate.

387. Although it is not common in violence against women surveys to offer an incentive to participate, the National Intimate Partner and Sexual Violence Survey in the United States of America did so with good results. Respondents were offered $10 to participate in the survey and could choose to have the incentive mailed to them or donated to the United Way on their behalf. Over half the respondents elected to have the money donated. Addresses were obtained to mail the incentive to those who requested it. This information was kept in a separate database and destroyed at the completion of data collection in order to protect the identity of respondents (Black and others, 2011). To further reduce non-response and sample bias, a random sample of non-respondents was recontacted and offered an incentive of $40 to participate in the survey. An overall participation rate of 81 per cent was achieved in this survey.

388. Interviewers have an important role to play in encouraging participation by creating a comfortable environment for respondents, presenting the survey objectives and benefits clearly, reassuring respondents that their confidentiality will be strictly guarded, showing flexibility in scheduling or rescheduling an interview at a time and place that is convenient for respondents (including taking a break and conducting the interview in stages) and demonstrating warmth and empathy for respondents in response to disclosures of violence.

389. An effort must be made, through callbacks or return visits to the sampled households, to ensure that groups typically overrepresented among non-responders or reluctant participants are not underrepresented in the survey. It is good practice to have the most experienced interviewers or field supervisors take on responsibility for persuading reluctant respondents to participate. Assurances of confidentiality and flexibility regarding the timing and location of interviews can help to alleviate respondents' concerns about participating and can help to reduce non-response.

390. Efforts to raise response rates by publicly announcing to the broader community that the survey will take place are not recommended. Some women may be placed in danger or their confidentiality violated if it is broadly known in the local community that the survey is taking place and neighbours or family members see them speaking with an interviewer.

391. Monitoring unit non-response is important from the perspective of field operations to ensure that field supervisors are able, at an early stage, to identify interviewers who are having

difficulty securing agreement from the first contact with the household and from the woman selected to respond to the survey. It is important to keep accurate records so that response rates can be calculated and reported in all public releases of the survey results. Response rates are estimated by calculating the number of completed questionnaires as a percentage of the total number of eligible sampling units. Reasons for non-response should also be recorded. These can include failure to find the selected respondent at home despite repeated attempts, outright refusal to participate, difficulty communicating because of language and the existence of logistical problems or security issues that prevent the inclusion of certain locations in the interviews. A complete accounting of the outcomes of all contacts with sampled households in terms of status as respondents, refusals or ineligible units is essential for calculating weights for the survey data.

392. One critical aspect of improving final response rates is rigorous oversight of sample selection. It is imperative that field supervisors pay close attention to the pace at which the sample is selected and released to interviewers in order to ensure that in all selected households an eligible respondent is identified and either interviews are completed or a legitimate non-response is recorded after concerted attempts have been made to secure participation. This is necessary in order to ensure that the sample is as representative as possible of the target population, thus minimizing non-response bias. Field supervisors will also be required to work closely with sampling specialists in order to monitor sample allocation and to ensure that a sufficient number of callbacks are made to selected households prior to new sample households being released. This issue also relates closely to the project budget since, if it is proving difficult to meet objectives related to the number of interviews within a specified time period, a decision can be made to extend the time spent in the field or to reduce the number of interviews that must be completed.

393. In larger jurisdictions, particularly those with sophisticated and automated sample selection processes, this task may be assigned to a specialist within the national statistical agency who will be required to collaborate with field supervisors. In jurisdictions where these processes are not automated, field supervisors may be responsible for overseeing both sample selection and release of sample. In face-to-face interviewing where a sampling frame is not available, field supervisors may be responsible for directly overseeing sample selection using a random walk method (UNODC and UNECE, 2010). In all situations, field supervisors will be required to monitor the sampling process closely.

394. Finally, a common strategy for adjusting for unit non-response occurs at the analysis stage, when responses are weighted to adjust for non-response among certain groups in order to render the sample more closely representative of the population. However, this is only a partial solution, since weighting can simply exacerbate the problem if women who are easily contacted at home or quickly accept to be interviewed are different in important respects from those who are less likely to be interviewed. It can be helpful, in order to engage hard-to-reach populations, to set quotas for respondents who are challenging to reach because of age or other characteristics such as race, ethnicity, language, or extreme poverty.

395. Efforts to maintain high response rates are an important consideration at all stages of planning and implementation in surveys on violence against women. However, field supervisors and interviewers must be aware of the risk that persistence on their part could pose to women who are living with a violent partner. Repeat calls or visits to households where either the selected respondent or another household member has refused to participate must be undertaken cautiously so that violent partners are not inadvertently alerted to the content of the survey and respondent safety is not put at risk as a result.

Reducing item non-response

396. A second source of non-sampling error results from missing information on some survey questions, referred to as item non-response. Non-response can occur in any question owing to ambiguity in the question wording or response categories, respondents' lack of knowledge about the topic of the question, non-exhaustive or overlapping response categories, respondent resentment at being asked certain questions, lack of rapport with the interviewer, lack of time, interviewers skipping questions, respondent boredom and dropping out and coding or data entry errors. Item non-response is a function of the questionnaire design, the quality of the interviewers' training and performance and the monitoring of interviewers' performance. It can be reduced by paying special attention to each of these phases of the project.

397. Taking into consideration that disclosing experiences of violence can be an emotional burden for respondents, there is a need to closely monitor disclosures of violence and responses to other sensitive questions. Non-response to specific questions should have been detected during the testing of the questionnaire but it is possible that some problems will not become evident until the fieldwork. Field supervisors must be able, at an early stage, to identify problems with question flow or wording or with interviewers who are unable to elicit disclosures of sensitive experiences at a rate similar to the rate at which other interviewers in similar settings and areas elicit disclosures.

398. For instance, in the Italian Citizen Safety Survey (1997), a higher level of non-response was observed in the case of specific questions in sections on violence against women and harassment. A detailed analysis of missing data revealed that certain respondent characteristics were associated with refusal to respond, including educational level, income, marital status and municipality of residence. Single women and women with higher family incomes and educational levels were more likely to provide a response to the questions. Item non-response was also associated with general difficulties in administering the questionnaire by some interviewers, which indicated a need for careful training of interviewers and sensitive administration of these questions (UNODC and UNECE, 2010).

399. The Italian Women's Safety Survey (2006), a dedicated survey that incorporated the major principles for conducting a survey on violence against women elaborated in these Guidelines, found that 45 per cent of women reporting violence by a current intimate partner were speaking about this violence for the first time to the interviewer. In a violence against women survey conducted in Turkey, 49 per cent of women reporting partner violence had thus far never spoken to anyone about it; in one part of the country, the figure was 63 per cent (Altinay and Arat, 2009). Thus, with appropriate measures in place, it is possible to reveal previously hidden experiences of violence that would otherwise be uncounted.

400. Quality control charts and indicators are useful for monitoring the overall survey processes and compliance with established targets and quality standards. Throughout the data collection period, each interviewer's activity should be monitored by analysing daily reports that include such quality control indicators as refusal and participation rates, interruption rates, non-contact rates, average length of interview and missing data for each survey question including reasons for the refusal and the age and other characteristics of the person who refused. Data obtained from answers to the questionnaire should be analysed on an ongoing basis and compared with external sources or previous surveys on the same topic, so that the response level for individual items is monitored continuously. This provides an additional check on data quality and consistency among interviewers and can help to identify both problems and necessary corrective measures (which may include direct intervention with individual interviewers or supervisors, group debriefings or additional training) early on in the data collection phase of the project.

401. An automated approach to monitoring quality control will help to ensure consistency among interviewers and is necessary in order to be able to immediately identify the need for additional or remedial training. The systems that can be put into place to ensure effective monitoring and quality control during the interviewing phase vary depending on the mode of interviewing. It is generally more straightforward for telephone surveys because of the centralization of the collection phase and the ability of supervisors and field managers to oversee the work of interviewers. In CATI data collection projects, indicators can be easily produced for each phase of the interviewer's work: contact with the household, selection of the person to be interviewed, follow-up contacts and all aspects of the conduct of the interview.

402. It can be expected that there will be variation among interviewers in the initial stages of the project in terms of their level of comfort with the subject matter and their ability to develop the rapport necessary to secure agreement from respondents to participate and to disclose personal information about their experiences of violence. These difficulties should be eliminated in the pilot testing phase of the project, during which all procedures, including interviewer training, are evaluated. Remedial training is typically effective in addressing problems promptly. In cases where additional training or coaching is not effective, interviewers may have to be removed from this role.

Pilot testing

403. Pilot testing involves testing all aspects of the project and can be thought of as a dress rehearsal of the fully fledged survey. The pilot test is more complex than the informal testing or pretesting of the questionnaire outlined in chapter IV (see paragraphs 311 to 316), since it is not limited to testing particular aspects of the data collection instrument but includes all survey processes from start to finish. It includes interviewer training, data capture and editing procedures, and the willingness of selected respondents to participate and to disclose sensitive information. The size of the sample required for pilot testing must be adequate so as to make it possible to identify problems with response rates and refusals to answer particular questions among targeted subgroups of interest. An accurate estimate of rates of disclosure in a survey on violence against women provides at the pilot test stage important information for knowing whether the sample size identified for the project is sufficient to yield statistically reliable estimates, particularly if the survey is being implemented for the first time.

404. Particular aspects of the procedures that need to be assessed or verified during pilot testing include the following (UNODC and UNECE, 2010):

- Aspects of respondents' willingness to participate, such as:
    ◊ Introduction to the survey and to particular sections
    ◊ Household and participant refusals and reasons for refusals
    ◊ Adequacy of techniques used to "convert" reluctant participants
    ◊ Number of contacts to the household and to the respondent required to complete the interview
    ◊ Consent and privacy assurances
    ◊ Item non-response and reactions to particular questions
    ◊ Rapport developed between the interviewer and the respondent

- Aspects of the questionnaire, such as:
    - ◊ Skip patterns and filter questions, in particular critical questions such as marital/relationship status questions
    - ◊ Redundant questions
    - ◊ Strong reactions to certain questions
    - ◊ Effectiveness of questions designed to obtain disclosures of violence
    - ◊ Complex definitions
    - ◊ Problems with the order and wording of questions, including issues surrounding the translation of questions into another language
    - ◊ Response categories and scales, especially for difficult-to-answer questions such as frequency of partner violence
    - ◊ Effectiveness of showcards and other visual aids
    - ◊ Problems with the length or structure of the questionnaire
    - ◊ Problems with translations
- Adequacy of criteria developed to select interviewers and adequacy of training provided to interviewers and field supervisors
- Frequency of situations in which respondent or interviewer safety is a concern and adequacy of procedures put in place to respond to safety concerns
- Frequency of situations in which emotional distress on the part of respondents or interviewers is a concern, and adequacy of procedures put in place to minimize and respond to concerns
- Procedures put in place to monitor interviewers' performance
- Procedures for replacing a sample household or sample respondent
- Problems encountered with the computer systems
- Problems encountered when recording and editing the data

405. All versions of the questionnaire (including those translated into different languages) and all aspects of the methodology should be pilot tested with individuals representing the target population in terms of age, race or ethnicity or other characteristics of interest.

406. Careful attention to the results of all aspects of pilot testing of the questionnaire, methods of data collection and data capture and editing processes will help to ensure that the questionnaire is properly finalized and that the method is sound and will yield the data needed to produce the core and additional indicators. From an ethical standpoint, it is critical to ensure, prior to implementing the fully fledged survey, that the procedures put in place to respond to safety, emotional trauma and confidentiality are sound. If during the pilot test weaknesses are found in any aspect of interviewing, coding or editing, time must be taken to revise or amend procedures accordingly. Depending on the magnitude of the changes required, a second pilot test may be required to ensure that all problems have been addressed.

Chapter VI
Data processing and analysis

407. Data processing refers to the stage when survey responses obtained through the administration of the questionnaire are transformed into a database that will be used for tabulation and analysis of the data. Data processing generally entails a combination of automated and manual activities and each step has an impact on the quality of the final results. Activities included at this stage are transfer of data collected through the questionnaire to data files, data coding, data editing and verification, data imputation, data analysis and tabulation, and dissemination of results.

408. Depending on how computer technology is used in the survey processes, the bulk of the data processing will occur either during the interviewing phase or once all the interviews have been completed. The rapid development of information technology has had a significant impact on the techniques available for designing and implementing systems for processing statistical survey data; consequently, all statistical sample surveys will utilize some degree of computer automation, though this will vary depending on the mode of interviewing and available technology and resources.

409. In computer-assisted telephone interviewing (CATI) or computer-assisted personal interviewing (CAPI) applications, interviewing and electronic data capture occur simultaneously. Data are processed and edited in batches on an ongoing basis and a data file is produced quickly thereafter. In surveys using paper questionnaires, data processing and editing are much more time-consuming and labour intensive, as the responses from each questionnaire must be entered into a database by data entry clerks as a separate step following the interviewing. The efficiency of data processing procedures will determine how quickly results will be obtained. Data processing for a first-time survey on violence against women is a complex task requiring coordination of computer technology specialists, statisticians and data analysts.

Data coding and editing

410. Data coding is established during the questionnaire design phase and entails assigning numerical values to each survey question and each response category on the questionnaire. Data editing, meanwhile, entails developing and implementing procedures to detect and correct errors made at the stage of entering data onto a questionnaire or into an electronic data file. Errors made at the data capture or coding stage can have serious impacts on the quality of the final survey results. This section will outline the procedures that need to be put in place to minimize errors in data capture and coding and in data editing and verification.

Data capture and coding

411. Data entry for a statistical sample survey on violence against women will follow the routine procedures pertinent to other surveys within the national statistical system. In surveys employing computer-assisted interviewing, detailed instructions will be provided in the inter-

viewer's manual in order to ensure that each survey question and the corresponding response categories are clearly understood. In the case of surveys employing paper questionnaires, a detailed manual will also be available to the data coders and data entry clerks responsible for entering each response into a data file. Explicit instructions are essential for ensuring that data entry errors are avoided. All open-ended questions will need to be coded into numeric format or retained in verbatim transcription, depending on the intended purpose of the question.

412. The precise nature of the activities associated with data capture and coding will vary according to the method by which the data are collected. Whether interviews are conducted over the telephone or face to face, computer-assisted data capture is preferable, since it allows data to be processed at the same time as the interview in a format compatible with the master data file. Much of the verification process occurs while the interview is taking place by way of procedures built into the data capture system that check for and disallow many inconsistencies and require errors to be corrected before proceeding to the next question. Simultaneous electronic data capture further avoids the costly and time-consuming process of manually coding data from paper questionnaires after the fact.

413. An additional advantage of using computer technology in the interviewing phase of the survey is that field supervisors and project managers are able to monitor the fieldwork in real time, thereby improving the quality of the data collected. Data are transferred directly to a central location at regular intervals, enabling project managers to monitor progress on key performance indicators, such as response rates, completion rates, responses to key variables (such as disclosures of various types of violence), performance of individual interviewers, and average length of interview, and thereby to ensure that project costs remain within budget. In addition, through close monitoring of the survey results, problems with built-in edits that were overlooked during pilot testing can be quickly identified and corrected, thereby ensuring that errors do not accumulate throughout the course of the fieldwork.

414. Data collected using CAPI is captured immediately, but an extra step is required to transfer data from each interviewer's laptop computer to a centrally held data file. Completed interviews using CAPI can be returned electronically by modem to the central office through an intranet arrangement or some other secure media such as a computer disk. Security measures are paramount for any type of electronic transfer. Unauthorized access to the data can be prevented by using user name and password protection systems and by limiting access to specific individuals. All personal details of respondents must be stored in files that are encrypted and transmitted separately from the main survey data in order to provide additional security and protection against breaches of confidentiality.

415. In face-to-face surveys where data are not captured electronically during the interviewing phase, extra care must be taken to train interviewers on accurate coding and skip and filter questions must be clearly specified and thoroughly tested. Paper questionnaires will require considerably more time and effort to process data following interviewing and this must be taken into account in the budget and time frame for the project.

416. In situations with manual data entry, double entry of data is a reliable way of ensuring data quality. Double entry involves entering the responses from each questionnaire twice by different data entry clerks then comparing the entries for discrepancies. Since this increases costs, one option is to use double entry at the beginning of data entry to identify and correct common mistakes. However, the experience of the Demographic and Health Surveys has shown that the increased cost associated with full double data entry reduces subsequent data editing so substantially that the benefits of double entry outweigh the extra cost of the second data entry entirely (United Nations, 2005a).

417. Field supervisors who oversee face-to-face interviews that are not aided by computer technology will be confronted with large quantities of questionnaires that must be systematically logged as they are sent into the field and received back as completed interviews. Field supervisors are required to visually scrutinize and edit completed questionnaires for accuracy and completeness on a daily basis and will need to take immediate corrective measures as needed, and to provide feedback to project managers as data are captured and analysed. This is a slow and labour-intensive process in manually conducted surveys and presents potential difficulties in terms of being able to detect and respond quickly to coding problems, missing data or problems with skip patterns or editing procedures. Developing a checklist that can be checked against each questionnaire will help to ensure consistency and ensure that some basic rules are followed. For example, in a survey on violence against women, the checklist should include verifying that data on key variables are not missed or skipped, such as age, marital/relationship status, disclosures of violence and follow-up questions pertaining to the consequences of that violence. Project managers must endeavour to ensure that data are captured as quickly as possible so that field supervisors can be supplied periodically with critical performance indicators, thereby ensuring that data quality can be monitored and follow-up action taken, where necessary.

418. Rigorous policies and practices regarding the physical security of completed questionnaires are important in terms of preventing loss of data and violations of confidentiality. All questionnaires and the data captured therein need to be anonymized by deleting all information that directly identifies respondents, such as name, address or telephone number, by substituting this information with a number or code and by ensuring that any documentation containing lists of households or respondents with identifying information is kept separately and can be assessed by the field supervisor only. Access to and control of all personal information must be rigorously protected. Completed questionnaires must be securely stored for the duration of the fieldwork and should eventually be destroyed, but only once data have been captured and edited and the data file finalized. If possible, paper questionnaires should also be scanned and stored electronically before being destroyed. However, the scanned copies would also need to be subjected to rigorous security protocols. These practices are essential for protecting both the safety and well-being of respondents and the integrity and reputation of the national statistical agency conducting the survey.

419. In addition, for all methods of data entry—both paper and computer-assisted—a backup copy must be created during each stage of the process and maintained separately from the main data file. Backup data files should be stored separately from the main CAPI or CATI servers or original paper questionnaires for added security and protection against loss of data.

Data editing and verification

420. Once responses have been entered into an electronic database, the data are again scrutinized for errors through editing and verification processes. During (using interactive checks) or after data entry, a series of checks are implemented in order to identify missing, invalid, illogical or inconsistent entries that point to possible errors in the data. Efforts are made to correct these errors, if possible, and consideration is given to substituting missing or invalid responses with replacement values through data imputation processes, a topic that will be addressed in the next section of this chapter.

421. Editing and verification processes performed with automated computer systems will have a higher degree of accuracy, though some manual oversight will also be necessary as it is not possible to build in all possible checks. These procedures are essential not only for enhancing the quality and accuracy of the survey data, but also for identifying weaknesses or

limitations in the data that will need to be considered when planning and conducting data analysis and communicating the survey results. Consistent errors would suggest problems with the questionnaire design, interviewing techniques or interviewer training. Once the reasons behind the errors have been identified, steps can be taken to correct them. The quicker data editing begins, the sooner problems can be detected and addressed.

422. There are many possible aspects of verification but the primary ones include: checks for range of responses, skip checks, checks for logic and consistency, and handling missing data.

423. Range checks are intended to ensure that every variable contains only data within a limited range of valid values (United Nations, 2008). Categorical variables can be coded as one (and sometimes several) of the values predefined for them and continuous variables can fall only within prescribed minimum and maximum values. For example, the range of values for the variable measuring respondent age should be no lower than 15 and no higher than 100, although the upper limit will vary according to site. Unusual, out-of-range or extreme values may indicate errors in data capture or problems associated with interviewer training. Survey managers and data entry clerks should be on the lookout for responses that are unusual or outliers (one useful rule is anything beyond three standard deviations above or below the mean). Such responses should be identified and verified for accuracy. Many variables can be expected to yield skewed distributions so this does not necessarily signify a problem with data quality. It should be checked, nonetheless, in order to be certain that this does not indicate an error in coding.

424. Skip checks are used to verify that skip patterns have been followed appropriately. For example, respondents who replied that children witnessed the violence perpetrated by their husbands or partners must have indicated either that they have children at the time of the interview or that they had children previously. If this is not the case, it would suggest a possible problem with the instructions in the questionnaire to follow a specific sequence of questions, with the interviewer training or interviewer's manual or with the data capture system in the case of a computer-assisted interview.

425. Filter questions are used to screen eligible respondents into subsequent questions. An example of a filter question used in violence against women surveys is the marital/relationship status question, which filters respondents into specific modules of questions about violence perpetrated by the current/most recent partner or former partners. Respondents who indicate that they are (or have been) married, living with a man but not married to him or involved with a man but not living together should be filtered into the module of questions asking about violence by the current or most recent partner. If a respondent has had more than one partner, she should also be administered the subsequent set of questions on preceding partners. In the event that the filter is not applied owing to a coding error, the information about experiences of violence by former partners may be lost.

426. In surveys using paper questionnaires, interviewers can easily make a mistake. Specific and detailed training in a variety of scenarios is needed in order to prevent errors that would be costly in terms of loss of data that are fundamental to the success of the survey. Good format and layout of the questionnaire can also help to minimize or reduce data entry errors. Such errors should not occur in computerized interviewing, since skip patterns are built into the computer program; if errors do occur, this is an indication of a problem with the computer program that must be corrected immediately upon detection.

427. Logic and consistency refer to the extent to which responses follow a coherent pattern. Consistency checks verify that values from one question are consistent with values from another. For example, if a respondent reports that she was injured but then reports that she

received no physical injuries, there may be a problem with the internal logic of her responses. Her responses, as they have been coded, are inconsistent. A decision will need to be made whether to leave the responses as they are, to recode her response to the type of injury question to indicate that she was injured or to recode her response to the type of injury question as missing data. Since type of injury is measured by many detailed questions concerning specific types of injury, the only possible correction would be to code her response as "other injury". Although it will not be possible to detect and address all inconsistencies in the data, project managers will need to develop guidelines with respect to correcting those inconsistencies that are anticipated to be the most commonly occurring or the most important in terms of weighting and meeting the survey objectives. Inconsistent data on important variables should be corrected where possible and where survey managers are confident that they can attribute a response with a good degree of accuracy.

428. Missing data can occur for a number of reasons apart from outright refusal to respond to a particular question, such as inability to answer owing to a lack of knowledge, inability to remember accurately or reluctance to respond owing to embarrassment or fear of reprisals from a violent partner.

429. Strategies for reducing the amount of missing data must be incorporated into the design of the questionnaire and interviewer training for violence against women surveys, as presented in previous chapters, in order to ensure that violence is not undercounted or the nature of the problem misrepresented. As a first step in addressing missing data, a review of the completed survey questionnaire should be conducted. In some situations, it may be appropriate to substitute the missing data for an estimate, a procedure known as imputation which will be addressed in the following section.

430. An important step/quality control measure in the editing process is that of accurately recording the number of errors detected, the number of errors corrected and the method of correction used. This information can be linked to individual interviewers and coders and problems conveyed back to them so that performance can be improved. A pattern of missing data on questions that are key to the survey objectives, such as experiences of violence, may indicate a problem with the approach followed when asking these questions. If so, this should be addressed by offering remedial training to the interviewer concerned.

Data imputation

431. Data imputation is a technique used to correct for item non-response; this results when some questions or entire sections of questions are omitted or skipped or when data are deemed to be invalid or incomplete. Possible reasons for item non-response include a feeling among respondents that questions are too personal or too intrusive, respondent fatigue owing to the length of the interview, confusing skip patterns, data entry errors and fatigue or a lack of attention on the part of interviewers. In the case of item, rather than unit, non-response, other information is available for those cases where certain items are missing. This provides an opportunity to both understand and analyse unit non-response patterns, as well as a possibility of using imputation to reduce missing data.

432. It is not usually possible in a survey on violence against women to recontact respondents owing to the danger that this might present to respondents. Therefore, decisions must be made and rules established about the extent to which missing data will be imputed or left as missing and what imputation procedures will be used. The grounds for imputing data must be clearly specified along with the method to be used to impute any data and the details of each imputed data point.

433. It is vital to ascertain the missing data mechanism before making decisions about imputation. Data may be Missing Completely At Random (MCAR), Missing At Random (MAR) or Missing Not At Random (MNAR). For data that are MCAR, the same analyses can be carried out on the data that have been observed as if there were no missing data at all; this is because data that are MCAR are not related to any observed or unobserved measurement. Data that are MAR may warrant imputation, as the missingness mechanism does not depend on the unobserved data. Compensating for data that are MNAR is hardest of all and imputation is likely to lead to invalid inferences. Unfortunately, it is often hard to distinguish between data that are MAR and data that are MNAR. In a survey on violence against women, missing data on the prevalence and experience of violence may well be MNAR since, intuitively, it seems likely that women who have experienced violence will be less likely to provide a response. Thus, imputing this sort of data is unlikely to be reliable. It may, however, be possible to impute data on items such as background characteristics. For more information, see Gower (2011), Little and Rubin (2002) or www.missingdata.org.uk.

434. Imputation involves replacing invalid or missing data with better artificial data points for individual survey variables. Imputation is generally used in surveys in order to ensure that key variables, such as age or marital/relationship status, have valid entries. This is particularly important for variables that are required for weighting or that form an integral part of the analyses. Care must be taken when considering imputing data and determining the method to be used because while some methods can improve the quality of the data, some can actually distort the results. A fuller review of imputation methodologies can be found in Brick and Kalton (1996) and Kalton and Kasprzyk (1986).

435. Examples of methods used to impute missing data for surveys on violence against women include deductive imputation, mean value imputation, "hot deck" imputation and regression imputation. Deductive imputation is the most straightforward and yields the most reliable results, since it involves assigning the one possible response, such as when all the numeric values are given but the total is missing. An example might be total number of children in the household. There is little risk of error in imputing a total number and this procedure should therefore be used, when necessary, to eliminate missing data.

436. In mean value imputation, the average value in the entire data set or in a subset of relevant characteristics is substituted for the missing data element. For example, if a respondent's level of education is missing, it could be imputed by finding the average number of years of education for all women in the respondent's province, income range and age group. In countries where a population register is available, these data could be used for the purposes of imputation.

437. In hot deck imputation, a missing value is replaced with a response from a similar unit. For example, if the respondent's level of education was not entered, a list of possible donors matching certain criteria, such as region, income range and age group, would be generated and one of them selected randomly. An alternative form of this method is to apply specific criteria in order to identify the respondent who is most like the respondent with the missing data element and to substitute the value of the education variable for the missing response. Hot deck imputation must be used with extreme caution in surveys with small samples or where the imputation is based on a rare occurrence. In addition, care must be taken not to overuse a particular case as a donor otherwise the precision of the estimates will be affected.

438. Regression imputation is a statistical procedure by which known characteristics of the respondent are regressed to predict the value of the missing response. Say, for example, that the variable Y contains some missing values. A model can be produced that attempts to predict Y from j other variables in the data—X_1 to X_j. The most straightforward model to use would then be:

$$Y_i = \beta_0 + \beta_1 X_{1i} + ... + \beta_j X_{ji} + \varepsilon_i$$

This model should be fitted for all cases where Y and X1 to Xi are non-missing. The predicted value of Y can then be estimated from this model for cases where it is missing using the following formula:

$$\hat{Y}_i = \hat{\beta}_0 + \hat{\beta}_1 X_{1i} + ... + \hat{\beta}_j X_{ji}$$

There are many variations on this technique; further information can be found elsewhere in, for example, Yansaneh, Wallace and Marker (1998).

439. Good imputation ensures that imputed records are internally consistent. It is good practice to flag imputed records on the data file so that, in the event that analysis reveals an unexpected result, the method of imputation can be verified in order to ensure that the result is not a product of a flaw in the method of imputation.

Weighting of data[25]

440. Estimates based on probability samples are assumed to represent the sampled population, but this assumption is valid only if complete coverage of the target population is achieved (i.e., there is zero non-response) or if the sampling units that were excluded due to non-response or non-coverage occurred randomly and independently of specific characteristics of the units, especially those related to the survey topic. However, some degree of non-response or refusal to participate can be expected and it should not be assumed that refusals are random. Bias due to non-coverage is often built into the sampling frame or interviewing procedures; for example, telephone surveys exclude households without landlines and, unless specific procedures are put in place to reach linguistic or cultural minorities, surveys risk excluding these groups. It is therefore almost assured that probability surveys will produce biased estimates unless steps are taken to adjust for known biases through weighting.

441. The objective of weighting is to produce estimates of violence against women that correspond as closely as possible to the real parameters in the target population. Weights are calculated to correct for unequal probabilities of selection, design effects caused by stratification or clustering, known differences between the sample and the target population, and non-response. If weights are not used to adjust for these factors, the estimates of the population parameters will be biased.

442. In addition to adjusting for design effects and biases in the sample, the data can be weighted up to the total target population in order to calculate the total number of women affected by violence (as opposed to the number in the sample), the number who were physically injured, the number who suffered psychological or economic abuse, and so forth. These estimates give an indication of the number of women affected by violence that is not clearly presented with the use of percentages, rates, means or sample counts.

443. Weighting can be a highly sophisticated exercise, depending on the complexity of the applied sampling design, and requires specific expertise. The first step in the construction of sample weights is to determine the probabilities of selection of the sampling units, which is determined by the sampling design. Most statistical sample surveys on violence against

---

25 Calculating the construction of sample weights for a variety of sampling design scenarios is beyond the scope of these Guidelines. There are numerous texts available on the subject. In particular, readers are directed to consult United Nations (2008).

women use multistage stratified sampling (see paragraphs 183 to 196). The base weight of a sampled unit is calculated as the reciprocal or inverse of its probability of selection. For multistage designs, the base weights must reflect the probabilities of selection at each stage of selection (including the last stage: the probability of a woman being selected among the eligible women in the household). The ability to make statistical adjustments to multistage stratified samples depends on the availability of totals for the entire population and specific strata used for sampling. The weights for the sample units can be adjusted to make the sum of weights match the totals within subgroups.

444. The second step in the construction of sample weights is to adjust for unit non-response and non-coverage. If this is not done, the estimates may be biased in some way by under inclusion of certain groups in the target population. The magnitude of bias due to non-response is associated with two factors: the overall non-response rate (the number of units that fail to respond calculated as a proportion of all eligible units) and the size of the difference in the characteristic of interest between the respondent group and the non-responding group. Differential non-response for subgroups of the population can be addressed by identifying the response rates for those groups and inflating the weight of respondents in each group by the inverse of their response rate. While this produces a more accurate weighting structure, the result is an increase in the design effect of the estimate. This must be taken into consideration when analysing the data (Kalton, Brick and Lê, 2005).

445. Biases associated with non-coverage also occur when the sampling frame fails to cover the target population with the results that some units have no chance of selection. This is a major concern in the case of surveys conducted face to face where logistical challenges, war or unrest, natural disasters or difficult terrain prevents interviewers from travelling to every selected household. Non-coverage is also present in sampling frames that are out-of-date, meaning that many new dwelling units are not listed, or sampling frames that fail to include certain types of households, such as nomadic households or people living on boats. An additional source of non-coverage occurs when certain individuals cannot be selected because they do not live in households, such as women living in institutions, military installations, shelters or refuges. It is essential to determine, in the planning stage, whether specific segments of the population will be systematically excluded from the sampling frame.

446. For instance, remote areas with sparse populations or other areas that are difficult to access may be intentionally excluded from the sampling frame for logistical or safety reasons. Exclusion of areas with small populations may have a small affect on the overall estimates, but if the residents represent unique characteristics (e.g., indigenous populations) their exclusion may result in important population segments being unrepresented in the survey results. It is important that, when the survey results are released, survey managers make very clear which segments of the population were excluded from the survey.

447. Surveys on violence against women will rely on variables such as age and marital/relationship status to weight for non-response. Age is a primary characteristic, since it correlates strongly with other sociodemographic factors, such as main occupation, lifestyle and education, and therefore helps to adjust for other personal characteristics when data for those variables are not available. Marital/relationship status is a key variable for weighting, since calculations of current and previous intimate partner violence form several of the core indicators. At a minimum, the survey sample should be compared to the age profile of the target population and adjusted accordingly. Data used for weighting should be retrieved from the most recent census of the population and updated using vital statistics or other reliable population survey data.

Computing sampling error

448. Reporting on the precision or accuracy of the estimates derived from the survey data requires sampling errors to be computed and reported.

449. Sampling error (or sampling variability) occurs as a result of selecting a sample rather than interviewing the entire population. All samples can be expected to differ from the target population simply by chance, but the magnitude of sampling error will also be affected by sample design, sample size and population variability. Sampling errors are calculated in order to provide an indication of the likely accuracy or precision of the estimate. Larger samples result in smaller sampling error and greater precision.

450. Key measures of precision of the estimates derived from probability samples are standard deviation, standard error, coefficient of variation and confidence intervals.

451. The standard deviation of the estimate measures the degree of variability or the spread of a group of observations around the mean and is useful for comparing the variability of different estimates. It provides an idea of whether a set of observations are loosely or tightly clustered around the mean and helps to identify the representativeness of the mean vis-a-vis all the data points. It is relatively easily interpreted because it is expressed in the same unit of measurement as the estimate.

452. The standard error (SE) is a measure of the sampling error and is calculated as the standard deviation of the estimate divided by the square root of the sample size. This means that SEs are directly affected by sample size. The smaller the SE, the more confident one can be that the estimate is an accurate representation of the population value.

453. Standard errors are often expressed as a coefficient of variation (CV), which is the SE of the estimate divided by the estimate itself. As with SEs, the smaller the CV, the more confident one can be that the estimate is an accurate representation of the population value. Many readers find CVs easier to interpret, as they can be expressed as a percentage of the estimate. CVs also help to standardize comparisons of standard errors across estimates with different scales (e.g., income and age will have very different scales compared to variables such as number of years of education or number of children in the household).

454. A question that frequently arises in the analysis of survey data is what size of standard error is considered acceptable. Using CVs, survey managers can establish a general rule that estimates with CVs exceeding a certain percentage are not sufficiently reliable to use for policy purposes.

455. A confidence interval is the estimated range of values for a population parameter based on a specified probability. A confidence interval is constructed with the estimate and its standard error. It specifies the probability that the true population value falls within a certain range. For instance, if the population value follows a normal distribution, there is a 95 per cent chance that the true population parameter would fall within the survey estimate plus or minus 1.96 times its standard error. Calculation of standard errors is complicated by the use of sample weights and different sample designs; more details on calculating standard errors can be found in United Nations (2005a).

456. The calculation of variance estimation and sampling errors requires the sample design to be taken into account. Complex sample designs, such as those involving stratification, clustering and unequal probability of selection, will require the computation of complex estimators. Surveys in developing and transition countries tend to cluster households in order to control costs, but households that are clustered tend to be alike on certain characteristics and this affects the precision of the survey estimates (by inflating the variance and thereby lowering precision). This results in a design effect, which is calculated as the ratio of the

variance of an estimate based on the complex design relative to the variance of an estimate based on a simple random sample of the same size. Failure to take account of the design effect when calculating standard errors can lead to misinterpretation of the survey results. For these reasons, statisticians with sophisticated knowledge of the complexities of variance estimation must be included in the project team in order to ensure that the survey results are accurately represented (United Nations, 2005a).

457. Information on the precision and accuracy of the estimates obtained from the survey needs to be made available to data users. Since the data produced by statistical surveys on violence against women will be used for policy and programming purposes, data analysts and researchers who have access to the data file must be well informed about the most appropriate way to present the data and about any limitations and restrictions that should be placed on their use.

Data analysis and tabulation

458. Once a complete data file has been prepared, analysis and tabulation of results can get under way. Data analysis, tabulation and dissemination are the steps involved in communicating the key findings and results to data users and stakeholders in Government, universities, non-governmental organizations, service providers, the media and the general public. Data analysis refers to the process of transforming raw data into statistics and statistics into useable information presented in the form of numbers, tables and graphics and interpreted in analytical articles that discuss the trends or patterns in the data and their significance for policy or programme formation. It involves organizing, summarizing and interpreting the data in a way that provides clear answers to policy-relevant questions.

459. Data analysis is the survey process that aims to provide answers to the overarching questions identified by stakeholders at the outset of the project. Data analysts engage in consultations with stakeholders in order to establish an analytical plan, to ensure that the results are presented in a way that is relevant to policy concerns and to discuss avenues for further exploration of the data. It is important to formulate an analytical plan early in the planning stages, because the structure of the questionnaire strongly influences the type and range of analysis that is possible. There must be a clear understanding among survey sponsors, survey managers, and stakeholders and data users concerning what types of analysis are required in order to ensure that the design of the questionnaire is able to meet these requirements. Limitations to the analysis posed by the questionnaire are often not obvious until the analytical plans are established.

460. The core indicators on violence against women identified by the Friends of the Chair of the United Nations Statistical Commission on indicators (see chap. II) call for the computation of new variables derived from survey variables.[26] For example, rates of intimate partner violence are calculated as the number of women who report one or more experiences of physical or sexual violence by an intimate partner divided by the number of women who have ever had an intimate partner, expressed as a percentage. What might appear to be a straightforward calculation requires a computer program that first calculates the number of women who have ever had an intimate partner based on the appropriate marital/relationship status question and then checks the responses to each separate question from within the module of questions on physical and sexual violence perpetrated by current/most recent partner or former partners. These are combined to find the percentage of women who have been in a relationship who have experienced physical or sexual violence by their partners.

---

[26] Online resources for computing indicators on violence against women can be found at www1.unece.org/stat/platform/display/VAW/Survey+module+for+measuring+violence+against+women.

461. The calculation of rates of physical, sexual, psychological and economic violence, considered separately, will follow a similar logic.

462. The calculation of prevalence rates of violence perpetrated by persons other than intimate partners is based on the number of women who report one or more experiences of physical or sexual violence by any person other than an intimate partner divided by all women, expressed as a percentage. Since all women are at risk of violence outside intimate relationships, all women are included in the denominator. The steps required to calculate rates of physical or sexual violence by non-partners are illustrated in figure VI.1.

Figure VI.1
Steps for calculating lifetime rates of physical or sexual violence by persons other than intimate partners

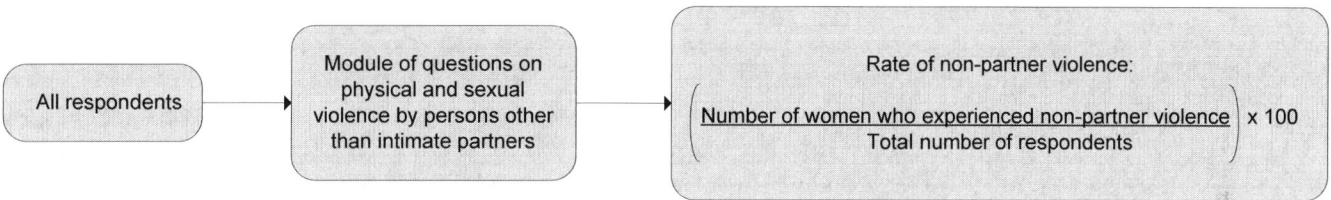

463. Similar calculations should be made for physical and sexual violence separately and subclassifications can be made for rape and other specific types of violence and for specific categories of perpetrators.

464. Each indicator on violence against women will require careful consideration as to the most appropriate denominator. For example, the calculation of the impacts and consequences of partner violence, such as injuries, will be based on the total number of women reporting violence, not total respondents. If additional variables include hospitalization, the prevalence rate of women hospitalized as a result of violence could be calculated based on the number of victims or the number of women who were injured. Examples of essential tabulations and their recommended denominators, according to each of the United Nations core indicators, are presented in annex VI.

465. Derived variables created for the calculation of the core indicators should be included in any data files in order to ensure consistency among data users. Apart from the core indicators, the depth and breadth of analysis and the format of the presentation of results will vary according to the audience that the output is intended to reach and the issues of concern. Great care must be taken to ensure that the conclusions presented in an analytical study, especially those that can affect public policy or stakeholder groups, are accurately portrayed and supported by the available data and that the precision of the estimates, definitions of concepts and limitations of the data are clearly specified.

466. Annex VI outlines the tabulations that are recommended as the minimum analytical results of a survey on violence against women. These tabulations are in accordance with the core indicators specified in chapter II

467. Identifying these key tabulations well in advance will help to expedite data analysis. An in-depth analysis of the data requires a considerable investment of time prior to the release of an analytical report. The costs of this must be considered in the planning stages of the project, as they influence resource requirements and budget allocation. In the first instance, analysis will involve an examination of the simple frequencies of each variable so that the basic properties of the sample are known prior to planning a more in-depth analysis. Bivariate analysis involves cross-tabulating variables of interest in order to identify factors that correlate with specific variables of interest, for example personal characteristics that correlate

with intimate partner violence, such as age of respondents and of perpetrators, or partners' economic activity. Chapter II describes the suggested minimum set of variables in more detail (see paragraphs 55, 56 and 70).

468. This level of analysis will satisfy the information needs of the majority of stakeholders. Academics and other researchers will be interested in more sophisticated multivariate analysis based, for instance, on logistic regression. This is needed to identify the unique influence of various predictors on outcome variables such as partner violence, non-partner violence and reporting to authorities. Researchers will also be interested in methodological reports with detailed descriptions of the sample design, weighting procedures, non-response and other features of the survey.

469. Analysts must take care to present their findings in a format that will be clearly understood and correctly interpreted by the media, service providers and others not trained in statistics. All estimates must be thoroughly evaluated for quality and accuracy prior to dissemination. Analytical reports and documentation that are released into the public domain must contain all relevant methodological information regarding sampling selection and must use sample weights and standard errors so that the data are accurately presented. It is paramount that the confidentiality of respondents is strictly guarded by presenting data in a format that is sufficiently aggregated so that no individual or community can be identified either because of small sample counts or unique characteristics.

Dissemination of results

470. The dissemination of data involves three distinct steps that require different areas of expertise: the release of the survey findings through various media outlets and other avenues; the production of metadata, and the creation and release of a data file.

Release of survey findings

471. Widespread dissemination of the results of the statistical analysis produced from surveys on violence against women ensures that the broadest possible benefit is gained from this work.

472. Prior to the official release of the survey results, the survey data should be subjected to verification in order to ensure that erroneous data are not released. This usually has to be done within tight timelines. A verification plan should therefore be set up in advance with a checklist of data quality and internal consistency checks. The survey data should be compared against other reliable data sources. It is also advisable to involve subject matter experts external to the national statistics agency so that they can verify the results in terms of how realistic they are. Further results will need to be discussed with stakeholders, who should be involved in their interpretation.

473. Communication specialists should be included in the project team as they can advise on the most cost-effective methods of communicating the survey results to a wide range of stakeholders. Depending on the local and national contexts, the range of statistical products available will include pamphlets, posters, short statistical reports and in-depth reports with details of the methodology. Dissemination strategies will include paper copies of reports, electronic copies accessible by Internet, web portals and products specifically tailored to the media.

474. The electronic dissemination of survey results is preferred because it is more efficient than other methods and broadens the access to users both nationally and internationally.

Many mailing lists have been established so that potential users of the data are informed when they become available. Data users are able to quickly share electronic documents across international and disciplinary borders. For the agency producing the output, the cost of printing reports is also eliminated.

475. Contacting various media outlets in order to draw attention to the release of this material in advance will help to ensure broad exposure and dissemination of the information. Involving stakeholders before and during media releases will ensure that experts are available to respond to media requests for viewpoints on the policy implications of the results and other insights that generally lie outside the knowledge and mandate of national statistical agencies. This is important for stimulating public debate about the issues addressed in the survey and for ensuring that policymakers and other stakeholders at the community level are aware of the results and the uses to which the data can be put.

476. Communication specialists and data analysts who will be responding to requests for media interviews will need to be prepared and trained to respond to potential misuse of the data. Efforts must be made to simplify and properly explain the survey outputs in order to avoid misinterpretation, but errors may nonetheless occur owing to a misunderstanding of denominators of specific estimates or technical terms such as sampling error and confidence intervals.

Production of metadata

477. Users of the data require detailed information about how the data was collected and how it is stored on data files. Metadata is "data about data". Metadata provides essential technical information to users about the records contained on a data file, including the data source and the method used to collect the data. Detailed metadata ensure appropriate use and accurate interpretation of the data.

478. Information contained in metadata includes data collection method, format of the file, sampling design, unit of count, relationships among records, reference period, aggregation of records, restrictions on the use of the data, indicators of data quality and names and definitions of all variables on the file, including derived variables that are essential for replicating the key survey outputs. Derived variables for a survey on violence against women will be extensive and may include the following:

- Respondents reporting physical or sexual violence by an intimate partner in the past 12 months
- Respondents reporting physical or sexual violence by an intimate partner during their lifetime
- Respondents reporting psychological violence by an intimate partner in the past 12 months
- Respondents reporting physical violence by a non-partner in addition to detailed types of perpetrators, such as acquaintances and strangers.

479. Indicators of data quality and accuracy will include response rates, item non-response, imputations, and sampling error and coefficients of variation which will determine the reliability of the estimates. Metadata should also be provided. Most national statistical agencies have developed standards and guidelines for producing metadata that should be followed for surveys on violence against women.

Creation of a data file

480. Survey managers should assume that there will be interest among researchers in a survey data file, since researchers will be interested in a more complex analysis. This file will typically be made available to interested parties (typically researchers and academics) by the national statistical agency. However, a data file can be made available to researchers only if the confidentiality and anonymity of survey respondents can be guaranteed (see paragraph 363 onwards).

481. The extent to which the data file will suppress identifying information depends on the sample size, the sample design and the complexity of the questionnaire. Of course, no information that could allow individuals to be indentified should ever be made available.

482. The creation of a data file for access by people outside the survey team requires an additional effort in order to produce high quality documentation and clean data files. Plans and policies for archiving, accessing and using the data should be discussed and agreed upon before data collection begins. If agreements about data release are not made at the beginning of the process, it will become increasingly difficult for this to happen.

Evaluation of the survey processes

483. At the end of the project, managers will be required to report on the outcome of the project in terms of meeting objectives and budgetary targets. This will involve planning in the early stages so that process information and quality control indicators are recorded throughout the life of the project. The ability to analyse and evaluate every aspect of the survey project from inception to release of data and to make recommendations for improvements to future cycles of the survey or for the development of other studies depends on the collection of accurate information at all stages of the project.

484. An evaluation should be developed in the planning stage of the survey and should cover a detailed list of aspects to be evaluated, including question wording, questionnaire flow, interviewer training and other aspects of fieldwork and data processing, analysis and dissemination. Responsibility for each portion of the evaluation should be assigned early in the project in order to ensure that relevant monitoring processes are implemented and appropriate data and indicators collected.

485. Data analysis is an important evaluation activity in terms of helping to identify data quality issues related to missing data and imputation procedures. The survey data should also be compared to other sources of data through a process of triangulation in order to assess the reliability and validity of the survey estimates and to identify where improvements can be made to future implementations of the survey. Potentially useful sources of data for evaluating data produced by a survey on violence against women include censuses and other demographic data, health surveys, crime victimization surveys and other data sources relevant to the topic.

Final Steps

486. Data processing, analysis and dissemination are key activities whereby responses to the survey are translated into statistics and presented to the public in a form that tells a story about the scope and the dimensions of various types of violence experienced by women in the particular country context. In addition to the standard practices for producing statistics, particular ethical and safety aspects of surveys on violence against women require atten-

tion. For instance, when presenting results, care must be taken not to reveal the identity of respondents, either directly or by publishing estimates based on small sample counts or rare events through which an individual can be identified. Violations of confidentiality can have potentially negative or even violent consequences for women participating in the survey.

487. It is essential that data are thoroughly verified and that missing data are minimized through built-in checks and manual verification. It is also essential that imputation is applied where necessary and where it can be verified that the method of imputation improves and does not reduce the accuracy of the data.

488. Dissemination of the survey findings is the step whereby the results of the survey are communicated broadly. Results will reach many audiences, some of whom will be satisfied with summary statistics while others will require more detailed analysis or access to the data file. In all aspects, the confidentiality and anonymity of survey responses must be protected.

Annex I

International instruments that aim to strengthen the collection of data on violence against women

Instrument	Directive regarding data collection
General Assembly resolution 64/139 of 18 December 2009 on violence against women migrant workers	19. *Encourages* concerned Governments, in particular those of the countries of origin, transit and destination, to avail themselves of the expertise of the United Nations, including the Statistics Division of the Department of Economic and Social Affairs of the Secretariat, the United Nations Development Fund for Women and the International Research and Training Institute for the Advancement of Women, to develop appropriate national data-collection and analysis methodologies that will generate comparable data and tracking and reporting systems on violence against women migrant workers;
General Assembly resolution 63/156 of 18 December 2008 on trafficking in women and girls	26: *Invites* States parties to the Convention on the Elimination of All Forms of Discrimination against Women, the Convention on the Rights of the Child and the International Covenants on Human Rights to include information and statistics on trafficking in women and girls as part of their national reports to their respective committees and to work towards developing a common methodology and statistics to obtain comparable data;
General Assembly resolution 63/155 of 18 December 2008 on the intensification of efforts to eliminate all forms of violence against women	16. Urges States to continue to develop their national strategy…, including…by using best practices…such as: *(e)* Ensuring the systematic collection and analysis of data to monitor all forms of violence against women, while ensuring and maintaining the privacy and confidentiality of the victims, including with the involvement of national statistical offices and, where appropriate, in partnership with other actors; *(f)* Establishing appropriate national mechanisms for monitoring and evaluating the implementation of national measures, including national action plans, taken to eliminate violence against women and girls, including through the use of national indicators;
The United Nations Secretary-General's UNiTE to End Violence against Women campaign, launched in 2008	By 2015, UNiTE aims to achieve the goal of strengthening data collection on the prevalence of violence against women and girls in all countries.
General Assembly resolution 62/134 of 18 December 2007 on eliminating rape and other forms of sexual violence in all their manifestations, including in conflict and related situations	2. *Calls upon* States and the United Nations system: (a) To support all efforts to address rape, including through the regular collection, analysis and dissemination of data, to facilitate such efforts and, in particular, to work towards overcoming the difficulties and challenges of capacity-building and collecting information on the practice;

Instrument	Directive regarding data collection
General Assembly resolution 62/133 of 18 December 2007 on the intensification of efforts to eliminate all forms of violence against women	7. *Requests* the Secretary-General to intensify his efforts to develop and propose a set of possible indicators on violence against women, building on the work undertaken by the Special Rapporteur on violence against women, its causes and consequences, in order to assist States in assessing the scope, prevalence and incidence of violence against women…;
General Assembly resolution 61/143 of 19 December 2006 on the intensification of efforts to eliminate all forms of violence against women	11. *Also urges* States to ensure the systematic collection and analysis of data on violence against women, including with the involvement of national statistical offices and, where appropriate, in partnership with other actors, taking note of the World Health Organization multi-country study on women's health and domestic violence against women and its recommendation to enhance capacity and establish systems for data collection to monitor violence against women;
General Assembly resolution 59/165 of 20 December 2004 on working towards the elimination of crimes against women committed in the name of honour	3. *Calls upon* all States: (k) To gather and disseminate statistical information on the occurrence [of crimes against women and girls committed in the name of honour], including information disaggregated by sex and age…;
General Assembly resolution 56/128 of 19 December 2001 on traditional or customary practices affecting the health of women and girls	3 *Calls upon* all States: (c) To collect and disseminate basic data about the occurrence of traditional or customary practices affecting the health of women and girls, including female genital mutilation;
Beijing Platform for Action adopted at the Fourth World Conference on Women, held in Beijing from 4 to 15 September 1995	Actions to be taken 129. By Governments, regional organizations, the Untied Nations, other international organizations, research institutions, women's and youth organizations and non-governmental organizations, as appropriate: (a) Promote research, collect data and compile statistics, especially concerning domestic violence relating to the prevalence of different forms of violence against women, and encourage research into the causes, nature, seriousness and consequences of violence against women…; (c) Support and initiate research on the impact of violence, such as rape, on women and girl children, and make the resulting information and statistics available to the public;
Declaration on the Elimination of Violence against Women, contained in General Assembly resolution 48/104 of 20 December 1993	States…should….: (k) Promote research, collect data and compile statistics, especially concerning domestic violence, relating to the prevalence of different forms of violence against women and encourage research on the causes, nature, seriousness and consequences of violence against women and on the effectiveness of measures implemented to prevent and redress violence against women; those statistics and findings of the research will be made public;

Annex II

Other sources of statistics on violence against women

In addition to statistical sample surveys, administrative data that are disaggregated by sex provide useful data for understanding the societal response to violence against women and women's use of services. Statistics that are collected in the day-to-day operation of services and agencies that provide support and assistance to women victimized by violence can in some cases provide much needed information that is not obtainable through sample surveys. Data concerning trafficking of women and femicide are two examples of cases where administrative data play an important role.

Administrative data are not usually intended for research purposes and cannot be used to estimate the prevalence of violence against women in the population owing to the severe underreporting of these experiences.

Beginning with the strengths of administrative data, detailed and rigorously collected data are useful in the following contexts:

- Monitoring the number of women seeking services as a result of experiencing violence.

- Identifying the scope of cases of a specific agency involving violence against women, e.g., the number of intimate partner violence calls to which the police respond as a percentage of all calls or the number of injuries caused by violence against women treated by hospital emergency services compared to other traumas.

- Estimating the financial and human resources costs of violence against women to society.

- Providing context vis-à-vis the need for additional education and sensitivity training for service providers such as police, court personnel and medical personnel.

- Contributing to evaluations of the effectiveness of the response of existing services to violence against women.

- Providing context to other projects examining the prevalence of violence against women.

- Identifying the extent to which various subpopulations access different services and identifying which groups are absent from service records, thereby possibly helping to identify which groups of women face barriers to receiving assistance and accessing services.

- Identifying the need for existing services to be expanded or additional services created.

The following sections outline the potential benefits and limitations specific to primary sources of administrative data.

Health services

While health services treat many women who have experienced violence and provide opportunities for identifying female victims of sexual assault, intimate partner violence and other forms of intentional injury, such women do not always readily disclose to health authorities either because they are afraid of the perpetrator or too ashamed to disclose the true nature of their injuries or because health and medical professionals fail to accurately identify them owing to a lack of training, a reluctance to intervene or a lack of services to which they can refer. Targeted approaches to identifying women treated by medical facilities or medical forensic departments have been used in some countries to monitor trends.[1] However, the surveillance of women in medical settings has raised a number of ethical issues. There is considerable debate concerning whether medical personnel have a duty or obligation to identify cases of violent victimization, particularly in settings where follow-up services are non-existent or experiencing overcapacity. It is argued by some that screening initiatives can breach confidentiality and the woman's autonomy, lead to psychological distress and retaliation from the violent partner and deter future disclosures, thereby increasing the risks of future violence and medical complications for victims.[2] Medical records are limited in their capacity to identify victims of violence, since they typically do not provide information about the cause of injuries or the relationship between victims and perpetrators. However, some medical units that offer support to victims of sexual assault or intimate partner violence collect potentially useful data in the course of their work.[3]

Criminal and civil justice services

Data collected by criminal justice systems tend to be more systematic owing to the operational and procedural nature of the tracking systems used and the organization of these data by codified law. These data are particularly useful in countries that are able to collect information about victims, perpetrators and the nature of the crime involved. Some more advanced systems are able to track repeat victimization and offending. However, police data are linked to court data collection systems in very few settings and it is rare for criminal and civil justice agency data to be linked. This results in an inability to count individual victims and perpetrators. The greatest limitation is that criminal justice system data is representative of a fraction of all violence against women that occurs and cannot be considered representative of the extent or nature of the violence occurring in the population, as victims tend to involve the police only as a last resort and after other strategies to end the violence have failed. Criminal justice system data are potentially useful for assessing the justice system's response to various forms of violence against women, including charges laid, plea bargaining and guilty

---

1 See World Health Organization, Expert Meeting on Health-sector Responses to Violence against Women, Geneva, Switzerland, 17-19 March 2009 (Geneva, 2010).

2 See H. L. MacMilland and others, "Screening for intimate partner violence in health-care settings: A randomized trial", Journal of American Medical Association, vol. 302, No. 5 (August 2009), pp. 493-501.

3 See M.C. Hofner and others, "Characteristics of victims of violence admitted to a specialized medico-legal unit in Switzerland", Journal of Forensic and Legal Medicine, vol. 16, No. 5 (July 2009), pp. 269-272.

pleas, cases that go to trial, trial outcomes, sentencing decisions, adherence to probation and parole conditions, and detected recidivism.[4]

The civil justice system may also be a source of data on violence against women. Some civil justice systems include civil injunctions or perform family law functions and issue orders to prevent the perpetrator from having contact with the victim through a peace bond, restraining order, or other such protection order. These various injunctions may also carry other conditions to assist in the protection of women, such as prohibitions against alcohol, drugs and weapons. The most serious limitation of police statistics is the fact that crimes of violence against women are among the most underreported of all crimes; police statistics therefore offer only a partial accounting of this phenomenon. Court statistics are often even more limited owing to the fact that police and prosecutors often use their discretion not to proceed with these cases.[5]

Other Government agencies/programmes

Numerous Government and community agencies exist to deal with victims of violence either directly or out of some other need. The variety and availability of these services varies widely from one setting to the next. Two common examples of services that deal with victims of violence indirectly are public housing services and social services. Public housing services are often involved in helping to find temporary or permanent housing solutions for victims of intimate partner violence. Data collected in jurisdictions where housing services have a legal obligation to prioritize housing for intimate partner violence victims often provide the best results. Social services such as child protective services and social assistance may intervene in cases of intimate partner violence. Often, children themselves are witnesses or victims when violence occurs in the home. Income assistance may be required by women who are forced to flee the family home owing to violence. Both of these sources represent only a small number of women victimized by violence.

Depending on the setting, numerous other agencies provide support to women who are victims of violence and may be sources for data. These are best conceptualized as either dedicated violence against women services or services that come into contact with victims of such violence. The availability of these services depends on a variety of factors including level of need, funding, political and economic situation at the national and local levels, and community motivation and support for such services. Other possible sources of service-based data include, but are not limited to the following:

- Women's groups/advocacy organizations
- Legal aid services
- Counselling services
- Crisis intervention
- Women's shelters/refuges
- Rape/sexual assault services
- Family services

---

4 See report of the Expert Group Meeting on the topic "Violence against women: A Statistical overview, challenges and gaps in data collection and methodology and approaches for overcoming them", Geneva, April 2005. Available from www.un.org/womenwatch/daw/egm/vaw-stat-2005/index.html.

5 See V. Jaquier, H. Johnson and B.S. Fisher, "Research methods, measures and ethics", in Sourcebooks on Violence against Women, 2nd ed., C.M. Renzetti, J.L. Edleson and R.K. Bergen, eds. (SAGE Publications, 2010).

- Community resource centres
- Faith-based or religious services
- Crime prevention programmes or agencies
- Disability services
- Immigrant and refugee services
- Programmes for abusive men
- Addiction centres
- Academics and researchers inside and outside government.

The quality, quantity, reliability and validity of the data collected by these agencies and organizations varies considerably and should be examined on a case-by-case basis. As data collection is typically not the primary mandate of these services, often there is no systematic data collection system in place or the agencies collect data in non-standardized form. As a result, data quality is often poor, inconsistent and/or unrepresentative of the women that these services serve. There have been attempts to standardize the data collected by services for abused women, such as Statistics Canada's biennial Transition Home Survey, which asks shelters across the country to report on the number of women and children who have used their services during the past 12 months, including the location of shelters and the type of services provided, and to provide a snapshot of the women and children admitted or turned away on a single day.

Problems can arise from a lack of collaboration on data collection. Women are often counted multiple times when data from multiple agencies are combined. Many victims seek assistance from more than one agency and therefore show up repeatedly in the combined data. Data collection mechanisms are rarely linked at this level. Nor are police and court data systems likely to be linked, making it difficult to estimate with precision how many individual victims or perpetrators of violence are represented in the totals recorded. In some countries, there are also concerns about the accuracy of record-keeping, for example in the case of murders of newborn babies, acid-throwing incidents and murders of women that are recorded as "accidents" or not recorded at all.[6]

Despite some potentially useful aspects of administrative data, most women victims of violence do not seek help from medical or health agencies, social service providers or criminal justice agencies owing to a range of factors, including shame, fear of the perpetrator, fear of the police, concerns about the reaction of family and friends, cultural and religious beliefs and a lack of community support, and therefore do not appear in administrative statistics. Additional limitations on utilizing administrative data occur when Government services are absent, limited in number or limited in capacity, when violence against women or any of its subtypes are not identified as criminal acts by that country's criminal code, when laws are poorly enforced and when social or cultural conventions fail to recognize the many forms of violence directed at women. International comparison of administrative data is difficult, as the availability of services and the availability and quality of data varies a great deal.

Although the statistical data collected from these agencies may be questioned, these services may be a rich source of qualitative data and may provide useful context to official statistical sources.

---

[6] See E.G. Krug and others, eds., World Report on Violence and Health (Geneva, 2002).

Table AII.1
Strengths and limitations of sources of data on violence against women

Data source	Strengths	Limitations
Health services	Data can be used to identify women seeking help for physical or sexual violence from health service providers.	Universal surveillance raises ethical concerns if health services are absent or limited. The majority of cases of violence against women do not reach health services. Injuries may not be acknowledged as resulting from violence. Data are not representative. Data cannot be used to measure prevalence of violence against women.
Criminal and civil justice systems	Data can be used: - to identify women seeking help for physical or sexual violence from the police or other justice authorities. - to evaluate police and court responses. Data are: - systematically collected in some countries. - The data are recorded according to legal codes.	The majority of cases of violence against women are not reported to the police. Data may not be disaggregated by sex. Data are not representative. Data cannot be used to measure prevalence of violence against women.
Other Government agencies/programmes/support services	Data can be used to identify victims of violence that come forward owing to other needs. Data can supplement police and health service data. These services can be a rich source of qualitative data.	Data may be incomplete. Data are not representative. Data cannot be used to measure prevalence of violence against women.
Population surveys	If the sample is representative of the population, population surveys can effectively measure prevalence, correlates (risk factors) and consequences of violence against women.	Data are of limited use in the case of small areas or subgroups unless large samples or stratification are used. Not all types of violence against women can be effectively measured. Data collected in this way raise ethical and safety concerns.

Annex III

Selected countries that have conducted violence against women surveys since 2000

Country	Source	Year of study[1]	Coverage	Sample size	Intimate partner violence	Non-partner violence
Albania	2	2002	National	5,697 women and 1,740 men	√	√
Armenia	3	2008-2009	National	2,763 women	√	√
Australia	4	2002-2003	National	6,677 women	√	√
Azerbaijan	5	2001	National	5,533 women	√	√
Azerbaijan	6	2006	National	8,444 women and 2,558 men	√	√
Bangladesh	7	2002-2003	City and province	3,130 women	√	√
Bangladesh	8	2007	National	10,996 women and 3,771 men	√	
Bolivia (Plurinational State of)	9	2008	National	16,939 women and 6,054 men	√	
Brazil	7	2001	City and province	2,128 women	√	√
Cambodia	10	2000	National	12,236 women	√	
Cambodia	11	2005	National	16,823 women and 6,731 men	√	√
Cameroon	12	2004	National	11,304 women	√	√
Canada	13	2004	National	13,162 women and 10,604 men	√	√
Canada	14	2009	National	19,422 households	√	√
Cape Verde	15	2005	National	5,505 women and 2,644 men	√	
Chile	16	2004	City	442 women	√	
China, Hong Kong Special Administrative Region	17	2005	National	1,297 women	√	√
Colombia	18	2004-2005	National	51,100 women	√	
Costa Rica	17	2003	National	908 women	√	√
Côte d'Ivoire	19	2005	National	5,183 women and 4,103 men	√	√
Czech Republic	17	2003	National	1,980 women	√	√
Democratic Republic of the Congo	20	2007	National	9,995 women and 4,757 men	√	√
Denmark	17	2003	National	3,589 women	√	√
Dominican Republic	21	2002	National	23,384 women	√	√
Dominican Republic	22	2007	National	27,195 women and 27,975 men	√	√
Ecuador	23	2004	National	10,184	√	
Egypt	16	2004	City	631 women	√	
Egypt	24	2005	National	19,474 women	√	

Country	Source**	Year of study*	Coverage	Sample size	Intimate partner violence	Non-partner violence
Egypt	25	2008	National	16,527 women	√	
El Salvador	26	2008	National	12,008 women	√	
Ethiopia	7	2002	Province	3,016 women	√	√
Finland	27	2005-2006	National	7,213 women	√	√
France	28	2000	National	6,970 women	√	√
Georgia	29	2005	National	6,376 women	√	
Germany	30	2003	National	10,264 women	√	√
Ghana	31	2008	National	4,916 women and 4,568 men	√	√
Guatemala	32	2002	National	6,595 women	√	
Haiti	33	2005-2006	National	10,757 women and 4,958 men	√	√
Honduras	34	2005-2006	National	19,948 women	√	
India	16	2004	City	1,922 women	√	
India	35	2005-2006	National	124,385 women and 74,369 men	√	√
Indonesia	36	2006	National	68,800 households	√	√
Ireland	37	2003	National	1,800 women and 1,500 men	√	
Ireland	38	2008	National	2,008 adults	√	
Italy	39	2006	National	25,000 women	√	√
Japan	7	2000-2003	City	1,371 women	√	√
Jordan	40	2007	National	10,876 women	√	√
Kenya	41	2003	National	8,195 women and 3,578 men	√	√
Kenya	42	2008-2009	National	8,444 women and 3,465 men	√	√
Kiribati	43	2008	National	1,501 women	√	√
Liberia	44	2007	National	7,092 women and 6,009 men	√	√
Lithuania	45	2000	National	517 women	√	
Malawi	46	2004	National	11,698 women and 3,261 men	√	√
Maldives	47	2006	National	2,584 households	√	√
Mexico	48	2003	National	34,184 women	√	√
Mexico	49	2006	National	133,398 women	√	√
Mexico	50	2011	National	152,636 women	√	√
Morocco	51	2009-2010	National	8,275 women	√	√
Mozambique	17	2004	National	2,015 women	√	√
Namibia	7	2002	City	1,367 women	√	√
New Zealand	50	2002	City	2,960 women	√	√
Nicaragua	53	2006	National	14,221 women	√	
Nigeria	54	2008	National	33,385 women and 15,486 men	√	
Norway	55	2008	National	2,407 women	√	
Paraguay	56	2004	National	7,321 women	√	
Peru	57	2009	National	24,213 women	√	
Philippines	17	2003	National	2,602 women	√	√
Philippines	16	2004	City	1,000 women	√	
Philippines	58	2008	National	13,594 women	√	
Poland	17	2004	National	2,009 women	√	√
Republic of Korea	59	2007	National	10,000 households	√	√
Republic of Moldova	60	2005	National	7,440 women and 2,508 men	√	√
Romania	61	2004	National	4,441 women and 2,361 men	√	√

Selected countries that have conducted violence against women surveys since 2000

Country	Source**	Year of study*	Coverage	Sample size	Intimate partner violence	Non-partner violence
Rwanda	62	2005	National	11,321 women and 4,820 men	√	√
Samoa	7	2000	National	1,640 women	√	√
Sao Tome and Principe	63	2008-2009	National	2,378 women and 2,110 men	√	
Serbia	7	2003	City	1,456 women	√	√
Slovakia	64	2008	National	827 women	√	√
Solomon Islands	65	2009	National	2,960 women	√	√
Spain	66	2005	National	32,426 women	√	
Sweden	67	2000	National	6,926 women	√	√
Switzerland	17	2003	National	1,973 women	√	√
Tajikistan	68	2005	Khatlon Region	400 women	√	
Thailand	7	2002/2005	Province and City	2,818 women	√	√
Timor-Leste	69	2009-2010	National	13,137 women and 4,076 men	√	√
Turkey	70	2008	National	12,795 women	√	√
Uganda	71	2006	National	8,531 women and 2,503 men	√	√
Ukraine	72	2007	National	6,841 women and 3,178 men	√	√
United Kingdom of Great Britain and Northern Ireland	73	2001	National	12,226 women and 10,237 men	√	√
United Kingdom of Great Britain and Northern Ireland	74	2005	National	24,498 individuals	√	√
United States of America	75	2000	National	8,000 women and 8,005 men	√	√
United Republic of Tanzania	7	2002	City and Province	1,820 women	√	√
Viet Nam	76	2009	National	4,838 women	√	√
Zambia	21	2001-2002	National	7,658 women	√	√
Zambia	77	2007	National	7,146 women and 6,500 men	√	√
Zimbabwe	78	2005-2006	National	8,907 women and 7,175 men	√	√

* Year of data collection. When not reported, the year of publication was used.
** Source

2 L. Morris and others, eds., "Albania Reproductive Health Survey, 2002: Final Report" (Tirana Institute of Public Health, Ministry of Health and Institute of Statistics, 2005).

3 Armenia, National Statistical Service and United Nations Population Fund (UNFPA), "Nationwide Survey on Domestic Violence against Women in Armenia 2008-2009" (Yerevan, 2010).

4 J. Mouzos and T. Makkai, Women's Experiences of Male Violence: Findings from the Australian Component of the International Violence against Women Survey (IVAWS), Research and Public Policy Series, No. 56 (Canberra, Australian Institute of Criminology, 2004).

5 F. Serbanescu and others, eds., "Reproductive Health Survey, Azerbaijan, 2001: Final Report" (Atlanta, Georgia, Centers for Disease Control and Prevention, 2003).

6   Azerbaijan, State Statistical Committee and Macro International, "Azerbaijan: Demographic and Health Survey 2006" (Baku; Calverton, Maryland, 2008).

7   C. Garcia-Moreno and others, WHO Multi-country Study on Women's Health and Domestic Violence against Women: Initial Results on Prevalence, Health Outcomes and Women's Responses (Geneva, World Health Organization, 2005).

8   Bangladesh, National Institute of Population Research and Training, Mitra and Associates and Macro International, "Bangladesh: Demographic and Health Survey 2007" (Dhaka; Calverton, Maryland, 2009).

9   R. Coa and L.H. Ochoa, Bolivia: "Encuesta Nacional de Demografía y Salud 2008" (La Paz, Ministry of Health and Sport and National Statistics Institute; Calverton, Maryland, Macro International, 2009).

10 Cambodia, National Institute of Statistics and Directorate General for Health, and ORC Macro, "Cambodia: Demographic and Health Survey 2000" (Phnom Penn; Calverton, Maryland, 2001).

11 Cambodia, National Institute of Public Health and National Institute of Statistics, and ORC Marco, "Cambodia: Demographic and Health Survey 2005" (Phnom Penn; Calverton, Maryland, 2006).

12 Cameroon, National Statistics Institute, and ORC Macro, "Cameroon: Enquête Démographique et de Santé"(Yaounde; Calverton, Maryland, 2005).

13 H. Johnson, Measuring Violence against Women: Statistical Trends 2006, Catalogue No. 85-570-XIE (Ottawa, Statistics Canada, 2006).

14 Statistics Canada, Family Violence in Canada: A Statistical Profile, Catalogue No. 85-224-X (Ottawa, 2011).

15 Cape Verde, National Statistics Institute and Ministry of Health, and Macro International, "Cape Verde: Inquérito Demográfico e de Saúde Reprodutiva (IDSR-II) 2005" (Praia; Calverton, Maryland, 2008).

16 F. Hassan and others, "Physical intimate partner violence in Chile, Egypt, India and the Philippines" International Journal of Injury Control and Safety Promotion, vol. 11, No. 2, pp. 111-116.

17 H. Johnson, N. Ollus and S. Nevala, Violence against Women: An International Perspective (New York Springer, 2008).

18 G. Ojeda, M. Ordóñez and L.H. Ochoa, "Salud sexual y reproductiva en Columbia: Encuesta Nacional de Demografía y Salud 2005" (Bogotá, Asociación Probienestar de la Familia Colombiana, Profamilia; Calverton, MD, Macro International, 2005).

19 Côte d'Ivoire, National Statistics Institute and Ministry for Fight against AIDS, and ORC Macro, "Côte d'Ivoire: Enquête sur les Indicateurs du Sida 2005" (Abidjan; Calverton, Maryland 2006).

20 Democratic Republic of the Congo, Ministry of Planning and Ministry of Health, and Macro International, "République Démocratique du Congo: Enquête Démographique et de Santé (EDS-RDC) 2007" (Kinshasa; Calverton, Maryland, 2008).

21 S. Kishor and K. Johnson "Domestic violence in nine developing countries: A comparative study" (Calverton, Maryland, Macro International, 2004).

22 Centre for Social and Demographic Studies and Macro International, "República Dominicana: Encuesta Demográfica y de Salud 2007" (Santo Domingo; Calverton, Maryland, 2008).

23 Centre for Population and Social Development Studies, "Informe final de la Encuesta Demográfica y de Salud Materna e Infantil (ENDEMAIN 2004)" (Quito, 2005).

24 F. El-Zanaty and A. Way, "Egypt: Demographic and Health Survey 2005" (Cairo: Ministry of Health and Population, National Population Council and El-Zanaty and Associates; Calverton, Maryland, ORC Macro, 2006).

25 F. El-Zanaty and A. Way, "Egypt: Demographic and Health Survey 2008" (Cairo, Ministry of Health and El-Zanaty and Associates; Calverton, Maryland, Macro International, 2009).

26 Salvadorian Demographic Association and Centers for Disease Control and Prevention, "Encuesta Nacional de Salud Familiar de 2008: Informe final" (San Salvadar; Atlanta, Georgia, 2009).

27 M. Piispa and others, "Violence against women in Finland" (Helsinki, National Research Institute of Legal Policy and the European Institute for Crime Prevention and Control, 2006).

28 M. Jaspard and others, "Les violences enver les femmes en France: Une enquete nationale" (Paris, 2001).

29 F. Serbanescu and others, eds., "Reproductive Health Survey Georgia 2005: Preliminary report" (Atlanta, Georgia, Centers for Disease Control and Prevention, 2005).

30 Germany, Federal Ministry for Family Affairs, Senior Citizens, Women and Youth, "Health, wellbeing and personal safety of women in Germany: A representative study of violence against women in Germany" (Berlin, 2004).

31 Ghana, Ghana Statistical Service and Ghana Health Service, and ICF Macro, "Ghana: Demographic and Health Survey 2008" (Accra; Calverton, Maryland, 2009).

32 Guatemala, Ministry of Public Health and Social Assistance, and Centers for Disease Control and Prevention, "Guatemala; Encuesta Nacional de Salud Materno Infantil 2002" (Guatemala City; Atlanta, Georgia, 2003).

33 M. Cayemittes and others, "Haiti: Enquête Mortalité, Morbidité et Utilisation des Services 2005-2006" (Port-au-Prince, Ministry of Public Health and Population and Haitian Children's Institute; Calverton, Maryland, Macro International, 2007).

34 Honduras, Ministry of Health and National Statistics Institute, and Macro International, "Honduras: Encuesta Nacional de Demografía y Salud (ENDESA) 2005-2006" (Tegucigalpa; Calverton, Maryland, 2006).

35 International Institute for Population Sciences and Macro International, "India: National Family and Health Survey (NHPS-3) 2005-06" (Mumbai; Calverton, Maryland 2007).

36 U. Suhaimi and D.R.W.W. Utami, "The 2006 Survey of Violence against Women and Children in Indonesia" (Jakarta, Statistics Indonesia, 2006).

37 D. Watson and S. Parsons, Domestic Abuse of Women and Men in Ireland: Report on the National Study of Domestic Abuse (Dublin, Stationery Office, 2005).

38 J. Horgan and others, "Attitudes to domestic abuse in Ireland: Report of a survey on perceptions and beliefs of domestic abuse among the general population of Ireland" (Dublin, National Office for the Prevention of Domestic, Sexual and Gender-based Violence, 2008).

39 M.G. Muratore (ISTAT), "Measuring violence: indicators from the Italian Violence against Women Survey", paper presented at the Expert Group Meeting on Indicators to Measure Violence against Women, Geneva, October 2007.

40 Jordan, Department of Statistics, and Macro International, "Jordan: Population and Family Health Survey 2007" (Amman; Calverton, Maryland, 2008).

41 Kenya, Central Bureau of Statistics and Ministry of Health, and ORC Macro, "Kenya: Demographic and Health Survey 2003" (Nairobi; Calverton, Maryland, 2004).

42 Kenya, National Bureau of Statistics and ICF Macro, "Kenya: Demographic and Health Survey 2008–2009" (Nairobi; Calverton, Maryland, 2010).

43 Secretariat of the Pacific Community, Kiribati Family Health and Support Study: A Study on Violence against Women and Children (Noumea, New Caledonia, 2010).

44 Liberia, Liberia Institute of Statistics and Geo-information Services, Ministry of Health and Social Welfare and National AIDS Control Programme, and Macro International, "Liberia: Demographic and Health Survey 2007" (Monrovia; Calverton, Maryland, 2008).

45 J. Reingardiene, "Gender politics in Lithuania: A case of gender-based violence against women in the family", Sociologija, Mintis ir Veiksmas No. 1 (2002), pp. 16-34.

46 Malawi, National Statistical Office and ORC Marco, "Malawi: Demographic and Health Survey 2004" (Zomba; Calverton, Maryland, 2005).

47 E. Fulu, The Maldives Study on Women's Health and Life Experiences: Initial Results on Prevalence, Health Outcomes and Women's Responses to Violence (Malé, Ministry of Gender and Family, 2007).

48 Mexico, National Institute of Statistics, Geography and Informatics, "Panorama de violencia contra las mujeres (ENDIREH 2006): Estados Unidos Mexicanos" (Aguascalientes, 2007).

49 Mexico, National Institute of Statistics, Georgraphy and Informatics. «Panorama de Violencia Contra las Mujeres (ENDIREH 2006) : Estado Unidos Méxicanos" (Aguascalientes, 2006).

50 Mexico, National Institute of Statistics, Georgraphy and Informatics, "Encuesta Nacional Sobre la Dinamica de las Relaciones en los Hogares 2011 (ENDIREH): Sintesis metodologica" (Aguascalientes, 2012).

51 Morocco, High Commission for Planning, "Enquête Nationale sur la Prévalence de la Violence à l'égard des femmes: Principaux résultats" (Rabat, 2011).

52 J. Fanslow and E. Robinson "Violence against women in New Zealand: Prevalence and health consequences", The New Zealand Medical Journal, vol. 117, No. 1206, pp. 1173-1184.

53 Nicaragua, National Institute of Development Information, and Centers for Disease Control, "Encuesta Nicaragüense de Demografía y Salud 2006/07: Informe Final" (Managua; Atlanta, Georgia, 2008).

54 Nigeria, National Population Commission and ICF Macro, "Nigeria: Demographic and Health Survey 2008" (Abuja; Calverton, Maryland, 2009).

55 A. Neroien and B. Schei, "Partner violence and health: Results from the first national study on violence against women in Norway" Scandinavian Journal of Public Health, vol. 36, No. 2, pp. 161-168.

56 Paraguayan Center for Population Studies, "Paraguay: Encuesta National de Demografia y Salud Sexual y Reproductiva 2004: Informe Final" (Asunción, 2005).

57 Peru, National Institute of Statistics and Informatics, and ORC Macro, "Peru: Encuesta Demográfica y de Salud Familiar 2009" (Lima; Calverton, Maryland, 2010).

58 Philippines, National Statistics Office and ICF Macro, "Philippines: 2008 National Demographic and Health Survey: Key Findings" (Manila; Calverton, Maryland, 2009).

59 Byun Wha Soon (Korean Women's Development Institute) "Korea's experience in the implementation of a survey on VaW", paper presented at the Expert Group Meeting on Gender Statistics and the Use of Violence against Women Indicators in Support of the CEDAW and the Beijing Platform for Action, Bangkok, October 2008.

60 Republic of Moldova, National Scientific and Applied Center for Preventive Medicine, and ORC Macro, "Moldova: Demographic and Health Survey 2005" (Chisinau; Calverton, Maryland, 2006).

61 Romania, Ministry of Health, Reproductive Health Survey Romania 2004: Summary Report (Buzau, 2005).

62 Rwanda, National Statistics Institute, and ORC Macro,"Rwanda: Demographic and Health Survey 2005" (Kigali; Calverton, Maryland, 2006).

63 Sao Tome and Principe, National Statistics Institute and Ministry of Health, and ICF Marco "São Tomé e Príncipe: Inquérito Demográfico e Sanitário 2008-2009" (Sao Tome; Calverton Maryland, 2010).

64 B. Bodnarova, J. Filadelfiova and B. Holubova, "Representative research on prevalence and experience of women with violence against women (VaW) in Slovakia" (Bratislava, Institute for Labour and Family Research, 2008).

65 Secretariat of the Pacific Community, Solomon Islands Family Health and Safety Study: A Study on Violence against Women and Children (Noumea, New Caledonia, 2009).

66 SIGMA DOS, "III Macroencuesta sobre la violencia contra las mujeres:Informe de resultados" (Madrid, 2006).

67 E. Lundgren and others, Captured Queen: Men's Violence against Women in "Equal" Sweden—A Prevalence Study (Umeå, Sweden, Åströms tryckeri, 2001).

68 R. N. Haarr, "Violence against women in marriage: A general population study in Khatlon Oblast, Tajikistan" (Dushanbe, NGO Social Development Group, 2005).

69 Timor-leste, National Statistics Directorate and Ministry of Finance and ICF Macro, "Timor-Leste: Demographic and Health Survey 2009-10" (Dili; Calverton, Maryland, 2010).

70 Turkey, Directorate General on the status of Women and ICON-Institut Public Sector, Hacettepe University Institute of Population Studies and BNB Consulting, "Domestic violence against women in Turkey" (Ankara, Elma Teknik Basim Matbaacihik, 2009).

71 Uganda, Uganda Bureau of Statistics and Macro International, "Uganda: Demographic and Health Survey 2006" (Kampala; Calverton, Maryland, 2007).

72 Ukraine, Ukrainian Center for Social Reforms, State Statistical Committee and Ministry of Health, and Macro International, "Ukraine: Demographics and Health Survey 2007" (Kyiv; Calverton, Maryland, 2008).

73 S. Walby and J. Allen, Domestic Violence, Sexual Assault and Stalking: Findings from the British Crime Survey, Research Study 276 (London, Home Office, 2004).

74 A. Finney, Domestic Violence, Sexual Assault and Stalking: Findings from the 2004/05 British Crime Survey (London, Home office, 2006).

75 P. Tjaden and N. Thoennes, "Full report of the prevalence, incidence, and consequences of violence against women: Findings from the National Violence against Women Survey" (National Institute of Justice, Washington, D.C.; Centers for Disease Control and Prevention, Atlanta, 2000).

76 Viet Nam, General Statistics Office, "'Keeping silent is dying': Results from the National Study on Domestic Violence against Women in Viet Nam" (Hanoi, 2010).

77 Zambia, Central Statistical Office and Ministry of Health, Tropical Diseases Research Centre, University of Zambia and Macro International, "Zambia: Demographic and Health Survey 2007" (Lusaka; Calverton, Maryland, 2009).

78 Zimbabwe, Central Statistical Office, and Macro International, "Zimbabwe: Demographic and Health Survey 2005-06" (Harare; Calverton, Maryland, 2007).

Annex IV

Example of a public campaign: Violence prevention in Italy

The Italian Women Safety's Survey provided the data needed to develop a national campaign to prevent violence against women. The posters below were intended to challenge common beliefs that tolerate violence against women in intimate relationships.

Annex V

Design components of selected surveys on violence against women

Country	Survey	Sample design	Mode of data collection
Australia	Women's Safety Survey, 1996	Multistage cluster sampling: Each state and territory was divided into geographical regions and subdivided into collector's districts (CDs). CDs were stratified by geographical region (metropolitan/non-metropolitan). In metropolitan areas, CDs were randomly selected from each stratum with probability of selection proportional to the number of dwellings. The total number of metropolitan CDs selected was determined by the size of the sample allocated to each metropolitan area in each state and territory. Non-metropolitan CDs had the added step of pairing adjacent CDs in order to minimize interviewing costs. The probability of selecting a pair of CDs was inversely proportionate to the cost of interviewing at that location (determined by distance from a major urban centre). Within CDs, a block of dwellings was randomly selected. Systematic sampling was utilized to select individual households from each block. A respondent was selected from each household.	Combination of face-to-face and telephone interviews
Australia	International Violence Against Women Survey, 2002-2003	Stratified random sample: Households were identified using the "White Pages plus one" method within geographical areas. A pre-survey letter was mailed to households whose telephone numbers were selected. A woman aged 18 to 69 years was selected from each household using the "next birthday" method.	Telephone Interviews
Bangladesh	WHO Multi-country Study on Women's Health and Domestic Violence against Women, 2000-2003	Multistage cluster sampling: Sampling was designed to select women aged 15 to 49 years from Dhaka and one rural area. Clusters were selected systematically and stratified by socio-economic level. Households within a cluster were selected in such a way that ensured that the sample was self-weighting.	Face-to-face interviews

Country	Survey	Sample design	Mode of data collection
Cambodia	Household Survey on Domestic Violence, 1996	Systematic sampling: From six provinces, 155 villages were systematically selected. Households were randomly selected from within those villages. Communes were considered unsafe and were therefore removed from the sampling frame.	Face-to-face interviews
Ethiopia	Butajira Rural Health Programme, 2002	Multistage cluster sampling: Ten kebeles (neighbourhoods) were selected for inclusion using the demographic registration of the Butajira Rural Health Programme. The study kebeles were then stratified based on location (urban and rural). A simple random sampling strategy was used to select a target respondent from the kebeles, with a higher proportion of urban residents selected. Based on the national census, the total sample was designed to ensure that 15 per cent of the study population came from urban kebeles and 85 per cent from rural kebeles.	Face-to-face interviews
Finland	Women's Safety Study, 1997	Systematic sampling: Every 259th Finnish woman was selected from the Central Population Register. Data were post-stratified by region and age.	Postal survey
Ireland	National Study of Domestic Abuse, 2003	Multistage cluster sampling: Sampling units were selected randomly from the National Electoral Register to produce a nationally representative sample. A set of 100 randomly generated telephone numbers was then derived for each cluster. One person from each household was interviewed and stratification controls were imposed to control for gender, age and broad socioeconomic status (at work/not at work), with a target number of individuals from each stratum being interviewed.	Telephone interviews
Kiribati	Kiribati Family Health and Support Study, 2008	Multistage cluster sampling: The sample was stratified by the most urbanized island and the outer islands. The outer islands were further stratified and one or two islands were selected from each stratum based on the size of the stratum and the costs associated with interviewing. The urban sample was stratified by enumeration areas (EAs). Households were allocated proportionately to each EA based on the overall number of households per area. The sample for the outer islands was proportionally allocated to each stratum based on the number of 15 to 49 year-old women counted during the 2005 census. Within each stratum, the sample was proportionally allocated to each island. The sample selected from each village was based on the proportion of households that the village contained.	Face-to-face interviews
`Mexico	National Survey on the Dynamics of Relationships in Homes, 2006	Stratified, multistage cluster sampling.	Face-to-face interviews

Design components of selected surveys on violence against women

Country	Survey	Sample design	Mode of data collection
New Zealand	New Zealand Violence against Women Study, 2002	Multistage cluster sampling: Randomly selected meshblocks (census areas) in Auckland and the rural area of Waikato were used as the primary sampling units. Within each meshblock, a starting point was chosen randomly. Interviewers then approached every second or fourth house (based on population density) from the starting point.	Face-to-face interviews
South Africa	Cross-sectional Study of Violence against Women, 1998	Random multistage cluster sampling: EAs from the 1996 Census were used as clusters that were stratified into urban and rural areas in three provinces. Fourteen households were randomly selected per cluster in urban areas and 28 in rural areas.	Face-to-face interviews
Sweden	Survey on Violence against Women, 2001	Simple random sampling: Respondents were randomly selected from the Register of Total Population.	Postal survey
Turkey	National Violence Against Women Survey, 2008	Stratified and multistage cluster sampling: In the first stage, up to five provinces were selected in each region representing urban and rural strata and using probability proportional to size (PPS) for a total of 51 provinces. In the second stage, settlements in selected provinces were selected by PPS corresponding to each stratum. Nationwide, 378 urban and 164 rural clusters were selected. The size of clusters was 48 households in urban areas and 36 households in rural settlements.	Face-to-face interviews
United States of America	National Violence against Women Survey, 1995-1996	Simple random sampling: A random 2-digit number was added to each selected telephone bank number to produce a full 10-digit telephone number. Separate banks of numbers were generated for male and female respondents. A simple random sample was drawn. The adult with the most recent birthday was selected.	Telephone interviews and computer-assisted telephone interviewing
United States of America	National Intimate Partner and Sexual Violence Survey, 2010	Dual-frame stratified random digit dialling sampling design: A list-assisted landline frame of working banks of residential telephone numbers and a cell phone frame of banks of active numbers currently in use for cell phones were created. State-level stratified disproportionate sampling was used. Males and females were eligible to be interviewed. Persons answering landlines were selected as the respondent in one-person households; random selection was used in households with two adults and the "most recent birthday" method in households with more than two adults. Persons answering cell phones were selected as the respondent because cell phones are personal devices.	Telephone interviews with landlines and mobile phones

Country	Survey	Sample design	Mode of data collection
Viet Nam	National Study on Domestic Violence against Women, 2009	Multistage cluster sampling: A total of 460 EAs were chosen from six geographical regions. The number of households selected in each area was proportionate to the square root of the total number of households in each region. The sample size of each region was allocated to the urban and rural areas of each region in a similar fashion (12 households per EA). Respondents were selected randomly from among eligible women.	Face-to-face interviews
Zimbabwe	Musasa Project, 1995-1997	Multistage cluster sampling: Census information was used to select locations and households randomly in one province. One woman was chosen randomly for an interview.	Face-to-face interviews

Annex VI

Recommended tabulations for the core indicators identified by the Friends of the Chair of the United Nations Statistical Commission on indicators on violence against women

This section outlines recommended tabulations that should be produced by a national survey on violence against women in accordance with the core set of indicators identified in chapter II. The extent of possible analyses from the survey results is extensive, depending on the sample size, the additional survey questions that are included, the local country conditions and the priorities of stakeholders. These are examples only of the main tabulations that could be produced using data as collected using the questions contained in the UN Economic Commission for Europe (UNECE) survey module on violence against women (see annex VII). More extensive dummy tables are provided on the UNECE website.[1]

The following tabulations are a suggested minimum breakdown. There are other breakdowns, such as by partnership status, that might be relevant to your national setting but not included in the core indicators or related tabulations. It is essential to ensure that the tabulations capture the total experience of violence women are subjected to in your society.

The recommended tabulations for each core indicator are as follows:

Indicator I: Total and age-specific rate of women subjected to physical violence in the past 12 months by severity of violence, relationship to the perpetrator and frequency

Table I-1. Women reporting physical violence in the past 12 months by age and relationship to perpetrator

Table I-2. Women reporting physical violence by non-partner perpetrators in the past 12 months by age and detailed relationship to perpetrator

Table I-3. Women reporting physical violence by partner or non-partner in the past 12 months by age and by severity of violence

Table I-4. Women reporting physical violence by partner or non-partner in the past 12 months by age and by frequency

---

[1] www1.unece.org/stat/platform/display/VAW/Survey+module+for+measuring+violence+against+women.

Table I-1
Women reporting physical violence in the past 12 months by age and relationship to perpetrator

Age group	Total women n	Type of perpetrator					
		Partner (percent)	n	Non-partner (per cent)	n	Any (per cent)	n
15-19							
20-24							
25-29							
30-34							
35-39							
40-44							
45-49							
50-54							
55-59							
60+							
Total							

Table I-2
Women reporting physical violence by non-partner perpetrators in the past 12 months by age and detailed relationship to perpetrator

Age group	Total women	Any type of non-partner violence		Family member							Non-family member									
				Parent				Other family member				Someone at work		Friend/ acquaintance		Teacher		Stranger		Other	
				Father		Mother		Male		Female											
	n	(per cent)	n	(per cent)	n	(per cent)	n	(per cent)	n	(per cent)	n	(per cent)	n	(per cent)	n	(per cent)	n	(per cent)	n	(per cent)	n
15-19																						
20-24																						
25-29																						
30-34																						
35-39																						
40-44																						
45-49																						
50-54																						
55-59																						
60+																						
Total																						

Table I-3
Women reporting physical violence by partner or non-partner in the past 12 months by age and by severity of violence

Age group	Total women	Type of perpetrator												
		Any				Partner						Non-partner		
		Moderate only		Severe		Moderate only		Severe				Moderate only		Severe
	n	(per cent)	n	(per cent)	n	(per cent)	n	(per cent)	n			(per cent)	n	(per cent)	n
15-19														
20-24														
25-29														
30-34														
35-39														
40-44														
45-49														
50-54														
55-59														
60+														
Total														

See paragraphs 71-76 for an in-depth discussion on severity.

Table I-4
Women reporting physical violence by partner or non-partner in the past 12 months by age and by frequency

Age group	Total women n	Type of perpetrator													
		Any							Partner						Non-partner					
		Once		Few		Many		Once		Few		Many		Once		Few		Many	
		(per cent)	n	(per cent)	n	(per cent)	n	(per cent)	n	(per cent)	n	(per cent)	n	(per cent)	n	(per cent)	n	(per cent)	n
15-19																			
20-24																			
25-29																			
30-34																			
35-39																			
40-44																			
45-49																			
50-54																			
55-59																			
60+																			
Total																			

The denominator is the number of respondents; therefore, if a respondent mentions multiple perpetrators in the same category she is included only once in the total.

Indicator II: Total and age-specific rate of women subjected to physical violence during their lifetime by severity of violence, relationship to the perpetrator and frequency

Table II-1. Women reporting physical violence during their lifetime by age and relationship to perpetrator

Table II-2. Women reporting physical violence by non-partner perpetrators during their lifetime by age and detailed relationship to perpetrator

Table II-3. Women reporting physical violence by partner or non-partner during their lifetime by age and by severity of violence

Table II-4. Women reporting physical violence by partner or non-partner during their lifetime by age and by frequency

Table II-1
Women reporting physical violence during their lifetime by age and relationship to perpetrator

Age group	Total women n	Type of perpetrator					
		Partner		Non-partner		Any	
		(per cent)	n	(per cent)	n	(per cent)	n
15-19							
20-24							
25-29							
30-34							
35-39							
40-44							
45-49							
50-54							
55-59							
60+							
Total							

Table II-2
Women reporting physical violence by non-partner perpetrators during their lifetime by age and detailed relationship to perpetrator

Age group	Total women	Any type of non-partner violence		Family member							Non-family member									
				Parent				Other family member				Someone at work		Friend/ acquaintance		Teacher		Stranger		Other	
				Father		Mother		Male		Female											
	n	(per cent)	n	(per cent)	n	(per cent)	n	(per cent)	n	(per cent)	n	(per cent)	n	(per cent)	n	(per cent)	n	(per cent)	n	(per cent)	n
15-19																						
20-24																						
25-29																						
30-34																						
35-39																						
40-44																						
45-49																						
50-54																						
55-59																						
60+																						
Total																						

Table II-3
Women reporting physical violence by partner or non-partner during their lifetime by age and by severity of violence

Age group	Total women	Type of perpetrator											
		Any				Partner				Non-partner			
		Moderate only		Severe		Moderate only		Severe		Moderate only		Severe	
	n	(per cent)	n	(per cent)	n	(per cent)	n	(per cent)	n	(per cent)	n	(per cent)	n
15-19													
20-24													
25-29													
30-34													
35-39													
40-44													
45-49													
50-54													
55-59													
60+													
Total													

See paragraphs 71-76 for an in-depth discussion on severity.

Table II-4
Women reporting physical violence by partner or non-partner during their lifetime by age and by frequency

Age group	Total women n	Type of perpetrator																	
		Any							Partner							Non-partner					
		Once		Few		Many		Once		Few		Many		Once		Few		Many	
		(per cent)	n	(per cent)	n	(per cent)	n	(per cent)	n	(per cent)	n	(per cent)	n	(per cent)	n	(per cent)	n	(per cent)	n
15-19																			
20-24																			
25-29																			
30-34																			
35-39																			
40-44																			
45-49																			
50-54																			
55-59																			
60+																			
Total																			

The denominator is the number of respondents; therefore, if a respondent mentions multiple perpetrators in the same category she is included only once in the total.

Indicator III: Total and age-specific rate of women subjected to sexual violence in the past 12 months by severity of violence, relationship to the perpetrator and frequency

Table III-1. Women reporting sexual violence in the past 12 months by age and relationship to perpetrator

Table III-2. Women reporting sexual violence by non-partner perpetrators in the past 12 months by age and detailed relationship to perpetrator

Table III-3. Women reporting sexual violence by partner or non-partner in the past 12 months by age and by severity of violence

Table III-4. Women reporting sexual violence by partner or non-partner in the past 12 months by age and by frequency

Table III-1
Women reporting sexual violence in the past 12 months by age and relationship to perpetrator

Age group	Total Women	Type of perpetrator					
		Partner		Non-partner		Any	
	n	(per cent)	n	(per cent)	n	(per cent)	n
15-19							
20-24							
25-29							
30-34							
35-39							
40-44							
45-49							
50-54							
55-59							
60+							
Total							

Table III-2
Women reporting sexual violence by non-partner perpetrators in the past 12 months by age and detailed relationship to perpetrator

Age group	Total women	Any type of non-partner violence		Family member							Non-family member							
				Parent				Other family member				Someone at work		Friend/ acquaintance		Teacher		Stranger		Other	
				Father		Mother		Male		Female											
	n	(per cent)	n	(per cent)	n	(per cent)	n	(per cent)	n	(per cent)	n	(per cent)	n	(per cent)	n	(per cent)	n	(per cent)	n	(per cent)	n
15-19																						
20-24																						
25-29																						
30-34																						
35-39																						
40-44																						
45-49																						
50-54																						
55-59																						
60+																						
Total																						

Table III-3
Women reporting sexual violence by partner or non-partner in the past 12 months by age and by severity of violence

Age group	Total Women n	Any				Type of perpetrator Partner				Non-partner			
		Moderate only		Severe		Moderate only		Severe		Moderate only		Severe	
		(per cent)	n	(per cent)	n	(per cent)	n	(per cent)	n	(per cent)	n	(per cent)	n
15-19													
20-24													
25-29													
30-34													
35-39													
40-44													
45-49													
50-54													
55-59													
60+													
Total													

See paragraphs 71-76 for an in-depth discussion on severity.

Table III-4
Women reporting sexual violence by partner or non-partner in the past 12 months by age and by frequency

Age group	Total women n	Type of perpetrator																	
		Any							Partner							Non-partner					
		Once		Few		Many		Once		Few		Many		Once		Few		Many	
		(per cent)	n	(per cent)	n	(per cent)	n	(per cent)	n	(per cent)	n	(per cent)	n	(per cent)	n	(per cent)	n	(per cent)	n
15-19																			
20-24																			
25-29																			
30-34																			
35-39																			
40-44																			
45-49																			
50-54																			
55-59																			
60+																			
Total																			

The denominator is the number of respondents; therefore, if a respondent mentions multiple perpetrators in the same category she is included only once in the total.

Indicator IV: Total and age-specific rate of women subjected to sexual violence during their lifetime by severity of violence, relationship to the perpetrator and frequency

Table IV-1. Women reporting sexual violence during their lifetime by age and relationship to perpetrator

Table IV-2. Women reporting sexual violence by non-partner perpetrators during their lifetime by age and detailed relationship to perpetrator

Table IV-3. Women reporting sexual violence by partner or non-partner during their lifetime by age and by severity of violence

Table IV-4. Women reporting sexual violence by partner or non-partner during their lifetime by age and by frequency

Table IV-1
Women reporting sexual violence during their lifetime by age and relationship to perpetrator

Age group	Total Women	Type of perpetrator					
		Partner		Non-partner		Any	
	n	(per cent)	n	(per cent)	n	(per cent)	n
15-19							
20-24							
25-29							
30-34							
35-39							
40-44							
45-49							
50-54							
55-59							
60+							
Total							

Table IV-2
Women reporting sexual violence by non-partner perpetrators during their lifetime by age and detailed relationship to perpetrator

Age group	Total women n	Any type of non-partner violence		Family member						Non-family member								
				Parent				Other family member				Someone at work		Friend/ acquaintance		Teacher		Stranger		Other	
				Father		Mother		Male		Female											
		(per cent)	n	(per cent)	n	(per cent)	n	(per cent)	n	(per cent)	n	(per cent)	n	(per cent)	n	(per cent)	n	(per cent)	n	(per cent)	n
15-19																						
20-24																						
25-29																						
30-34																						
35-39																						
40-44																						
45-49																						
50-54																						
55-59																						
60+																						
Total																						

Table IV-3
Women reporting sexual violence by partner or non-partner during their lifetime by age and by severity of violence

Age group	Total Women	Type of perpetrator											
		Any					Partner					Non-partner			
		Moderate only		Severe		Moderate only		Severe		Moderate only		Severe	
	n	(per cent)	n	(per cent)	n	(per cent)	n	(per cent)	n	(per cent)	n	(per cent)	n
15-19													
20-24													
25-29													
30-34													
35-39													
40-44													
45-49													
50-54													
55-59													
60+													
Total													

See paragraph 71-76 for an in-depth discussion on severity.

Table IV-4
Women reporting sexual violence by partner or non-partner during their lifetime by age and by frequency

Age group	Total women	Type of perpetrator																	
		Any							Partner							Non-partner					
		Once		Few		Many		Once		Few		Many		Once		Few		Many	
	n	(per cent)	n	(per cent)	n	(per cent)	n	(per cent)	n	(per cent)	n	(per cent)	n	(per cent)	n	(per cent)	n	(per cent)	n
15-19																			
20-24																			
25-29																			
30-34																			
35-39																			
40-44																			
45-49																			
50-54																			
55-59																			
60+																			
Total																			

The denominator is the number of respondents; therefore, if a respondent mentions multiple perpetrators in the same category she is included only once in the total.

Indicator V: Total and age-specific rate of ever-partnered women subjected to sexual and/or physical violence by a current or former intimate partner in the past 12 months by frequency

For these indicators, total women refers only to those women who have ever had a partner.

Table V-1. Women reporting physical, sexual, physical or sexual violence by a current or former intimate partner in past 12 months by age

Table V-2. Women reporting physical violence by a current or former intimate partner in the past 12 months by age and frequency

Table V-3. Women reporting sexual violence by a current or former intimate partner in the past 12 months by age and frequency

Table V-4. Women reporting sexual and/or physical violence by a current or former intimate partner in the past 12 months by age and frequency

Table V-1
Women reporting physical, sexual, physical or sexual violence by a current or former intimate partner in past 12 months by age

Age group	Any partner (most recent and/or former partner)							Current/most recent partner							Total with more than one partner	Former partner					
	Total ever partnered	Physical violence		Sexual violence		Physical or sexual violence		Total ever partnered	Physical violence		Sexual violence		Physical or sexual violence			Physical violence		Sexual violence		Physical or sexual violence	
	n	(per cent)	n	(per cent)	n	(per cent)	n	n	(per cent)	n	(per cent)	n	(per cent)	n	n	(per cent)	n	(per cent)	n	(per cent)	n
15-19																						
20-24																						
25-29																						
30-34																						
35-39																						
40-44																						
45-49																						
50-54																						
55-59																						
60+																						
Total																						

Table V-2
Women reporting physical violence by a current or former intimate partner in the past 12 months by age and frequency

Age group	Total ever partnered n	Any partner (most recent and/or former partner)						Total ever partnered n	Current/most recent partner						Total with more than one partner n	Former partner					
		Once		Few		Many			Once		Few		Many			Once		Few		Many	
		(per cent)	n	(per cent)	n	(per cent)	n		(per cent)	n	(per cent)	n	(per cent)	n		(per cent)	n	(per cent)	n	(per cent)	n
15-19																						
20-24																						
25-29																						
30-34																						
35-39																						
40-44																						
45-49																						
50-54																						
55-59																						
60+																						
Total																						

Table V-3
Women reporting sexual violence by a current or former intimate partner in the past 12 months by age and frequency

Age group	Total ever partnered n	Any partner (most recent and/or former partner)							Current/most recent partner							Total with more than one partner	Former partner					
		Once		Few		Many		Total ever partnered n	Once		Few		Many			n	Once		Few		Many	
		(per cent)	n	(per cent)	n	(per cent)	n		(per cent)	n	(per cent)	n	(per cent)	n			(per cent)	n	(per cent)	n	(per cent)	n
15-19																						
20-24																						
25-29																						
30-34																						
35-39																						
40-44																						
45-49																						
50-54																						
55-59																						
60+																						
Total																						

Table V-4
Women reporting sexual and/or physical violence by a current or former intimate partner in the past 12 months by age and frequency

Age group	Total ever partnered n	Any partner (most recent and/or former partner)						Total ever partnered n	Current/most recent partner						Total with more than one partner n	Former partner					
		Once		Few		Many			Once		Few		Many			Once		Few		Many	
		(per cent)	n	(per cent)	n	(per cent)	n		(per cent)	n	(per cent)	n	(per cent)	n		(per cent)	n	(per cent)	n	(per cent)	n
15-19																						
20-24																						
25-29																						
30-34																						
35-39																						
40-44																						
45-49																						
50-54																						
55-59																						
60+																						
Total																						

Indicator VI: Total and age-specific rate of ever-partnered women subjected to sexual and/or physical violence by a current or former intimate partner during their lifetime by frequency

Table VI-1. Women reporting physical, sexual, physical or sexual violence by a current or former intimate partner during their lifetime by age

Table VI-2. Women reporting physical violence by a current or former intimate partner during their lifetime by age and frequency

Table VI-3. Women reporting sexual violence by a current or former intimate partner during their lifetime by age and frequency

Table VI-4. Women reporting sexual and/or physical violence by a current or former intimate partner during their lifetime by age and frequency

Table VI-1
Women reporting physical, sexual, physical or sexual violence by a current or former intimate partner during their lifetime by age

Age group	Any partner (most recent and/or former partner)						Total ever partnered	Current/most recent partner						Total with more than one partner	Former partner					
	Total ever partnered	Physical violence		Sexual violence		Physical or sexual violence			Physical violence		Sexual violence		Physical or sexual violence			Physical violence		Sexual violence		Physical or sexual violence	
	n	(per cent)	n	(per cent)	n	(per cent)	n	n	(per cent)	n	(per cent)	n	(per cent)	n	n	(per cent)	n	(per cent)	n	(per cent)	n
15-19																						
20-24																						
25-29																						
30-34																						
35-39																						
40-44																						
45-49																						
50-54																						
55-59																						
60+																						
Total																						

Table VI-2
Women reporting physical violence by a current or former intimate partner during their lifetime by age and frequency

Age group	Total ever partnered n	Any partner (most recent and/or former partner)						Total ever partnered n	Current/most recent partner						Total with more than one partner n	Former partner					
		Once		Few		Many			Once		Few		Many			Once		Few		Many	
		(per cent)	n	(per cent)	n	(per cent)	n		(per cent)	n	(per cent)	n	(per cent)	n		(per cent)	n	(per cent)	n	(per cent)	n
15-19																					
20-24																					
25-29																					
30-34																					
35-39																					
40-44																					
45-49																					
50-54																					
55-59																					
60+																					
Total																					

Table VI-3
Women reporting sexual violence by a current or former intimate partner during their lifetime by age and frequency

Age group	Any partner (most recent and/or former partner)							Current/most recent partner								Former partner					
	Total ever partnered n	Once		Few		Many		Total ever partnered n	Once		Few		Many		Total with more than one partner n	Once		Few		Many	
		(per cent)	n	(per cent)	n	(per cent)	n		(per cent)	n	(per cent)	n	(per cent)	n		(per cent)	n	(per cent)	n	(per cent)	n
15-19																					
20-24																					
25-29																					
30-34																					
35-39																					
40-44																					
45-49																					
50-54																					
55-59																					
60+																					
Total																					

Table VI-4
Women reporting sexual and/or physical violence by a current or former intimate partner during their lifetime by age and frequency

Age group	Total ever partnered n	Any partner (most recent and/or former partner)						Total ever partnered n	Current/most recent partner						Total with more than one partner n	Former partner					
		Once		Few		Many			Once		Few		Many			Once		Few		Many	
		(per cent)	n	(per cent)	n	(per cent)	n		(per cent)	n	(per cent)	n	(per cent)	n		(per cent)	n	(per cent)	n	(per cent)	n
15-19																						
20-24																						
25-29																						
30-34																						
35-39																						
40-44																						
45-49																						
50-54																						
55-59																						
60+																						
Total																						

Indicator VII: Total and age-specific rate of ever-partnered women subjected to psychological violence in the past 12 months by an intimate partner

Women reporting emotional abuse, controlling behaviors and emotional abuse and/or controlling behaviours by any intimate partner in the past 12 months by age

Age group	Total ever-partnered women n	Type of psychological abuse					
		Emotional abuse (per cent)	n	Controlling behaviours (per cent)	n	Emotional abuse and/or controlling behaviours (per cent)	n
15-19							
20-24							
25-29							
30-34							
35-39							
40-44							
45-49							
50-54							
55-59							
60+							
Total							

Indicator VIII: Total and age-specific rate of ever-partnered women subjected to economic violence in the past 12 months by an intimate partner

Women reporting economic violence by a current or former intimate partner in the past 12 months by age

Age group	Total ever partnered n	Any partner (per cent)	n	Current/most recent partner (per cent)	n	Former partner (per cent)	n
15-19							
20-24							
25-29							
30-34							
35-39							
40-44							
45-49							
50-54							
55-59							
60+							
Total							

Annex VII

A model questionnaire for producing statistics on the core indicators identified by the Friends of the Chair of the United Nations Statistical Commission on indicators on violence against women

Survey Module on Violence against Women[1]
Developed for the United Nations Economic Commission of Europe
by Henrica A.F.M. Jansen
20 March 2011

Questions in this module are grouped as follows:

R - Relationship information from respondent

V - Partner violence

N - Non-partner violence

Z - Completion of interview

The following documents have been developed to accompany this module:

1. Question-by-question explanation of the module

2. Facilitator's manual for workshops for training interviewers

3. Interviewer's manual (including ethical and safety recommendations)

4. Codebook and analysis plan for the violence against women indicators

5. Recode and analysis syntaxes (SPSS) to compute the UN violence against women indicators

The most recent version of the UNECE survey module and accompanying materials are available from www1.unece.org/stat/platform/display/VAW (regularly updated).

---

1 This survey module has been developed by Henrica A.F.M. Jansen to address the set of indicators developed by the Friends of the Chair of the United Nations Statistical Commission on statistical indicators on violence against women. This module builds on the violence against women instrument that was developed for the WHO Multi-country Study on Women's Health and Domestic Violence against Women and incorporates suggestions offered by the UNECE Expert Group Meetings on Measuring Violence against Women (Geneva, September 2009 and November 2010), the ESCWA Training of Trainers on Violence against Women (Beirut, May 2010) and the 2010 pilot testing in Armenia, Georgia, Mexico and the Republic of Moldova.

CHECK HH SELECTION FORM	WOMAN SELECTED FOR THIS MODULE [ ] ↓	WOMAN NOT SELECTED [ ] →	GO TO NEXT SECT.
Informed consent and privacy	READ TO RESPONDENT Now I would like to ask you questions about some other important aspects of a woman's life. Some of the topics may be difficult to discuss, but many women have found it useful to have the opportunity to talk. You do not have to answer any questions that you do not want to. I want to assure you that all of your answers will be kept strictly private and will not be told to anyone. And no one else will know that you were asked these questions. Do you have any questions? Do you agree to be interviewed? It is very important that we talk in private. Is this a good time and place to hold the interview, or is there somewhere else that you would like to go to? CHECK FOR PRESENCE OF OTHERS. DO NOT CONTINUE UNTIL EFFECTIVE PRIVACY IS ENSURED. PRIVACY OBTAINED.... 1 ↓	PRIVACY NOT POSSIBLE ... 2 →	GO TO [NEXT MODULE]
START	TIME OF STARTING THIS SECTION OF THE INTERVIEW (24h) [ ][ ]h [ ][ ]min		
R01	Are you at the moment married, living together or *involved in a relationship with a man without living together?*[2] *IF NEEDED PROBE: such as a regular boyfriend or a fiancé?* *THE OPTION IN ITALICS MAY NOT BE APPROPRIATE FOR ALL COUNTRIES*	CURRENTLY MARRIED......................................1 LIVING WITH MAN, NOT MARRIED............ .2 *CURRENTLY HAVING A REGULAR PARTNER (INVOLVED IN A RELATIONSHIP), WITHOUT LIVING TOGETHER*....................3 NOT CURRENTLY MARRIED OR LIVING WITH A MAN, *NOT INVOLVED IN A RELATIONSHIP WITH A MAN*......................4	→ R04 → R04 → R04

---

[2] The partner concept should be wide: married, cohabitating and dating with (sexual) relationship. Exclude occasional or sporadic dating as this would fall under "others". Note that including dating relationship may not be appropriate in all cultures, for example because it may not be appropriate to ask questions on sex to non-married women, or because the nature of engagements may be such that the woman is never spending time alone with her future husband until she is married. Partnership questions may need to be adapted to the country's specific situation. In general, same-sex relationships are not included here. Some countries may decide to adapt the questionnaire for same-sex partner violence and include a question on the sex of the partner.

R02	Previously were you married, living together or *involved in a relationship with a man without living together*? MARK ONLY THE ONE OPTION THAT APPLIES TO THE MOST RECENT RELATIONSHIP *THE OPTION IN ITALICS MAY NOT BE APPROPRIATE FOR ALL COUNTRIES*	PREVIOUSLY MARRIED..................................1 PREVIOUSLY LIVING WITH MAN, NOT MARRIED..2 *PREVIOUSLY HAVING A REGULAR PARTNER (INVOLVED IN A RELATIONSHIP), WITHOUT LIVING TOGETHER*...................3 NEVER MARRIED OR LIVING WITH A MAN AND NEVER *INVOLVED IN A RELATIONSHIP WITH A MAN*.....................4	→N01
R03	**Did your last partnership with a man** end in divorce or separation, or did your husband/partner die? *COUNTRY-SPECIFIC CODES CAN BE ADDED*	DIVORCED ....1 SEPARATED/BROKEN UP ....2 WIDOWED/PARTNER DIED ....3 DON'T KNOW/DON'T REMEMBER ....8 REFUSED/NO ANSWER 9	
R04	In your life, how many times have you been married and/or lived together with a man *and/or had a relationship with a man*? INCLUDE CURRENT PARTNER —COUNT EVERY PERSON ONLY ONCE, ACCORDING TO MOST RECENT SITUATION *THE OPTION IN ITALICS MAY NOT BE APPROPRIATE FOR ALL COUNTRIES*	(a) MARRIED NUMBER OF TIMES ....[ ][ ] (b) LIVING WITH MAN, NOT MARRIED NUMBER OF TIME................................... [ ][ ] (c) *REGULAR PARTNER WITHOUT LIVING TOGETHER* NUMBER OF TIMES ....[ ][ ]	

	V. PARTNER			
V01	**READ TO RESPONDENT:** When two people marry or live together, they usually share both good and bad moments. I would now like to ask you some questions about how your current (or most recent) husband/partner treats (treated) you. If anyone interrupts us, I will change the topic of conversation.			

V02[3]	I am now going to ask you about some situations that are true for many women. These questions are about your (current or most recent) husband/partner.
	
	 Would you say it is generally true that:
	
	 (a) He tries to keep you from seeing your friends?
	 (b) He tries to restrict contact with your family of birth?
	 (c) He insists on knowing where you are at all times?
	 (d) He ignores you and treats you indifferently?
	 (e) He gets angry if you speak with another man?
	 (f) He is often suspicious that you are unfaithful?
	 (g) He expects you to ask his permission before seeking health care for yourself?
		(A)
		
		 YES NO
		 (a) SEEING FRIENDS 1 2
		 (b) CONTACT FAMILY 1 2
		 (c) WANTS TO KNOW 1 2
		 (d) IGNORES YOU 1 2
		 (e) GETS ANGRY 1 2
		 (f) SUSPICIOUS 1 2
		 (g) HEALTH CENTRE 1 2
				(B) ONLY ASK IF "YES" IN V02A
				
				 Has this happened **in the past 12 months**?
				
				 YES NO
				  1 2
				  1 2
				  1 2
				  1 2
				  1 2
				  1 2
				  1 2

V03[4]	Again, this question is about your (current or most recent) husband/partner. Would you say it is generally true that: (a) He refuses to give you enough money for household expenses, even when he has money for other things?	(A) YES NO (a) REFUSES MONEY 1 2		(B) ONLY ASK IF "YES" IN V03A Has this happened **in the past 12 months**? YES NO 1 2

---

[3] Questions V02 and V04 on emotional abuse and controlling behaviour address the indicator on psychological violence. The items in these questions are still undergoing methodological developments.

[4] Question V03 on economic violence will need to be further developed to capture more aspects of economic violence. These aspects will need to be context specific.

		(A) **(If YES, continue with B. If NO, skip to next item.)**	(B) Has this happened **in the past 12 months**? **(If YES, ask C and D. If NO, ask D only.)**	(C) **In the past 12 months**, would you say that this has happened once, a few times or many times?	(D) Did this happen **before the past 12 months**? IF YES: would you say that this has happened once, a few times or many times?
V04	The next questions are about things that happen to many women and that your (current/most recent) husband/ partner may have done to you.				
	Has your (current or most recent) husband/partner ever…	YES NO	YES NO	One Few Many	NO One Few Many
	(a) Insulted you or made you feel bad about yourself?	1 2	1 2	1 2 3	0 1 2 3
	(b) Belittled or humiliated you in front of other people?	1 2	1 2	1 2 3	0 1 2 3
	(c) Done things to scare or intimidate you on purpose (e.g., by the way he looked at you, by yelling and smashing things)?	1 2	1 2	1 2 3	0 1 2 3
	(d) Verbally threatened to hurt you or someone you care about?	1 2	1 2	1 2 3	0 1 2 3

V05	Has your (current or most recent) husband/partner ever…	(A) (If YES, continue with B. If NO, skip to next item.) YES NO	(B) Has this happened **in the past 12 months**? (If YES, ask C and D. If NO, ask D only). YES NO	(C) **In the past 12 months**, would you say that this has happened once, a few times or many times? One Few Many	(D) Did this happen **before the past 12 months**?[5] IF YES: would you say that this has happened once, a few times or many times? NO One Few Many
	(a) Slapped you or thrown something at you that could hurt you?	1 2	1 2	1 2 3	0 1 2 3
	(b) Pushed you or shoved you or pulled your hair?	1 2	1 2	1 2 3	0 1 2 3
	(c) Hit you with his fist or with anything else that could hurt you?	1 2	1 2	1 2 3	0 1 2 3
	(d) Kicked you, dragged you or beat you up?	1 2	1 2	1 2 3	0 1 2 3
	(e) Choked or burnt you on purpose?	1 2	1 2	1 2 3	0 1 2 3
	(f) Threatened with or actually used a gun, knife or other weapon against you?	1 2	1 2	1 2 3	0 1 2 3
V06	CHECK V05C			**IF AT LEAST ONE "2" OR "3"** [_] ↓	**ALL OTHER SKIP TO V08**

---

[5] The answer options in column D were modified compared to the WHO questionnaire to enable them to be asked of all women who report the act. (In the WHO questionnaire, column D was asked only if the act had NOT occurred in the past 12 months.)

V07a[6]	For the things we just talked about (IF MORE THAN ONE TYPE MENTIONED, REFER TO THE ACTS MENTIONED), can you please tell me how often it happened in the past 12 months? Would you say: 1. Every day or nearly every day, all the time 2. Once or twice a week 3. Once or twice a month 4. Less than once a month PROBE: We are interested in separate incidents, not each time each individual act occurred.		EVERY DAY OR NEARLY EVERY DAY............1 ONCE OR TWICE A WEEK.........................2 ONCE OR TWICE A MONTH.......................3 LESS THAN ONCE A MONTH......................4 DON'T KNOW/DON'T REMEMBER..................8 REFUSED/NO ANSWER..............................9
V07b	Can you give me a number for how many times these things happened in the past 12 months? PROBE: More or less. It does not need to be precise. I would like to remind you that we are interested in separate incidents, not each time each individual act occurred.		NUMBER OF TIMES.........................[ ][ ][ ] MANY TIMES, CANNOT GIVE A NUMBER......995 REFUSED/NO ANSWER...........................999
V08		(A) (If YES, continue with B. If NO, skip to next item.) YES NO	(B) Has this happened in the past 12 months? (If YES, ask C and D. If NO, ask D only.) YES NO	(C) **In the past 12 months**, would you say that this has happened once, a few times or many times? One Few Many	(D) Did this happen **before the past 12 months**? IF YES: would you say that this has happened once, a few times or many times? NO One Few Many
	(a) Did your (current or most recent) husband/partner ever force you to have sexual intercourse when you did not want to?	1 2	1 2	1 2 3	0 1 2 3
	(b) Did you ever have sexual intercourse you did not want to because you were afraid of what your (current or most recent) husband/partner might do?	1 2	1 2	1 2 3	0 1 2 3
	(c) Did your (current or most recent) husband/partner ever force you to do something else sexual that you did not want or that you found degrading or humiliating?	1 2	1 2	1 2 3	0 1 2 3
V09	**CHECK V08C**		**IF AT LEAST ONE "2" OR "3"** [ ] ↓		**ALL OTHER SKIP TO V11**

---

[6] A more detailed question on frequency was added for physical and sexual violence in the past 12 months to test whether this information can be easily collected.

V10a	For the things we just talked about (IF MORE THAN ONE TYPE MENTIONED, REFER TO THE ACTS MENTIONED), can you please tell me how often it happened in the past 12 months? Would you say: 1. Every day or nearly every day, all the time 2. Once or twice a week 3. Once or twice a month 4. Less than once a month PROBE: We are interested in separate incidents, not each time each individual act occurred.	EVERY DAY OR NEARLY EVERY DAY...............1 ONCE OR TWICE A WEEK..................................2 ONCE OR TWICE A MONTH................................3 LESS THAN ONCE A MONTH..............................4 DON'T KNOW/DON'T REMEMBER.....................8 REFUSED/NO ANSWER.......................................9	
V10b	Can you give me a number for how many times these things happened in the past 12 months? PROBE: More or less. It does not need to be precise. I would like to remind you that we are interested in separate incidents, not each time each individual act occurred.	NUMBER OF TIMES...............................[ ][ ][ ] MANY TIMES, CANNOT GIVE A NUMBER......995 REFUSED/NO ANSWER...................................999	
V11	CHECK WHETHER ANSWERED YES TO ANY QUESTION ON PHYSICAL VIOLENCE **SEE V05A: AT LEAST ONE "1" (YES)**	YES, PHYSICAL VIOLENCE................................1 NO PHYSICAL VIOLENCE 2	
V12	CHECK WHETHER ANSWERED YES TO ANY QUESTION ON SEXUAL VIOLENCE **SEE V08A: AT LEAST ONE "1" (YES)**	YES, SEXUAL VIOLENCE ....1 NO SEXUAL VIOLENCE 2	
V13	IF "YES" TO V11 AND/OR V12 [ ] ↓	IF "NO" TO BOTH V11 AND V12 [ ] **SKIP TO V16**	
V14[7]	Did the following ever happen as a result of what your (current or most recent) husband/partner did to you? (a) You had cuts, scratches, bruises or aches. (b) You had injuries to eye or ear, sprains, dislocations or burns. (c) You had deep wounds, broken bones, broken teeth, internal injuries, or any other similar injury. (d) You had a miscarriage.	(A) YES NO 1 2 1 2 1 2 1 2	(B) ONLY ASK IF YES IN V14 A: Has this happened **in the past 12 months**? YES NO 1 2 1 2 1 2 1 2

---

7 Question V14 is being asked for those who reported physical or sexual violence. From the WHO experience, we learned that we miss out on injuries if the question is asked for physical violence only. The question is phrased differently from the WHO questionnaire. In this module, instead of asking first whether the respondent was ever injured, there are direct questions giving examples of injuries. The severity of physical violence could be operationalized by the nature of the acts of violence, as well as by the injuries. For the calculation of the indicator, we need to decide if we also include those who report injuries for only sexual violence without including physical violence. It should be noted that one case of victimization can include several acts and that, in the case of repeated victimizations, one severe incident raises the overall severity of all victimizations.

V15[8]	Would you say that your (current or most recent) husband/partner's behaviour towards you has affected your physical or mental well-being? Would you say that it has had no effect, a little effect or a large effect? REFER TO SPECIFIC ACTS OF **PHYSICAL AND/OR SEXUAL VIOLENCE** SHE DESCRIBED EARLIER	NO EFFECT ....1 A LITTLE ....2 A LOT ....3 DON'T KNOW/DON'T REMEMBER ....8 REFUSED/NO ANSWER 9	
V16[9]	Are you ever afraid of your (current or most recent) husband or partner? Would you say never, sometimes, many times, most/all of the time?	NEVER ....1 SOMETIMES ....2 MANY TIMES ....3 MOST/ALL OF THE TIME ....4 DON'T KNOW/DON'T REMEMBER ....8 REFUSED/NO ANSWER 9	
V17	**CHECK R04 a, b and c (TOTAL NUMBER OF PARTNERS)**	IF 2 OR MORE | | ↓	IF ONLY 1 | | **SKIP TO V43**

---

[8] The self-perceived impact of partner violence on physical and mental well-being is a measure of the subjective experience of the severity of the violence that the respondent is living (modified from WHO questionnaire where the question is in the coping section, Section 9). The way this module was set up is to ask this only of respondents who report physical or sexual partner violence (because it refers to the violent acts).

[9] Question V16 (not in the WHO instrument) addresses whether the respondent is living in constant fear (an alternative question could be "fearing for her life"), which is a measure of their subjective experience of the severity of the violence they are living. The way the module was set up is to ask this of all respondents, whether reporting acts of physical or sexual violence or not.

READ TO RESPONDENT:

I would now like to ask you some questions about how (any of) your <u>previous</u> husband/partner treated you (any partner that you may have had before the partner that we just talked about).

IF IT IS EVIDENT THAT THERE COULD HAVE BEEN NO CONTACT WITH THIS PREVIOUS PARTNER IN THE PAST 12 MONTHS, YOU DO NOT NEED TO ASK ALL THE QUESTIONS ABOUT THE PAST 12 MONTHS, BUT YOU WILL STILL NEED TO FOLLOW THE SKIP PATTERNS AND MARK 'NO' IN ALL THE QUESTIONS ABOUT THE PAST 12 MONTHS AND, WHEN INDICATED, ASK ABOUT THE PERIOD BEFORE THE PAST 12 MONTHS.

		(A)			(B) ONLY ASK IF "YES" IN V18A	
					Has this happened **in the past 12 months?**	
V18	Remember, these questions are about (any of) your previous husband/partner(s). Would you say it is generally true that:		YES	NO	YES	NO
	(a) He tried to keep you from seeing your friends?	(a) SEEING FRIENDS	1	2	1	2
	(b) He tried to restrict contact with your family of birth?	(b) CONTACT FAMILY	1	2	1	2
	(c) He insisted on knowing where you were at all times?	(c) WANTS TO KNOW	1	2	1	2
	(d) He ignored you and treated you indifferently?	(d) IGNORES YOU	1	2	1	2
	(e) He got angry if you spoke with another man?	(e) GETS ANGRY	1	2	1	2
	(f) He was often suspicious that you were unfaithful?	(f) SUSPICIOUS	1	2	1	2
	(g) He expected you to ask his permission before seeking health care for yourself?	(g) HEALTH CENTRE	1	2	1	2
V19	CHECK V18 A	IF AT LEAST ONE "1" (YES) [↓]			IF ONLY "2" (NO) [ ] SKIP TO V21	
V20	Could you please tell me about the type of relationship with the previous partner that did this to you. Were you married with him, living together *or involved in a relationship without living together*? IF MORE THAN 1 PREVIOUS PARTNER VIOLENT, MARK ALL THAT APPLY. *THE OPTION IN ITALICS MAY NOT BE APPROPRIATE FOR ALL COUNTRIES*	MARRIED ....A LIVING TOGETHER ....B *REGULAR PARTNER WITHOUT LIVING TOGETHER*..........................C NO ANSWER ....Z				

V21	Again, this question is about (any of) your previous husband/partner(s). Would you say it is generally true that: (a) He refused to give you enough money for household expenses, even when he had money for other things?	(A) YES NO (a) REFUSED MONEY 1 2	(B) ONLY ASK IF "YES" IN V21A Has this happened **in the past 12 months**? YES NO 1 2
V22	CHECK V21A	IF "1" (YES) | | ↓	IF "2" (NO) | | SKIP TO V24
V23	Could you please tell me about the type of relationship with the previous partner that did this to you. Were you married with him, living together *or involved in a relationship without living together*? IF MORE THAN 1 PREVIOUS PARTNER VIOLENT, MARK ALL THAT APPLY. *THE OPTION IN ITALICS MAY NOT BE APPROPRIATE FOR ALL COUNTRIES*	MARRIED..A LIVING TOGETHER ....B *REGULAR PARTNER WITHOUT LIVING TOGETHER...C* NO ANSWER..Z	

		(A) (If YES, continue with B. If NO, skip to next item.) YES NO	(B) Has this happened **in the past 12 months**? (If YES, ask C and D. If NO, ask D only.) YES NO	(C) **In the past 12 months**, would you say that this has happened once, a few times or many times? One Few Many	(D) Did this happen **before the past 12 months**? IF YES: would you say that this has happened once, a few times or many times? NO One Few Many
V24	Has (any of) your previous husband/partner(s), ever…				
	(a) Insulted you or made you feel bad about yourself?	1 2	1 2	1 2 3	0 1 2 3
	(b) Belittled or humiliated you in front of other people?	1 2	1 2	1 2 3	0 1 2 3
	(c) Done things to scare or intimidate you on purpose (e.g., by the way he looked at you, by yelling and smashing things)?	1 2	1 2	1 2 3	0 1 2 3
	(d) Verbally threatened to hurt you or someone you cared about?	1 2	1 2	1 2 3	0 1 2 3

V25	CHECK V24A	IF AT LEAST ONE "1" (YES) [ ] ↓	IF ONLY "2"(NO) [ ] SKIP TO V27			
V26	Could you please tell me about the type of relationship with the previous partner that did this to you. Were you married with him, living together *or involved in a relationship without living together*? IF MORE THAN 1 PREVIOUS PARTNER VIOLENT, MARK ALL THAT APPLY. *THE OPTION IN ITALICS MAY NOT BE APPROPRIATE FOR ALL COUNTRIES*	MARRIED ....A LIVING TOGETHER ....B *REGULAR PARTNER WITHOUT LIVING TOGETHER* ..C NO ANSWER ....Z				
V27	Has (any of) your previous husband/ partner(s) ever… (a) Slapped you or thrown something at you that could hurt you? (b) Pushed you or shoved you or pulled your hair? (c) Hit you with his fist or with anything else that could hurt you? (d) Kicked you, dragged you or beat you up? (e) Choked or burnt you on purpose? (f) Threatened with or actually used a gun, knife or other weapon against you?	(A) (If YES, continue with B. If NO, skip to next item.) YES NO 1 2 1 2 1 2 1 2 1 2 1 2	(B) Has this happened **in the past 12 months**? (If YES, ask C and D. If NO, ask D only.) YES NO 1 2 1 2 1 2 1 2 1 2 1 2	(C) **In the past 12 months**, would you say that this has happened once, a few times or many times? One Few Many 1 2 3 1 2 3 1 2 3 1 2 3 1 2 3 1 2 3	(D) Did this happen **before the past 12 months**? IF YES: would you say that this has happened once, a few times or many times? NO One Few Many 0 1 2 3 0 1 2 3 0 1 2 3 0 1 2 3 0 1 2 3 0 1 2 3	
V28	CHECK V27C			IF AT LEAST ONE "2" OR "3" [ ] ↓	ALL OTHER SKIP TO V30	

V29a	For the things we just talked about (IF MORE THAN ONE TYPE MENTIONED, REFER TO THE ACTS MENTIONED), can you please tell me how often it happened in the past 12 months? Would you say: 1. Every day or nearly every day, all the time 2. Once or twice a week 3. Once or twice a month 4. Less than once a month PROBE: We are interested in separate incidents, not each time each individual act occurred.		EVERY DAY OR NEARLY EVERY DAY ....1 ONCE OR TWICE A WEEK ....2 ONCE OR TWICE A MONTH ....3 LESS THAN ONCE A MONTH ....4 DON'T KNOW/DON'T REMEMBER ....8 REFUSED/NO ANSWER 9
V29b	Can you give me a number for how many times these things happened in the past 12 months? PROBE: More or less. It does not need to be precise. I would like to remind you that we are interested in separate incidents, not each time each individual act occurred.		NUMBER OF TIMES ....[ ][ ][ ] MANY TIMES, CANNOT GIVE A NUMBER ....995 REFUSED/NO ANSWER 999
V30	**CHECK V27A**	IF AT LEAST ONE "1" (YES) | | ⬇	IF ONLY "2" (NO) | | SKIP TO V32
V31	Could you please tell me about the type of relationship with the previous partner that did this to you. Were you married with him, living together *or involved in a relationship without living together*? IF MORE THAN 1 PREVIOUS PARTNER VIOLENT, MARK ALL THAT APPLY. *THE OPTION IN ITALICS MAY NOT BE APPROPRIATE FOR ALL COUNTRIES*		MARRIED ....A LIVING TOGETHER ....B *REGULAR PARTNER WITHOUT LIVING TOGETHER* ..C NO ANSWER ....Z

		(A) (If YES, continue with B. If NO, skip to next item.)	(B) Has this happened in the past 12 months? (If YES, ask C and D. If NO, ask D only.)	(C) **In the past 12 months**, would you say that this has happened once, a few times or many times?	(D) Did this happen **before the past 12 months**? IF YES: would you say that this has happened once, a few times or many times?
V32		YES NO	YES NO	One Few Many	NO One Few Many
	(a) Did (any of) your previous husband/partner(s) ever force you to have sexual intercourse when you did not want to?	1 2	1 2	1 2 3	0 1 2 3
	(b) Did you ever have sexual intercourse you did not want to because you were afraid of what (any of) your previous husband/partner(s) might do?	1 2	1 2	1 2 3	0 1 2 3
	(c) Did (any of) your previous husband/partner(s) ever force you to do something else sexual that you did not want or that you found degrading or humiliating?	1 2	1 2	1 2 3	0 1 2 3
V33	CHECK V32C			IF AT LEAST ONE "2" OR "3" ↓	ALL OTHER SKIP TO V35
V34a	For the things we just talked about (IF MORE THAN ONE TYPE MENTIONED, REFER TO THE ACTS MENTIONED), can you please tell me how often it happened in the past 12 months? Would you say: 1. Every day or nearly every day, all the time 2. Once or twice a week 3. Once or twice a month 4. Less than once a month PROBE: We are interested in separate incidents, not each time each individual act occurred.			EVERY DAY OR NEARLY EVERY DAY ....1 ONCE OR TWICE A WEEK ....2 ONCE OR TWICE A MONTH ....3 LESS THAN ONCE A MONTH ....4 DON'T KNOW/DON'T REMEMBER ....8 REFUSED/NO ANSWER 9	
V34b	Can you give me a number for how many times these things happened in the past 12 months? PROBE: More or less. It does not need to be precise. I would like to remind you that we are interested in separate incidents, not each time each individual act occurred.			NUMBER OF TIMES ....[ ][ ][ ] MANY TIMES, CANNOT GIVE A NUMBER ....995 REFUSED/NO ANSWER 999	

V35	CHECK V32A	IF AT LEAST ONE "1" (YES) | | ↓	IF ONLY "2" (NO) | | SKIP TO V37	
V36	Could you please tell me about the type of relationship with the previous partner that did this to you. Were you married with him, living together *or involved in a relationship without living together*? IF MORE THAN 1 PREVIOUS PARTNER VIOLENT, MARK ALL THAT APPLY. *THE OPTION IN ITALICS MAY NOT BE APPROPRIATE FOR ALL COUNTRIES*		MARRIED ....A LIVING TOGETHER ....B *REGULAR PARTNER WITHOUT LIVING TOGETHER ..C* NO ANSWER ....Z	
V37	CHECK WHETHER ANSWERED YES TO ANY QUESTION ON PHYSICAL VIOLENCE **SEE V27A: AT LEAST ONE "1" (YES)**		YES, PHYSICAL VIOLENCE ....1 NO PHYSICAL VIOLENCE 2	
V38	CHECK WHETHER ANSWERED YES TO ANY QUESTION ON SEXUAL VIOLENCE **SEE V32A: AT LEAST ONE "1" (YES)**		YES, SEXUAL VIOLENCE ....1 NO SEXUAL VIOLENCE 2	
V39	IF "YES" TO V37 AND/OR V38 | | ↓		IF "NO" TO BOTH V37 AND V38 | | SKIP TO V42		
V40	Did the following ever happen as a result of what (any of) your previous husband/partner(s) did to you? (a) You had cuts, scratches, bruises or aches. (b) You had injuries to eye or ear, sprains, dislocations or burns. (c) You had deep wounds, broken bones, broken teeth, internal injuries or any other similar injury. (d) You had a miscarriage.	(A) YES NO 1 2 1 2 1 2 1 2		(B) ONLY ASK IF YES IN V40A Has this happened **in the past 12 months**? YES NO 1 2 1 2 1 2 1 2	

V41	Would you say that (any of) your previous husband/partner's behaviour towards you affected your physical or mental well-being? Would you say, that it had no effect, a little effect or a large effect? REFER TO SPECIFIC ACTS OF **PHYSICAL AND/OR SEXUAL VIOLENCE** SHE DESCRIBED EARLIER	NO EFFECT ....1 A LITTLE ....2 A LOT ....3 DON'T KNOW/DON'T REMEMBER ....8 REFUSED/NO ANSWER 9
V42	Were you ever afraid of (any of) your previous husband or partner(s)? Would you say never, sometimes, many times, most/all of the time?	NEVER ....1 SOMETIMES ....2 MANY TIMES ....3 MOST/ALL OF THE TIME ....4 DON'T KNOW/DON'T REMEMBER ....8 REFUSED/NO ANSWER 9
V43	**ANY PARTNER VIOLENCE: IF "YES" TO V13 AND/OR V39 [ ] ⬇**	**IF "NO" TO BOTH V13 AND V39 [ ] SKIP TO NO1**
V44	Who have you told about your (current, most recent or previous) husband/partner's behaviour? REFER TO THE PARTNER WHO WAS VIOLENT AND IF NEEDED REFER TO THE ACTS MENTIONED PROBE: Anyone else? DO NOT READ OUT THE LIST MARK ALL MENTIONED	NO ONE ....A HER PARENTS ....B HIS PARENTS ....C OTHER RELATIVES ....D FRIENDS ....E NEIGHBOURS ....F POLICE ....G DOCTOR/HEALTH WORKER ....H PRIEST ....I COUNSELLOR ....J NGO/WOMEN'S ORGANIZATION ....K LOCAL LEADER ....L OTHER (specify):_____.........X

	N. OTHERS (NON-PARTNERS)		
N01	**READ TO RESPONDENT:** **In their lives, many women have unwanted experiences and experience different forms of maltreatment and violence from all kinds of people, men or women. These may be relatives, other people that they know, and/or strangers. If you don't mind, I would like to briefly ask you about some of these situations. Everything that you say will be kept private. I will first ask about what has happened since you were 15 years old, and thereafter during the past 12 months.**[10] **FOR WOMEN WHO WERE EVER PARTNERED ADD: These questions are about people other than your husband/partner(s).**		
N02[11]	**Since the age of 15**, has anyone ever hit, beaten, kicked or done anything else to hurt you physically? Thrown something at you? Pushed you or pulled your hair? Choked or burnt you on purpose? Threatened with or actually used a gun, knife or other weapon against you?	YES............................1 NO 2	☐ **N06**

---

[10] We suggest to focus first on perpetrators, then on specific acts with a question on injuries to operationalize severity. Alternatively, the focus could be on acts followed by a question on perpetrators, but this could result in losing the link between the specific acts and the perpetrators. A modification compared to the WHO questionnaire is to ask first about the period since the age of 15, followed by the past 12 months, in order to be able to address the indicators.

[11] Question N02 includes more acts than the WHO questionnaire. This is to ensure that the same acts are covered as for partner violence, even if we are not asking about them one by one to avoid that the questionnaire becomes too long.

N03	(a) Who did this to you? PROBE: Anyone else? How about a relative? How about someone at school or work? How about a friend or neighbour? A stranger or anyone else? DO NOT READ OUT THE LIST MARK ALL MENTIONED	(b) ASK ONLY FOR THOSE MARKED in (a). How many times did this happen **since you were 15**? Once, a few times, or many times?			(c) ASK ONLY FOR THOSE MARKED in (a). How many times did this happen **in the past 12 months**? Once, a few times, or many times?			
		Once	A few times	Many times	NO	Once	A few times	Many times
	FATHER/STEPFATHER ....A	1	2	3	0	1	2	3
	MOTHER ....B	1	2	3	0	1	2	3
	MOTHER-IN-LAW C	1	2	3	0	1	2	3
	OTHER MALE FAMILY MEMBER ....D	1	2	3	0	1	2	3
	OTHER FEMALE FAMILY MEMBER ....E	1	2	3	0	1	2	3
	SOMEONE AT WORK—MALE ....F	1	2	3	0	1	2	3
	SOMEONE AT WORK—FEMALE ....G	1	2	3	0	1	2	3
	FRIEND/ACQUAINTANCE—MALE ....H	1	2	3	0	1	2	3
	FRIEND/ACQUAINTANCE—FEMALE I	1	2	3	0	1	2	3
	RECENT ACQUAINTANCE—MALE ....J	1	2	3	0	1	2	3
	RECENT ACQUAINTANCE—FEMALE ....K	1	2	3	0	1	2	3
	COMPLETE STRANGER—MALE..................L	1	2	3	0	1	2	3
	COMPLETE STRANGER—FEMALE............M	1	2	3	0	1	2	3
	TEACHER—MALE ....N	1	2	3	0	1	2	3
	TEACHER—FEMALE ....O	1	2	3	0	1	2	3
	DOCTOR/HEALTH STAFF—MALE ....P	1	2	3	0	1	2	3
	DOCTOR/HEALTH STAFF—FEMALE ....Q	1	2	3	0	1	2	3
	RELIGIOUS LEADER—MALE.......................R	1	2	3	0	1	2	3
	POLICE/ SOLDIER—MALE ....S	1	2	3	0	1	2	3
	OTHER—MALE (specify) _____........W	1	2	3	0	1	2	3
	OTHER—FEMALE (specify) _____...X	1	2	3	0	1	2	3
N04	INDICATE BELOW THE LETTERS FOR THE PERPETRATORS THAT WERE MENTIONED. IF MORE THAN 3 PERPETRATORS HAVE BEEN MENTIONED, ASK WHICH 3 WERE THE MOST SERIOUS AND INDICATE THE LETTERS AS IN ABOVE LIST HERE: ....PERPETRATOR 1 [ ] ....PERPETRATOR 2 [ ] ....PERPETRATOR 3 [ ] ASK N05 a, b, and c, FIRST FOR PERPETRATOR 1, THEN FOR PERPETRATOR 2 AND FINALLY FOR PEPETRATOR 3. WHEN NO MORE PERPETRATORS, GO TO N06.							

N05[12]	Did the following ever happen as a result of what .... (USE SAME WORDS TO REFER TO THE PERPETRATOR AS RESPONDENT) did to you?	(A) PERPETRATOR 1		(B) PERPETRATOR 2		(C) PERPETRATOR 3	
		YES	NO	YES	NO	YES	NO
	(a) You had cuts, scratches, bruises or aches.	1	2	1	2	1	2
	(b) You had injuries to eye or ear, sprains, dislocations or burns.	1	2	1	2	1	2
	(c) You had deep wounds, broken bones, broken teeth, internal injuries or any other similar injury.	1	2	1	2	1	2
	IF AT LEAST ONE "YES" to (a)(b) or (c): ASK (d)						
	(d) Did the injury (injuries) happen in the past 12 months?	1	2	1	2	1	2
	ONLY ASK FOR THE PERTRATORS INDICATED IN N04.	IF MORE THAN 1 PERPETRATOR, GO TO B		IF MORE THAN 2 PERPETRATORS GO TO C			
N06[13]	Now I would like to ask you about other unwanted experiences you may have had. Again, I want you to think about any person, man or woman. FOR WOMEN WHO EVER HAD A PARTNER ADD IF NECESSARY: except your husband/male partner. **Since the age of 15,** has anyone ever **forced you into sexual intercourse** when you did not want to, for example by threatening you, holding you down, or putting you in a situation where you could not say no. Remember to include people you have known as well as strangers. Please at this point exclude **attempts** to force you. IF NECESSARY: We define sexual intercourse as oral sex, anal or vaginal penetration.	YES ....1 NO 2				→**N08**	

---

[12] In the WHO questionnaire, there is no question on injuries for non-partners. Note that for non-partners, we ask about physical violence only (for the severity classification). If there are more than three different perpetrators, the question is asked only for the most serious three.

[13] In the WHO questionnaire, there is only one question on sexual violence after the age of 15. In this module, there are two: one for rape (unwanted and forced sexual intercourse) and another for all other unwanted sexual acts.

N07[14]	(a) Who did this to you? PROBE: Anyone else? How about a relative? How about someone at school or work? How about a friend or neighbour? A stranger or anyone else? DO NOT READ OUT THE LIST MARK ALL MENTIONED	(b) ASK ONLY FOR THOSE MARKED in (a). How many times did this happen **since you were 15**? Once, a few times, or many times?			(c) ASK ONLY FOR THOSE MARKED in (a). How many times did this happen **in the past 12 months**? Once, a few times, or many times?			
		Once	A few times	Many times	NO	Once	A few times	Many times
	FATHER/STEPFATHER ....A	1	2	3	0	1	2	3
	MOTHER ....B	1	2	3	0	1	2	3
	MOTHER-IN-LAW C	1	2	3	0	1	2	3
	OTHER MALE FAMILY MEMBER ....D	1	2	3	0	1	2	3
	OTHER FEMALE FAMILY MEMBER ....E	1	2	3	0	1	2	3
	SOMEONE AT WORK—MALE ....F	1	2	3	0	1	2	3
	SOMEONE AT WORK—FEMALE................G	1	2	3	0	1	2	3
	FRIEND/ACQUAINTANCE—MALE...........H	1	2	3	0	1	2	3
	FRIEND/ACQUAINTANCE—FEMALE I	1	2	3	0	1	2	3
	RECENT ACQUAINTANCE—MALE ....J	1	2	3	0	1	2	3
	RECENT ACQUAINTANCE—FEMALE ....K	1	2	3	0	1	2	3
	COMPLETE STRANGER—MALE L	1	2	3	0	1	2	3
	COMPLETE STRANGER—FEMALE ....M	1	2	3	0	1	2	3
	TEACHER—MALE ....N	1	2	3	0	1	2	3
	TEACHER—FEMALE ....O	1	2	3	0	1	2	3
	DOCTOR/HEALTH STAFF—MALE ....P	1	2	3	0	1	2	3
	DOCTOR/HEALTH STAFF—FEMALE ......Q	1	2	3	0	1	2	3
	RELIGIOUS LEADER—MALE ....R	1	2	3	0	1	2	3
	POLICE/ SOLDIER—MALE ....S	1	2	3	0	1	2	3
	OTHER—MALE (specify) _____ ....W	1	2	3	0	1	2	3
	OTHER—FEMALE (specify) _____ X	1	2	3	0	1	2	3
N08	Again, I want you to think about any person, man or woman. FOR WOMEN WHO EVER HAD A PARTNER ADD: except your husband/male partner. Apart from anything you may have mentioned, can you tell me if, **since the age of 15**, any of the following has happened to you? Has anyone **attempted to force** you to perform a sexual act you did not want, attempted to force you into sexual intercourse (which did not take place), touched you sexually, or did anything else sexually that you did not want. Remember to include people you have known as well as strangers.	YES...........................1 NO............................2						→N10 or Z01

---

14 The list of perpetrators for non-partner violence is modified compared to the WHO instrument.

N09	(a) Who did this to you? PROBE: Anyone else? How about a relative? How about someone at school or work? How about a friend or neighbour? A stranger or anyone else? DO NOT READ OUT THE LIST MARK ALL MENTIONED	(b) ASK ONLY FOR THOSE MARKED in (a). How many times did this happen **since you were 15**? Once, a few times, or many times?			(c) ASK ONLY FOR THOSE MARKED in (a). How many times did this happen **in the past 12 months?** Once, a few times, or many times?			
		Once	A few times	Many times	NO	Once	A few times	Many times
	FATHER/STEPFATHER ....A	1	2	3	0	1	2	3
	MOTHER ....B	1	2	3	0	1	2	3
	MOTHER-IN-LAW C	1	2	3	0	1	2	3
	OTHER MALE FAMILY MEMBER ....D	1	2	3	0	1	2	3
	OTHER FEMALE FAMILY MEMBER ....E	1	2	3	0	1	2	3
	SOMEONE AT WORK—MALE ....F	1	2	3	0	1	2	3
	SOMEONE AT WORK—FEMALE ....G	1	2	3	0	1	2	3
	FRIEND/ACQUAINTANCE—MALE..............H	1	2	3	0	1	2	3
	FRIEND/ACQUAINTANCE—FEMALE I	1	2	3	0	1	2	3
	RECENT ACQUAINTANCE—MALE ....J	1	2	3	0	1	2	3
	RECENT ACQUAINTANCE—FEMALE........K	1	2	3	0	1	2	3
	COMPLETE STRANGER—MALE L	1	2	3	0	1	2	3
	COMPLETE STRANGER—FEMAE...............M	1	2	3	0	1	2	3
	TEACHER—MALE ....N	1	2	3	0	1	2	3
	TEACHER—FEMALE ....O	1	2	3	0	1	2	3
	DOCTOR/HEALTH STAFF—MALE ....P	1	2	3	0	1	2	3
	DOCTOR/HEALTH STAFF—FEMALE ....Q	1	2	3	0	1	2	3
	RELIGIOUS LEADER—MALE ....R	1	2	3	0	1	2	3
	POLICE/ SOLDIER—MALE ....S	1	2	3	0	1	2	3
	OTHER—MALE (specify) _____ ......W	1	2	3	0	1	2	3
	OTHER—FEMALE (specify) _____ X	1	2	3	0	1	2	3
N10	COUNTRIES MAY WANT TO ADD ONE ADDITIONAL COUNTRY-SPECIFIC QUESTION HERE[15]							

---

[15] Countries may include an additional question on a form of violence against women that is important in their context, but is not covered by this module, such as FGM.

	Z. COMPLETION OF INTERVIEW	
Z01	We have now finished the interview. Is there anything else that happened to you and that I have not asked? Do you have any comments, or is there anything else you would like to add?	
Z02	I have asked you about many difficult things. How has talking about these things made you feel? WRITE DOWN ANY SPECIFIC RESPONSE GIVEN BY RESPONDENT	GOOD/BETTER..............................1 BAD/WORSE..................................2 SAME/NO DIFFERENCE 3
Z03	***FINISH ONE - IF RESPONDENT HAS DISCLOSED PROBLEMS/VIOLENCE*** I would like to thank you very much for helping us. I realize that these questions may have been difficult for you to answer, but it is only by hearing from women themselves that we can really understand about their experiences of violence. From what you have told us, I can tell that you have had some very difficult times in your life. No one has the right to treat someone else in that way. However, from what you have told me, I can also see that you are strong and have survived through some difficult circumstances. Here is a list of organizations that provide support, legal advice and counselling services to women in STUDY LOCATION. Please do contact them if you would like to talk over your situation with anyone. Their services are free and they will keep anything that you say private. You can go whenever you feel ready to, either soon or later on. ***FINISH TWO - IF RESPONDENT HAS NOT DISCLOSED PROBLEMS/VIOLENCE*** I would like to thank you very much for helping us. I realize that these questions may have been difficult for you to answer, but it is only by hearing from women themselves that we can really understand about women's experiences in life. In case you ever hear of another woman who needs help, here is a list of organizations that provide support, legal advice and counselling services to women in STUDY LOCATION. Please do contact them if you or any of your friends or relatives need help. Their services are free and they will keep anything that anyone says to them private.	
FIN	**TIME FINISH INTERVIEW (24H)** |__|__|h |__|__|min	

Z04	WAS ANYBODY PRESENT AT THE INTERVIEW?	YES 1
		NO 2
	IF YES, INDICATE HOW MANY PEOPLE, WHO THEY WERE AND APPROXIMATE AGES:	

Z05	DID YOU ENCOUNTER ANY DIFFICULTIES IN OBTAINING PRIVACY?	YES 1
		NO 2
	IF YES, PLEASE SPECIFY:	

Z06	DO YOU HAVE THE IMPRESSION THE ANSWERS WERE TRUTHFUL?	YES 1
		NO 2
	IF NO, PLEASE SPECFIFY:	

Z07	DID YOU DETECT ANY SPECIFIC PROBLEMS WITH THE WORDING OR TRANLSATION?	
		YES 1
		NO 2
	IF YES, PLEASE INDICATE WITH WHICH QUESTIONS:	

Z08	WAS IS IT DIFFICULT TO OBTAIN ANSWERS ON QUESTIONS ABOUT FREQUENCY OF VIOLENCE? YES .... 1 NO .... 2 IF YES, PLEASE SPECIFY: _____ _____ _____ _____ _____ _____
Z09	DO YOU FEEL ANY QUESTIONS ARE MISSING? YES .... 1 NO .... 2 IF YES, PLEASE SPECIFY: _____ _____ _____ _____ _____ _____
Z10	ANY OTHER COMMENTS _____ _____ _____ _____ _____ _____

IF MORE THAN ONE HOUSEHOLD IN SELECTED DWELLING: FILL OUT SEPARATE HOUSEHOLD SELECTION FORM FOR EACH ONE[16]

	HOUSEHOLD SELECTION FORM				
	Hello, my name is _____. I am calling on behalf of CENTRE FOR SURVEY RESEARCH. We are conducting a survey in STUDY LOCATION on XXXXX.				
1	Please can you tell me how many people live here and share food? PROBE: Does this include children (including infants) living here? Does it include any other people who may not be members of your family, such as domestic servants, lodgers or friends who live here and share food? MAKE SURE THESE PEOPLE ARE INCLUDED IN THE TOTAL.			TOTAL NUMBER OF PEOPLE IN HOUSEHOLD [ ][ ]	
2	Is the head of the household male or female?			MALE ....1 FEMALE ....2 BOTH 3	
3	FEMALE HOUSEHOLD MEMBERS	RELATIONSHIP TO HEAD OF HOUSEHOLD	RESIDENCE	AGE	ELIGIBLE
	[For some of the questions] we would like to talk to only one woman from your household. To enable me to identify whom I should talk to, would you please give me the first names of all girls or women who usually live in your household (and share food)?	What is the relationship of NAME to the head of the household?* USE CODES BELOW	Does NAME usually live here? SPECIAL CASES: SEE (A) BELOW. YES NO	How old is NAME? (YEARS- more or less)	SEE CRITERIA BELOW (A + B) YES NO
1			1 2		1 2
2			1 2		1 2
3			1 2		1 2
4			1 2		1 2
5			1 2		1 2
6			1 2		1 2
7			1 2		1 2
8			1 2		1 2
9			1 2		1 2
10			1 2		1 2

---

[16] Only one woman per household can be interviewed. The way it will be done depends on sampling strategy and vehicle survey. The household selection presented here is an example of a possible way to select one eligible woman in a household (as used in the WHO multi-country study). It does not form part of the module.

CODES	06 MOTHER	12 DOMESTIC SERVANT
01 HEAD	07 MOTHER-IN-LAW	13 LODGER
02 WIFE (PARTNER)	08 SISTER	14 FRIEND
03 DAUGHTER	09 SISTER-IN-LAW	98 OTHER NOT RELATIVE:
04 DAUGHTER-IN-LAW	10 OTHER RELATIVE	_____
05 GRANDDAUGHTER	11 ADOPTED/FOSTER/ STEPDAUGHTER	

(A) SPECIAL CASES TO BE CONSIDERED MEMBER OF HOUSEHOLD:[17]

- <u>DOMESTIC SERVANTS</u> IF THEY SLEEP 5 NIGHTS A WEEK OR MORE IN THE HOUSEHOLD.
- <u>VISITORS</u> IF THEY HAVE SLEPT IN THE HOUSEHOLD FOR THE PAST 4 WEEKS.

(B) ELIGIBLE: ANY <u>WOMAN 15 YEARS AND OLDER</u> LIVING IN HOUSEHOLD.

MORE THAN ONE ELIGIBLE WOMEN IN HOUSEHOLD:

RANDOMLY SELECT ONE ELIGIBLE WOMAN FOR INTERVIEW. TO DO THIS, WRITE THE LINE NUMBERS OF ELIGIBLE WOMEN ON PIECES OF PAPER, AND PUT IN A BAG. ASK A HOUSEHOLD MEMBER TO PICK OUT A NUMBER – SO SELECTING THE PERSON TO BE INTERVIEWED.[18]

- **PUT CIRCLE AROUND LINE NUMBER OF WOMAN SELECTED.** ASK IF YOU CAN TALK WITH THE SELECTED WOMAN. IF SHE IS NOT AT HOME, AGREE ON DATE FOR RETURN VISIT.
- **CONTINUE WITH HOUSEHOLD QUESTIONNAIRE**

NO ELIGIBLE WOMAN IN HOUSEHOLD:[19]

- SAY "I cannot continue because I can only interview women 15 and over. Thank you for your assistance."
- **FINISH HERE**.

* If both (male and female) are the head, refer to the male.

---

[17] These selection criteria for whom belongs to the "household" (including live-in domestic workers and long term visitors—as used in the WHO study) may not be feasible for surveys on other subjects.

[18] Random selection could be done by this or any other method such as first birth date or Kish table.

[19] Whether the interview ends here or not depends on the purpose of the vehicle survey.

Annex VIII

Good practice for survey questions on additional variables/topics

The following tables contain examples from United Nations and international standards as well as country practices. Where there are no guidelines or principles and recommendations, country examples have been included. The included questions are only examples of possible wording to be considered when constructing questions for inclusion in a national survey. It should be noted and emphasized that these examples need to be adapted to the national context.

Table A.VIII.1
a. Personal characteristics of respondents

Additional variables	Suggested question(s)	Source	Note
a.i. Age at first marriage	a.i.1. How old were you when you (first) were married? _____ years	*Principles and Recommendations for Population and Housing Censuses, Revision 2*, Statistical papers, Series M, No. 67/Rev.2 (United Nations publication, Sales No. E.07.WVIII.8). http://unstats.un.org/unsd/publication/SeriesM/Seriesm_67rev2e.pdf	See paragraph 2.192 of the source document.
a.ii. Educational attainment and literacy	a.ii.1. How would you rate your current reading skills in (own language). Are they…? 1. Cannot read (own language) 2. Poor 3. Fair 4. Good 5. Very good 6. Don't know/refused a.ii.2. How would you rate your current writing skills in (own language). Are they…? 1. Cannot write in (own language) 2. Poor 3. Fair 4. Good 5. Very good 6. Don't know/refused a.ii.3. What is the highest level of education you have completed? 1. No formal education 2. Some primary school 3. Completed primary school 4. Some secondary school 5. Secondary school diploma 6. Some trades or apprenticeship training 7. Trade or apprenticeship certificate 8. Some college or university 9. College diploma 10. University degree—Bachelor's 11. Advanced university degree—Master's, Ph.d., professional (e.g., law, medicine, dentistry)	International Adult Literacy Survey coordinated by the Organization for Economic Co-operation and Development, adapted from the survey conducted in Canada by Statistics Canada. See www23.statcan.gc.ca/imdb-bmdi/instrument/4406_Q1_V1-eng.pdf	Corresponding question(s) in the source document: a.ii.1 corresponds to B5 a.ii.2 corresponds to B6 a.ii.3 corresponds to A6C
a.iii. Economic activity status	a.iii.1. Last week, how many hours did you work (not including volunteer work, housework, maintenance or repairs for your own family)? Include as work: • *Working without pay in a family farm or business (e.g., assisting in seeding, doing accounts);* • *Working in your own business, farm or professional practice, alone or in partnership;* • *Working for wages, salary, tips or commissions.* Number of hours (to the nearest hour) OR • None	*Measuring the Economically Active in Population Censuses: A Handbook, Studies in Methods*, Series F, No. 102 (United Nations publication, Sales No. E.09.XVII.7). http://unstats.un.org/unsd/publication/seriesf/Seriesf_102e.pdf	Corresponding question(s) in the source document: a.iii.1 corresponds to Example A.5.1 a.iii.2 corresponds to Example A.5.2

Good practice for survey questions on additional variables/topics 199

	a.iii.2. Last week were you on temporary layoff or absent from your job or business? *Mark one circle only* • No • Yes, on temporary layoff from a job to which expect to return • Yes, on vacation, ill, on strike, or locked out or absent for other reasons a.iii.3. During the past 30 days did … work for cash? 1. Yes, for someone else --> Go to X.X 2. Yes for self --> Go to X.X 3. No -->Go to a.iii.4 a.iii.4. Then what did … do during the past 30 days? 1. Family business 2. Work at lands/farms/cattle post 3. Actively seeking work 4. Housework 5. Student 6. Retiree (Other specify)	*Measuring the Economically Active in Population Censuses: A Handbook*, Studies in Methods, Series F, No. 102 (United Nations publication, Sales No. E.09.XVII.7). http://unstats.un.org/unsd/publication/seriesf/Seriesf_102e.pdf	Corresponding question(s) in the source document: a.iii.3 corresponds to Example A.6.1 a.iii.4 corresponds to Example A.6.2
a.iv. Place of residence	Recommended classification of localities by size: 500,000 or more inhabitants 100,000 – 499,999 inhabitants 50,000 – 99,999 inhabitants 20,000 – 49,999 inhabitants 10,000 – 19,999 inhabitants 5,000 – 9,999 inhabitants 2,000 – 4,999 inhabitants 1,000 – 1,999 inhabitants 500 – 999 inhabitants 200 – 499 inhabitants Less than 200 inhabitants Population not in localities	*Principles and Recommendations for a Vital Statistics System, Revision 2*, Series M, No. 19/Rev. 2 (United Nations publication, Sales No. E.01.XVII.10). http://unstats.un.org/unsd/demographic/sconcerns/densurb/densurbmethods.htm http://unstats.un.org/unsd/publication/SeriesM/SeriesM_19rev2E.pdf	See paragraphs 96-99 of the source document. Categories may be collapsed or expanded as national circumstances dictate and depending on the level of disaggregation required and permitted by the sample size.
a.v. Ethnicity, religion and language	Question wording depends on national context.		See paragraphs 266 to 275 above for an in-depth discussion of this.

Table A.VIII.2
b. Experience of violence

Additional topic	Suggested question(s)	Source	Note
b.i. Attitudes towards violence against women	b.i.1. Sometimes a husband is annoyed or angered by things that his wife does. In your opinion, is a husband justified in hitting or beating his wife in the following situations: 1. If she goes out without telling him 2. If she neglects the children 3. If she argues with him 4. If she refuses sex with him 5. If she burns the food	Both the MICS and DHS surveys have standardized modules for measuring attitudes towards domestic violence. See www.childinfo.org/attitudes_methodology.html.	Corresponding question(s) in the source document: b.i.1 corresponds to DV1
b.ii. Reporting to authorities/seeking help	b.ii.1. Did you or somebody else report this incident to the police or other judicial authorities? 1 Yes 2 No 98 Don't know/Can't remember 99 Refused/No answer If b.ii.1=1, go to b.ii.3 If b.ii.1=2, go to b.ii.2 Else go to b.ii.10 b.ii.2. Why did you not report this incident to the police? <<MARK ALL THAT APPLY>> 1 Dealt with it herself / Involved a friend / Family matter 2 Too minor / Not serious enough /Never occurred to her 3 Did not think the police would do anything 4 Did not think the police could do anything 5 Fear of offender / Fear of reprisals 6 Shame, embarrassment / Thought it was her fault 7 Didn't want anyone to know / Kept it private 8 Did not want offender arrested / in trouble with police 9 Would not be believed 10 Part of job / Goes with the job 11 Reported to someone else (specify) _____ 12 Other (specify) _____ 98 Don't know/Can't remember 99 Refused/No answer b.ii.3. What did the police do? <<MARK ALL THAT APPLY>> 1 Took a report 2 Arrested the man 3 Gave a warning 4 Suggested services to the respondent 5 Provided protection to the respondent 6 Followed through with the court procedure 7 Police did nothing 8 Something else (specify) _____ 98 Don't know/Can't remember 99 Refused/No answer	Heuni, UNICRI and Statistics Canada. International Violence against Women Survey. Rev 7.	Corresponding question(s) in the source document: b.ii.1 corresponds to E15 b.ii.2 corresponds to E16 b.ii.3 corresponds to E17 b.ii.4 corresponds to E18 b.ii.5 corresponds to E19 b.ii.6 corresponds to E20 b.ii.7 corresponds to E21

Good practice for survey questions on additional variables/topics

Question	Source
b.ii.4. Were charges ever brought against him (them) as a result of this incident? 1 Yes 2 No 98 Don't know/Can't remember 99 Refused/No answer *If b.ii.4 =1, go to b.ii.5.* *Else go to b.ii.6.* b.ii.5. Did these charges lead to a conviction in court? 1 Yes 2 No 3 The court process is still continuing 98 Don't know/Can't remember 99 Refused/No answer b.ii.6. How satisfied are you with the way the police handled the case? Were you: <<READ OUT>> 1 Very satisfied 2 Satisfied 3 Dissatisfied 4 Very dissatisfied 98 Don't know/Can't remember 99 Refused/No answer b.ii.7. Is there anything else the police should have done to help you? <<MARK ALL THAT APPLY>> 1 Informed her about what was going on 2 Provided information about legal procedures or services 3 Responded more quickly 4 Charged him / arrested him 5 Given him a warning 6 Taken complaint more seriously / listened to me / been more supportive / helped me more 7 Taken him away / out of the house / should have given restraining order 8 Referred her to a service or shelter 9 Provided her with some protection / helped her leave the house 10 Taken her to hospital / medical care 11 Other (specify) _____ 12 No, nothing 98 Don't know/Can't remember 99 Refused/No answer b.ii.8. (In some countries agencies have been set up to help women with similar experiences.) In relation to this incident, did you contact a specialized agency, such as: <<READ OUT>> <<MARK ALL THAT APPLY>> <<MODIFY NATIONALLY ACCORDING TO EXISTING SERVICES—SO THAT THEY ROUGHLY CORRESPOND TO THE GIVEN CATEGORIES>> 1 Shelter or transition house 2 Crisis centre/crises line 3 Another counsellor 4 Women's centre 5 Community/family centre 6 Other (specify) (DO NOT READ) _____ 7 Did not contact any agency (DO NOT READ) 98 Don't know/Can't remember (DO NOT READ) 99 Refused/No answer (DO NOT READ)	Heuni, UNICRI and Statistics Canada. International Violence against Women Survey. Rev 7. Corresponding question(s) in the source document: b.ii.8 corresponds to E11 b.ii.9 corresponds to E12 Questions will depend on the country context as there is vast variation in the availability of these services.

Additional topic	Suggested question(s)	Source	Note
	If b.ii.8=7, 98 or 99, go to question after b.ii.9. Else go to b.ii.9. b.ii.9 How helpful was the service in the shelter or transition house/crisis centre/…etc? <<ASK SEPARATELY FOR EACH OF THOSE MENTIONED AT b.iii.8>> 		Very helpful	Somewhat helpful	Not at all helpful	DK/CR	Ref/NA
---	---	---	---	---	---
1 Shelter or transition house	1	2	3	98	99
2 Crisis centre/crisis line	1	2	3	98	99
3 Another counsellor	1	2	3	98	99
4 Women's centre	1	2	3	98	99
5 Community/family centre	1	2	3	98	99
6 Other (specify)	1	2	3	98	99 | b.ii.10. Apart from people already mentioned did you ever talk to anyone about what happened, such as: <<READ OUT>> <<MARK ALL THAT APPLY>> 1 Immediate family members 2 Other relative 3 Friend/neighbour 4 Co-worker/boss/co-student 5 Religious leader/worker 6 Doctor, nurse 7 Psychologist, psychiatrist 8 Someone else (specify) (DO NOT READ) _____ 9 None of the above (DO NOT READ) 98 Don't know/Can't remember (DO NOT READ) 99 Refused/No answer (DO NOT READ)	Heuni, UNICRI and Statistics Canada. International Violence against Women Survey. Rev 7.	Corresponding question(s) in the source document: b.ii.10 corresponds to E22 It is also important to enquire about the extent to which victims of violence sought help or support from informal sources of support such as family or friends in the local community.
b.iii. Location of violence	b.iii.1. Where did this (the most recent) incident occur? 1 Your own home or yard 2 His home or yard 3 Someone's else home or yard 4 Street, alley 5 Parking lot 6 Car 7 Work 8 Bar, dance club, pool hall 9 Rural areas, woods, park, campground 10 Other public building 11 School, college, campus 12 Public transit 13 Other (specify) _____ 98 Don't know/Can't remember 99 Refused/No answer	Heuni, UNICRI and Statistics Canada. International Violence against Women Survey. Rev 7.	Corresponding question(s) in the source document: b.iii.1 corresponds to D4

Table A.VIII.3
c. Personal characteristics of intimate partners

Additional variables	Suggested question(s)	Source	Note
c.i. Age	c.i.1. In which year was your husband or partner born? ___ Year 98 Don't know/Can't remember 99 Refused/No answer c.i.2. Would you mind telling me his approximate age please? <<READ OUT IF REQUIRED >> 1 18 – 24 2 25 – 29 3 30 – 34 4 35 – 39 5 40 – 44 6 45 – 49 7 50 – 54 8 55 – 59 9 60 – 64 10 65 and over 98 Don't know/Can't remember (DO NOT READ) 99 Refused/No answer (DO NOT READ)	Heuni, UNICRI and Statistics Canada. International Violence against Women Survey. Rev 7.	Corresponding question(s) in the source document: c.i.1 corresponds to G5 c.i.2 corresponds to G6
c.ii. Educational attainment and literacy	See a.ii above.		
c.iii. Economic activity status	See a.iii above.		
c.iv. Substance abuse	c.iv.1. Most people drink sometimes—either beer, wine or other alcohol. How often does your husband/partner/boyfriend drink so much that he gets drunk? 1 Never drinks 2 Drinks, but never gets drunk 3 Gets drunk a couple of times a year 4 Gets drunk a couple of times a month 5 Gets drunk once or twice a week 6 Gets drunk every day or almost every day 7 Other (specify) _____ 98 Don't know/Can't remember 99 Refused/No answer	Heuni, UNICRI and Statistics Canada. International Violence against Women Survey. Rev 7.	Corresponding question(s) in the source document: c.iv.1 corresponds to G14
c.v. Witnessing partner violence in the family of origin	c.v.1. To the best of your knowledge, was your partner's father (or father figure) ever violent towards your partner's mother, or any of the women he lived with? 1 Yes / think so 2 No / don't think so 3 Father did not live with the family 4 Mother did not live with the family 98 Don't know/Can't remember 99 Refused/No answer	Heuni, UNICRI and Statistics Canada. International Violence against Women Survey. Rev 7.	Corresponding question(s) in the source document: c.v.1 corresponds to H1

Table A.VIII.4
d. Personal characteristics of non-intimate partners

Additional topic	Suggested question(s)	Source	Note
d.i. Relationship to victim/Sex	See UNECE Survey Module on Violence against Women, question N03	UNECE Survey Module on Violence against Women (Annex VII).	

References

Altinay, A.G. and Y. +Arat (2009). *Violence against Women in Turkey: A Nationwide Survey.* Istanbul: Punto Publishing Solutions.

Andersson, N. and others (2009). Collecting reliable information about violence against women safely in household interviews: Experience from a large-scale national survey in South Asia. *Violence against Women,* vol. 15, No. 4 (April), pp. 482-496.

Black, M.C. and others (2011). National Intimate Partner and Sexual Violence Survey: 2010 summary report. Atlanta, Georgia: National Center for Injury Prevention and Control, Centers for Disease Control and Prevention.

Blumberg, S.J. and J.V. Luke (2011). Wireless substitution: Early release of estimates from the National Health Interview Survey, January-June 2011. Hyattsville, Maryland: National Center for Health Statistics, Division of Health Interview Statistics.

Brick, J.M. and G. Kalton (1996). Handling missing data in survey research. *Statistical Methods in Medical Research*, vol. 5, No. 3 (September), pp. 215-238.

Claramunt, M.C. (1999). Helping ourselves to help others: Self-care guide for those who work in the field of family violence. Gender and Public Health Series 7. San Jose, Costa Rica: Pan American Health Organization/World Health Organization, Women, Health and Development Program.

Coker, A.L. and E.A. Stasny (1995). Adjusting the National Crime Victimization Survey's estimates of rape and domestic violence for "gag" factors, 1986-1990. ICPSR version, Columbia, South Carolina: University of South Carolina, School of Public Health, Department of Epidemiology and Biostatistics [producer]; Ann Arbor, Michigan: Inter-university Consortium for Political and Social Research [distributor].

de Leeuw, E.D. (1992). *Data Quality in Mail, Telephone and Face-to-Face Surveys.* Amsterdam: TT-Publikaties.

de Leeuw, E.D., J. Hox and S. Kef (2003). Computer-assisted self-interviewing tailored for special populations and topics. *Field Methods*, vol. 15, No. 3 (August), pp. 223-251.

Ellsberg, M. and others (2007). WHO Multi-country Study on Women's Health and Domestic Violence: Facilitator's manual—Workshop for Training Fieldworkers. Geneva: World Health Organization.

Ellsberg, M. and others (2001). Researching domestic violence against women: Methodological and ethical considerations. *Studies in Family Planning,* vol. 32, No. 1 (March), pp. 1-16.

Ellsberg M. and L. Heise (2005). *Researching Violence against Women: A Practical Guide for Researchers and Activists. Geneva: World Health Organization (WHO);* Washington, D.C.: Programme for Appropriate Technology in Health (PATH).

Fisher, B., F.T. Cullen and M.G. Turner (2000). The sexual victimization of college women. NCJ 182369. Washington, D.C.: National Institute of Justice and Bureau of Justice Statistics.

Garcia-Moreno, C. and others (2005). *WHO Multi-country Study on Women's Health and Domestic Violence against Women: Initial Results on Prevalence, Health Outcomes and Women's Responses.* Geneva: World Health Organization.

Gower, K. (2011). Book review (of *Missing Data: A Gentle Introduction*). *Organizational Research Methods*, vol.14, No. 3 (July), pp. 577-580.

Heiskanen, M. and M. Piispa (1998). *Faith, Hope, Battering: A Survey of Men's Violence against Women in Finland.* Helsinki: Statistics Finland.

Hindin, M.J., S. Kishor and D.L. Ansara (2008). Intimate partner violence among couples in 10 DHS countries: Predictors and health outcomes. DHS Analytical Studies No. 18. Calverton, Maryland: Macro International.

Holbrook, A.L., M.C. Green and J.A. Krosnick (2003). Telephone versus face-to-face interviewing of national probability samples with long questionnaires: Comparisons of respondent satisficing and social desirability response bias. *Public Opinion Quarterly*, vol. 67, No. 1, pp. 79-125.

Jansen, H.A.F.M. (2012). Prevalence surveys on violence against women: Challenges around indicators, data collection and use. Expert paper presented at the Expert Group Meeting on Prevention of Violence against Women and Girls. Bangkok, September.

_____ (2011). Survey module on violence against women: Interviewer's manual. Available from www1.unece.org/stat/platform/display/vaw/survey+module+for+measuring+violence+against+women.

_____ (2010). *Swimming against the Tide: Lessons Learned from Field Research on Violence against Women in the Solomon Islands and Kiribati.* Suva, Fiji: United Nations Population Fund (UNFPA) Subregional Office.

Jansen, H.A.F.M. and others (2007). WHO Multi-country Study on Women's Health and Domestic Violence: Supervisors's and Field Editor's Manual. Geneva: World Health Organization.

_____ (2004). Interviewer training in the WHO Multi-country Study on Women's Health and Domestic Violence. *Violence against Women* vol. 10, No. 7 (July), pp. 831-849.

_____ (2003). Questionnaire for the WHO Multi-country Study on Women's Health and Domestic Violence. Version 10. Geneva: World Health Organization.

Jaquier, V., B.S. Fisher and M. Killias (2006). Cross-national survey designs: Equating the National Violence against Women Survey and Swiss International Violence against Women Survey. *Journal of Contemporary Criminal Justice*, vol. 22, No. 2 (May), pp. 90-112.

Johnson, H. (1996). *Dangerous Domains: Violence against Women in Canada.* Toronto: Nelson Canada.

Johnson, H., N. Ollus and S. Nevala (2008). *Violence against Women: An International Perspective.* New York: Springer.

Kalton, G., J.M. Brick and T. Lê (2005). Estimating components of design effects for use in sample design. *Household sample Surveys in Developing and Transition Countries.* Studies in Methods, Series F, No. 96. United Nations publication, Sales No. E.05.XVII.6.

Kalton, G. and D. Kasprzyk (1986). The treatment of missing survey data. *Survey Methodology*, vol. 12, pp. 1-16.

Killias, M., M. Simonin and J. de Puy (2005). *Violence Experienced by Women in Switzerland over their Lifespan: Results of the International Violence against Women Survey (IVAWS).* Berne: Stämpfli.

Kish, L. (1965). *Survey Sampling.* New York: John Wiley & Sons.

Little, R.J.A. and D.B. Rubin (2002). *Statistical Analysis with Missing Data*, 2nd ed. Wiley

Series in Probability and Statistics. Hoboken, New Jersey: John Wiley & Sons.

Lundgren, E. and others (2001). *Captured Queen: Men's Violence against Women in "Equal" Sweden—A Prevalence Study*. Umeå, Sweden: Åströms tryckeri.

Mirrlees-Black, C. (1999). *Domestic Violence: Findings from a New British Crime Survey Self-completion Questionnaire*. Research Study 191. London: Home Office.

Mouzos, J. and T. Makkai (2004). *Women's Experiences of Male Violence: Findings from the Australian component of the International Violence against Women Survey (IVAWS)*. Research and Public Policy Series, No. 56. Canberra: Australian Institute of Criminology.

Paletta, A. and K. Mihorean (1998). Cognitive testing of questions to measure family violence. Ottawa: Statistics Canada.

Percy, A. and P. Mayhew (1997). Estimating sexual victimization in a national crime survey: A new approach. *Studies on Crime and Crime Prevention*, vol. 6, No. 2, pp. 125-150.

Saltzman, L. E. and others (1999). Intimate partner violence surveillance: Uniform definitions and recommended data elements. Atlanta, Georgia: National Center for Injury Protection and Control, Centers for Disease Control and Prevention.

Secretariat of the Pacific Community (2010). *Kiribati Family Health and Support Study: A Study on Violence against Women and Children*. Noumea, New Caledonia.

Statistics Canada (2003). *Survey Methods and Practices*. Ottawa.

Tourangeau, R. and T.W. Smith (1996). Asking sensitive questions: The impact of data collection mode, question format and question context. *Public Opinion Quarterly*, vol. 60, No. 2, pp. 275-304.

United Nations (2008). *Designing Household Survey Samples: Practical Guidelines*. Studies in Methods, Series F, No. 98. Sales No. E.06.XVII.13.

_____ (2006). *Ending Violence against Women: From Words to Action. Study of the Secretary-General*. Sales No. E.06.IV.8.

_____ (2005a). *Household Sample Surveys in Developing and Transition Countries*. Studies in Methods, Series F, No. 96. Sales No. E.05.XVII.6.
(INTRODUCTION, and Chapter VI)

_____ (2005b). Report of the Expert Group Meeting on the topic "Violence against women: A statistical overview, challenges and gaps in data collection and methodology and approaches for overcoming them". Geneva, April. Available from www.un.org/womenwatch/daw/egm/vaw-stat-2005/index.html.
(CHAPTER 3)

United Nations Economic Commission for Europe (2011, 2012). Survey module on violence against women and accompanying manuals and other materials. Available from www1.unece.org/stat/platform/display/VAW/Survey+module+for+measuring+violence+against+women.

United Nations Office on Drugs and Crime and United Nations Economic Commission for Europe (2010). Manual on victimization surveys. Geneva: ECE/CES/4.

University of Iowa (2003). Protocol outline. Available from http://hso.research.uiowa.edu/Protocol-outline.

van de Wijgert, J. and others (2000). Is audio computer-assisted self-interviewing a feasible method of surveying in Zimbabwe? *International Journal of Epidemiology*, vol. 29, No. 5, pp. 885-890.

Walby, S. and J. Allen (2004). *Domestic Violence, Sexual Assault and Stalking: Findings from the British Crime Survey*. Research Study 276. London: Home Office.

Walby, S. and A. Myhill (2001). New survey methodologies in researching violence against women. *British Journal of Criminology,* vol. 41, No. 3, (June), pp. 502-522.

Watts, C. and others (2007a). WHO Multi-Country Study on Women's Health and Domestic Violence: Interviewer's manual. Geneva: World Health Organization.

_____ (2007b). WHO Multi-Country Study on Women's Health and Domestic Violence: Study protocol. Geneva: World Health Organization.

World Health Organization (2001). Putting women first: Ethical and safety recommendations for research on domestic violence against women. Geneva, WHO/FCH/GWH/01.1. Available from www.who.int/gender/violence/womenfirtseng.pdf.

Yansaneh, I.S. (2005). Overview of sample design issues for household surveys in developing and transition countries. *Household Sample Surveys in Developing and Transition Countries.* Studies in Methods, Series F, No. 96. United Nations publication, Sales No. E.05.XVII.6.

Yansaneh, I.S., L.S. Wallace and D.A. Marker (1998). Imputation methods for large complex datasets: An application to the NEHIS. *Proceedings of the Survey Research Methods Section of the American Statistical Association.* pp. 314-319.